CLIFFS OF D

CLIFFS OF DESPAIR

A Journey to the Edge

TOM HUNT

RANDOM HOUSE

New York

Although *Cliffs of Despair* is a work of nonfiction, the names of a few
of the individuals who appear in these pages, along with certain descriptions
and identifying details, have been changed.

Published in the United States by Random House,
an imprint of The Random House Publishing Group,
a division of Random House, Inc., New York.

RANDOM HOUSE and colophon are registered
trademarks of Random House, Inc.

Grateful acknowledgment is made to the following for permission to reprint
previously published material:

Graywolf Press for an excerpt from "Having It Out with Melancholy" from
Collected Poems by Jane Kenyon, copyright © 2005 by the Estate of Jane Kenyon.
Reprinted by permission of Graywolf Press, St. Paul, Minnesota.

Dr. Robert E. Litman for an excerpt from a private conversation with
George Howe Colt. Reprinted by permission of Dr. Litman.

LIBRARY OF CONGRESS CATALOGING-IN-PUBLICATION DATA
Hunt, Tom.
Cliffs of despair: a journey to the edge / Tom Hunt.
p. cm.
Includes bibliographical references.
ISBN 0-375-50715-9
1. Suicidal behavior.   I. Title.
RC569.H886 2006   616.85'8445—dc22   2005052068

Printed in the United States of America on acid-free paper

www.atrandom.com

2 4 6 8 9 7 5 3 1

FIRST EDITION

Book design by Dana Leigh Blanchette

For Mom and Dad

CONTENTS

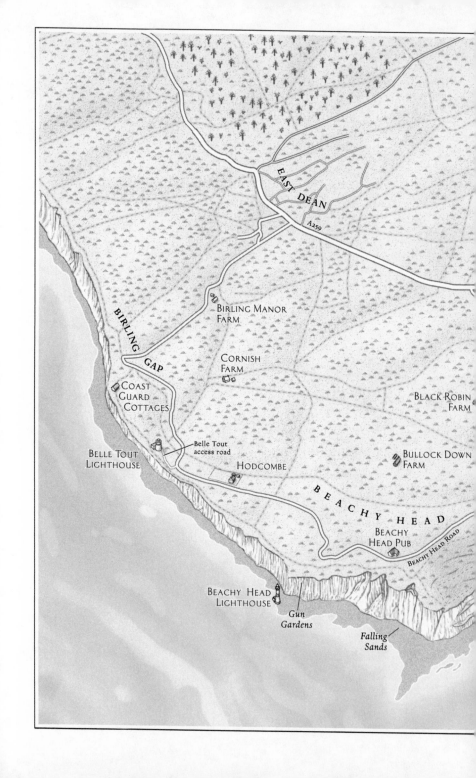

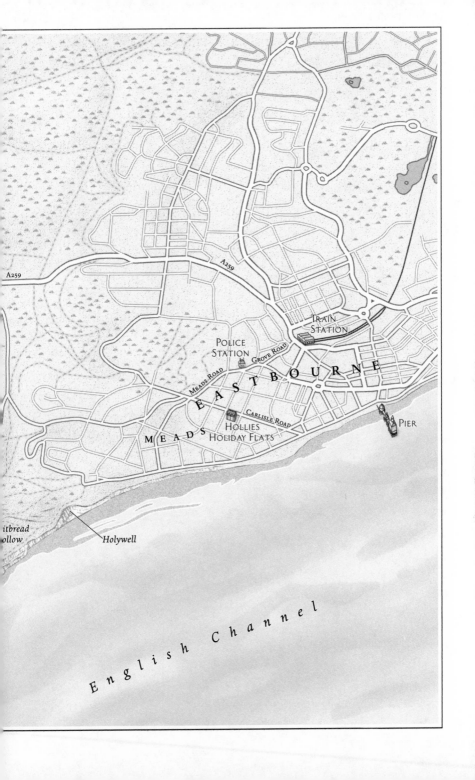

CLIFFS OF DESPAIR

1

The Last Stop Pub

A bearded man with black-rimmed glasses sits on the edge of a towering cliff, staring vacantly at a sea glimmering with the last remains of sunlight. Clouds drift above his head like barroom smoke. The stiff Channel wind ripples his lightweight jacket and shivers his scruffy hair. He presses his hands against the spongy turf, leans forward, and studies the rocks below. The foam-marbled sea has receded, leaving pools of water around the chalk rubble scattered across the beach.

Thirty feet behind the man, a woman in a bulky sweater gazes inland, a male companion by her side. Sheep and cows graze on hills dotted with yellow cowslips. Crows speckle red slate farmhouse roofs and strips of freshly plowed earth. A rabbit emerges from a nearby gorse patch and scampers across the cliff top. The woman's eyes follow it to the man, whose hands now grip the cliff edge. His back is framed by a pewter sea. He raises his head, turns, and flashes her a heart-stopping smile.

He turns back to the sea. The woman taps her partner's shoulder. They whisper and watch. Abruptly, the man stands and takes a large step away from the edge, as if suddenly repulsed by it. He glances at the woman. This time he isn't smiling. She averts her gaze and affects a casual stroll. When she glances over her shoulder, the man is back at the edge, peering over. She and her companion confer. They watch the man take a step backward. He begins to pace along the cliff top like a mad professor contemplating a problem. Then he stops, strides to the edge, and stands perfectly still. The woman and her partner turn to each other and make a decision. When they turn back to the cliff edge, the man is gone.

I ROUND THE CORNER of Eastbourne's town hall, on the fringe of the city's business district. My shadow stretches El Greco–like across the last bit of flatland for sixty miles, toward a smartly dressed woman closing her shop across the street. Hunched by a backpack stuffed with microwaveable Indian dinners, bananas, bread, and beer, I turn and begin the steep two-mile ascent to Beachy Head, a borough of Eastbourne known for its majestic chalk cliffs and for the number of people who jump off them.

The hill is the first in a chain that ripples across most of the length of the south coast county of Sussex, and it is interminable. One besotted English scribe compared the South Downs to the soft, gentle breasts of a sleeping girl; fully freighted, jet-lagged, and hungry, I feel like an ant lugging an oversize crumb up the backside of a Rubenesque nude. I trudge past charming homes tucked behind flint walls, and cross traffic intersections as confusing as exchange rates. What do the passing motorists think when they see a flagging, disheveled man with a backpack walking toward a famous suicide spot? It's my fifth day in England, and already I'm beginning to wonder if the fifteen hundred dollars I withdrew from my retirement fund to finance this trip was a good idea. I'll think differently, I hope, after a hearty dinner in my cozy bungalow at the farm on top of the hill.

I hear a siren. Seconds later, a police car careens around the corner, and I think, "Beachy Head." I pick up the pace. The grade steepens as Meads Road becomes Beachy Head Road, barren woods replace houses, and the sidewalk turns to a dirt path dotted with chalk. Minutes later, the top of the hill comes into view. I lean in to the steepening grade as though gravity were a headwind. Soon, crossing onto the coast road, my body straightens, and I'm blasted by gale-force winds. The hill protects Eastbourne from the foul weather blowing east, and now I'm at the top of it, exposed.

I pass a sign for Beachy Head and stop at a smaller sign announcing the entrance to Black Robin Farm. I gaze down the dirt drive and imagine taking off my sneakers, cracking open a beer, and watching television in my brick cocoon. I turn and look down the lonely coast road. I tell myself I have only a mile to go, if, in fact, there is anything to go to. I keep walking.

The coast road inclines gently and, running as it does along a ridge, offers a unique view of two different worlds: to the east below, the shimmering orange lights of a Victorian seaside resort; to the west, undulating hills and dusky farmhouses. The road humps, blocking the southern view ahead, but soon enough I see the Beachy Head Pub and flashing police lights.

I run. Past a farm, past stunted sycamores, past a couple in a parked car. Approaching the driveway to the Beachy Head Pub, I slow to a stroll so as not to look like the ambulance chaser I am.

A roadside phone booth installed by a local suicide-prevention group casts a faint glow on the sign planted next to it: THE SAMARITANS—ALWAYS THERE DAY AND NIGHT—PHONE 735555 OR 0345 90 90 90. At the driveway entrance, another sign, this one sprouting from a pole, announces BREWERS FAYRE AT BEACHY HEAD. A floodlight illuminates the pub's entrance, and the lights of Black Robin Farm glimmer in the distance beyond. I cross the road and pass a woman in a baggy sweater who leans like a felled tree into the tangle of her partner's arms.

I step onto the windswept Downs and plod toward the cliff edge, toward the din of helicopter rotors and two bystanders silhouetted against the sky. A police radio crackles across the cliff top. Some hundred feet away, a constable, backlit by strobes of red and blue, paces in front of a patrol car.

I join the two men. We watch the chopper hover over the Channel. I step up to the cliff edge and look down. The chalk boulders scattered along the shore look phosphorescent in the spray of searchlight. Despite the long drop, my legs remain steady; darkness fills the space with substance.

I step back and ask what happened. The larger of the two men turns to me. His nose is as ruggedly askew as his wool beret. He tells me, "Someone jumped about forty-five minutes ago. The police've been searching for, oh, I'd say twenty minutes now." He says his name is Shane; his friend is Simon.

I glance at the sea. The helicopter looks like a confused dragonfly, making several passes over the beach, banking back to the ocean between each pass, and hovering there before trying again. Simon watches, mesmerized, his leather flight jacket drooping over narrow shoulders.

"On holiday?" Shane asks.

"Yes." The truth is too complicated. I shift my gaze inland, but there isn't much to see at dusk. "It's beautiful here—a lot more open than I expected."

"It's like the stereotypical English flowing countryside. You know, makes you want to have a cup of tea, stiff upper lip, and let's go beat the Germans again."

I nod in agreement, though actually the land only makes me want to look.

The chopper continues to jab and feint above the Channel.

"Loud, isn't it?" I say.

"It's as much a part of Beachy Head as the wind and orchids." Shane turns to me and smiles. "It's a crowded sky here at Beachy Head: jackdaws, gulls, wheatears—and the police helicopter."

"I think they found it." Simon points below. The chopper lowers onto the beach. Two figures emerge from the hulk in a concentrated beam of white light. They clamber across floodlit shingle, stopping at a huddle of boulders, and there the light lingers. One of the figures spreads out an orange bag; the other reaches behind a boulder and tugs on a dark clothed body, flopping it onto the bag. They pack it, drag it, and shove it into the helicopter. When they're aboard as well, the chopper lifts and turns, rippling the sea with its wash.

I say goodbye to Shane and Simon and head across the cliff top, galvanized by this anonymous death. I negotiate clusters of gorse and stop at the top of the coast road embankment. Across the street, two police constables examine a car in the pub's parking lot. One appears to be taking down the license plate number; the other peers through the windshield on the driver's side. Then they head toward the pub, and I follow.

Brewers Fayre at Beachy Head, also known as the Beachy Head Pub, is a sprawl of contiguous ranch-style buildings a hundred yards from the sea. It was called the Queen's when it opened as a restaurant in 1880 and the Beachy Head Hotel when eight bedrooms were added in the 1890s. After World War II, it was a jumble of shacks where the fare was, according to one local, "an unending supply of mince followed by bread-and-butter pudding, with no choice, of course." It burned to the ground in the fall of 1966, the result of a kitchen fire fanned by gale-force winds, and again in 1994, nine months after being purchased by Whitbread, one of England's largest breweries.

Undaunted, Whitbread built an enlarged restaurant and pub on the charred site, as well as a quaint museum showcasing the area's natural wonders. In summer, camera-toting tourists pack the pub's picnic benches, and children invade its candy-colored playground as an ice-cream truck idles in the parking lot.

But the pub has a darker side. In some circles, it's known as the Last Stop Pub, a place where "suspicious ones" go for a little Dutch courage before heading to the cliffs. The pub's employees are instructed to keep their eyes open for solemn, solitary drinkers, and to suss out their intentions. Sometimes they call the police; other times they follow them out the building and, if necessary, physically restrain them.

I'm about to witness one of the pub's post-suicide rituals. The constables remove their hats in the entryway. They pass a pinball machine, then veer toward the bar, radios crackling. Two men turn on their stools. The bartender looks up as he draws a pint of ale. He doesn't wait for the officers to ask the usual question: the manager, he offers quietly, is working the till.

The constables continue on, and I follow. I stop at a dessert display some fifteen feet from the till and scan the dining area. Potted plants, antique lanterns, and ceramic mobiles of farm animals dangle from thick oak beams. Spinning wheels and burlap bags marked WOOL and FLOWER SEED sit on slatted platforms chained to a timber-frame ceiling. Silky pop music floats above tables occupied mostly by couples focused unwaveringly on their plates or each other. It's a surreal scene, these strapping police officers with their staticky radios moving urgently through a space so thick with the clinking languor of a weekday evening that it seems to blot them out. Either they've become such a familiar presence in the pub that they register as a peripheral blip in the consciousness of the diners, or the diners choose not to see them so they can continue to drink and eat, unencumbered by the tragedy that just transpired outside the darkened windows.

I peer into the brightly lit showcase of waxen cakes and pies, then cast a sidelong glance at the till. A ruddy-faced man with a dish towel slung over his shoulder listens to the constables and nods. He abandons his post and disappears with them through a doorway. They emerge minutes later. One of the constables utters a grim "We'll be in touch."

I stop at the bar, order a beer, and find a corner table. I molt my backpack and sit down, affecting a pose of self-assured watchfulness. A waiter walks by carrying a birthday cake to a table of giggling German schoolgirls.

"Will you be having dinner, sir?"

I turn to see a young man clutching a coffeepot and smiling politely. STEVE is pinned to his shirt pocket.

"No, I don't think so."

"Right." He glances at my backpack. "On holiday?"

"A working holiday."

"What do you do?"

"I'm a teacher."

"A professor?"

"No, a high school teacher."

He nods, like one of my students pretending to get it. Steve, if you have a few hours, pull up a chair, and I'll attempt to explain why I'm here, try to explain why, while my winter-worn prep school colleagues spend their spring break lounging on tropical beaches, I'm indulging in England's suicide package. "I'm here to research the Beachy Head suicides."

He seems momentarily stunned by my admission. "Really?"

I nod.

He glances at the bar, leans forward, and lowers his voice, as if he's about to tell a dirty joke. "We get some suicides coming here, you know. You probably saw the police come in."

"Yes, I did." I pause. "Have you come across any yourself?"

It's a long shot. Months before my visit, the pub's previous managers, a married couple, made the mistake of describing on national television their encounters with suicidal patrons; they're now laboring in a Brewers Fayre on the outskirts of Eastbourne. When I phoned the couple, James Cunningham said they couldn't talk about their tenure at the Beachy Head Pub unless I got Whitbread's permission. He gave me the number for the brewery's public relations representative, who told me that an interview with the Cunninghams regarding their employment at the Beachy Head Pub would not be possible.

The waiter says, "I haven't myself, but some of the other waiters have. We're not supposed to talk about the suicides, though."

I decide not to pursue it. I ask for another beer, forgetting that I'm supposed to get it myself; he takes my glass anyway. I watch the birthday girl open her gifts as her friends break into periodic bursts of laughter. I can see why Whitbread doesn't want it known that the pub's employees watch for suspicious ones or that it offers its conference room for mass police interviews, as was the case when a member of a school group accidentally stumbled backward over the cliffs. To know the pub's hidden curriculum is to experience it differently, to see a vaguely sinister quality in the sepia photographs of men in top hats, in the wooden rocking horses, in the teeth-baring laughter. Not the kind of dining experience Whitbread has in mind for customers in a family-style pub.

Steve returns with my beer. "So people in the States know about Beachy Head, do they?"

"Few Americans know about Beachy Head, actually."

He tilts his head in surprise. "Really?" He clasps his forearm with the hand that once held a coffeepot and a pint, as if grasping things is a compulsion. "How did you find out about it?"

I DISCOVERED BEACHY HEAD on the back page of *The Philadelphia Inquirer*. It was the title of the article that caught my attention: "Keeping an Eye on the Suspicious Ones." It began, "The last line of defense falls to bartender James Cunningham. Drawing pints of ale as coastal winds whip and swirl across the barren Downs outside, he keeps an eye on strangers in his cliffside pub, especially those who eschew the bar stools or fireside to sit alone in a corner." I read on, utterly captivated by the incongruity of a pub situated near a world-famous suicide spot. I pictured a timber-frame hovel with brightly lit windows and rattling shutters. I imagined an entire community affected by the suicides, and I wanted to know how. What was it like for the cabdriver who suspected he had a suicidal passenger? For the rescue worker who discovered the body? For the police officer who delivered the news and for the family members who received it? I'd read accounts of living in war zones; what was it like living in a suicide zone? I cut out the article and filed it away with my other unfulfilled writing intentions.

Two and a half years later, my wife and I were awakened at dawn by the heart-quickening sound of a ringing telephone. It was Moses, my father-in-law, informing me as best he could that his youngest son, Conrad, had shot himself in the head. "He's dead" are the only words I remember exactly.

I now found myself asking the same question from a different perspective: What is it like living in a suicide zone, in that place in the mind that borders on self-destruction? Is suicide an act of madness or reason? Of ambivalence or resolve? Of courage or cowardice? Why do people do it?

After Conrad's death, the pub grew larger in my imagination, as if it somehow contained the answers to these questions. On the anniversary of his suicide, I booked a flight to London. Six months later, on a tempestuous March midnight, five evenings before watching the helicopter recovery, I arrived at the East-bourne train station, took a cab to the entrance of a working farm a mile from the cliffs, and trudged down a long dirt drive, past an inquisitive donkey and a dark farmhouse, to a brick bungalow where I fell asleep in clouds of frozen breath, wondering what I'd gotten myself into.

2

Southern Hospitality

I awake some six hours later. The conditions are still medieval. The bungalow creaks and whistles as I lay in bed, regarding my cloudy exhalations. Maybe this is the way it's supposed to be. If I'd grown up on this damp, squally island, I might be so inured to the cold that I'd think the temperature was actually quite pleasant.

I finally summon the courage to throw off my pillowy comforter and shed my stale clothes. I grab a pair of wrinkled underwear from the duffel bag. When it takes three tries to thread my trembling feet through the leg holes, I come to my senses. No way is this normal. Fully clothed at last, I search for a thermostat. On the kitchen wall, I discover some sort of timing device, but I'm afraid to mess with it. I'll talk to the owners when I get back from the cliffs. I shuffle into the den and look out a window blasted with mist. The Channel is barely visible. A plowed field specked with chunks of upturned chalk runs to the base of a whale-backed hill under an ashen sky. Westward, the land billows toward distant farmhouses, the green broken here and there by strips of tilled soil and clusters of sheep. "I'm here," I whisper.

Derived from the French *beau chef* ("beautiful headland"), Beachy Head is a four-mile bulge on England's southeastern flank, its chalk face zigzagging from Eastbourne, a staid midsize city known for its preponderance of retirees, to Birling Gap, a sleepy hamlet and former smugglers' haunt. Undulating and meandering across Beachy Head, skirting cliff edges here and there, is a hundred-mile hiking trail known as the South Downs Way.

I study a map and decide to pick up the path where it begins. I take the coast road seaward, scud eastward across windblown fields, and sidestep down a plummeting slope. The air is calmer now, but the Channel churns. In the distance, proud hotels crowd the Eastbourne seafront, their creamy ornate exteriors dulled by mist. Below, a tree-lined road runs along the base of the hill, then curves sharply in front of a secluded cottage. At the road's edge, a wooden sign with an arrow pointing seaward announces the entrance to the South Downs Way.

The path starts close to sea level, then rises along the rim of a cove; an iron-railed fence guards the edge, imprisoning an angry sea. A quarter mile farther, I come to a stadium-size bowl with shrubby sides and a flat green bottom that was once the site of a convalescent camp for injured World War I soldiers and, later, a soccer field for brave schoolchildren. The plain ends abruptly, 120 feet above the sea.

Farther on, the trail dips through terraced slopes covered with thickets of hawthorn. I stop at the memorialized remains of concrete gun emplacements and try to imagine the soldiers who once stood watch on days like today, their hands clutching cold metal as their eyes scanned the skies for Messerschmitts. To stumble upon such relics is to feel a vague sense of inadequacy. I can't claim membership in that international club of adults who've fought on native soil and who would probably regard my Beachy Head trip as a morbid indulgence.

I pass a set of rickety stairs to the beach. Impatient to reach Beachy Head's summit, I get off the main trail and take a shortcut along scree-covered capillaries snaking up a series of ledges. Soon I begin to feel I've made a terrible mistake. The cliff face between shelves is deceptively steep and crumbly, the paths end without warning, and the cumulative danger of the slope is impossible to appreciate until I'm well past the first ledge and turn seaward. The slope seems much steeper, looking down. If I slipped, I'd tumble like a doll down a staircase. I start to panic. What do I do? Push my luck and keep climbing? Wait for help? Rewind the adventure—slowly? The choice is between foolhardiness, embarrassment, and caution. I choose caution and rewind, dislodging chunks of chalk as I go, until I'm back on the main trail, relieved and humbled.

The cliffs angle east to south and rise sharply as I near the main headland. I soon find myself gazing up a steep, bowed hill, contemplating the crumbly trail that runs along its sea-sliced edge. I begin the long trudge up, forgoing the dirt trail for a turfier route farther away from the edge. The rabbit holes are no longer nuisances but footholds, and stinging gusts blast across the exposed slope, sending my Red Sox cap flying.

The hill seems interminable, but up ahead, nestled into the slope just below the crest of the hill, is a sight for sore toes and burning calves: a viewing platform with a bench. Several rabbit holes later, I collapse onto the bench and, doubled over, consider for the first time at any length the insensibility of my footwear, a pair of worn canvas sneakers.

When I finally get up, I realize I was sitting on the carved names of suicides. IN MEMORY OF A. E. WRAMPLING, 1954. IN LOVING MEMORY OF GREG NOBLE, 2/8/67–23/1/96: WISH YOU WERE HERE. It's hard to empty your mind here. Something always impinges: pain, fear, history, the epigraph of a man not much older than Conrad.

I push on to the summit, and after another forty feet or so, I'm there. The Beachy Head Pub lies directly across the road, its parking lot virtually empty. On the cliff top, a couple of tourists stand before a granite monument near a knoll I later learn is the entryway to a mothballed bunker built during the Cold War. When they move on, I take their place. Engraved in the stone is a prayer that, in its imperative first-person parallelism, seems determined to insinuate itself into the mind of a potential jumper:

Lead me from death to life
From falsehood to truth
Lead me from despair to hope
From fear to trust
Lead me from hate to love
From war to peace
Let peace fill our hearts
Our world, our universe
Peace.

It is, I imagine, like the Samaritan phone booth across the road, a noble but largely futile gesture.

"The glory of these glorious Downs," gushed one Victorian scribbler in an essay on Beachy Head, "is the breeze. . . . The great headland and the whole rib of the promontory is windswept and washed with air." This "breeze" shoves me around and stings my cheeks as I pass a stone tablet bearing another message of hope: MIGHTIER THAN THE THUNDERS OF MANY WATERS. MIGHTIER THAN THE WAVES OF THE SEA, THE LORD ON HIGH IS MIGHTY. GOD IS ALWAYS GREATER THAN ALL OF OUR TROUBLES.

Continuing westward, I come to yet another monument, this one an octagonal sitting area honoring the Canadian troops stationed at Beachy Head during World War II. As I read the inscription, it occurs to me that this section of the cliff top, the highest point on England's southern edge, is one big memorial to resistance. The plaque on the sitting area—a converted watchtower— is a reminder that Beachy Head was once the first line of defense against foreign invaders; the other monuments, with their words of hope, are the last line of defense against potential jumpers.

I watch a dog chase his old man's tennis ball. The ball veers into a gorse patch, sending the dog into a sniffing frenzy. The man turns to me and smiles, and I return the gesture. I head toward a DANGER: CLIFF EROSION sign planted near the cliff edge. The terrain gets ugly as I draw closer to the sign. Springy turf turns to packed dirt littered with chalk and riddled with rabbit holes. The sign fronts a spindly wire fence cordoning off gaping fissures near the cliff edge. I walk along the fence until it ends at more stable ground, then fix my eye on the horizon, hoping that if I look hard enough, the French coast will materialize. All I see is white sky against a gray sea, and a lonely seagull flying high above a candy-striped lighthouse on the lapping foreshore. I realize that, standing some five hundred feet above the sea, I'm trespassing on the gull's territory. It glides westward and crosses the cliff top and then arcs eastward, flapping across a backdrop of rolling farmland and— He's watching me. The man with the dog. Am I striking too pensive a pose or too solitary a figure? Is he worried I'll jump? I put on a happy face, which seems to reassure him; he smiles, turns away, then gives the ball another fling, and I turn back to the sea. Torn between curiosity and fear, I hesitantly step up to the edge and look down, unaware that a gust once blew a coast guard off this cliff top. The sea froths and tosses against chalk boulders scattered along the shore. How easy it would be to go over—a little lean would do it—and how impossibly courageous. How many jumpers change their minds in midflight? I'm trying to imagine the horror of living for a few seconds with that regret when a rogue gust slams me from behind, pitching me forward. For a terrifying instant, my head crosses the plane of the cliffs as my hips struggle to hold anchor. Then my weight shifts from my toes to my heels; I straighten up and back away. I turn around to see if anybody was watching, but the cliff top is empty except for the retreating image of the man and dog. Jelly-kneed, I turn and stare at the edge, which now assumes an even greater air of malevolence.

But I'm drawn to it with the force of an addiction. I step closer and, throwing dignity to the winds, get down on my belly and inch across the spongy turf until my chin slips over the cliff edge. I look straight down. Huge chalk boulders pile against the base of the cliff. I push farther over the edge until my chest is on it, and crane my neck far enough to look Beachy Head in the face. But I'm too close to see anything other than a featureless white wall; my instinct is to inch farther out, but if I do, I risk losing my balance. I move a smidge, compelled by some inexplicable force stronger than mere curiosity. "This beautiful place," writes novelist Louis de Bernières, "openly invites you to die."

People have been accepting the invitation for centuries. Legend has it that in the seventh century, a shipwrecked Christian missionary named Saint Wilfrid observed the natives throwing themselves off the cliffs to placate the gods for years of crop failure. The first documented death off Beachy Head is found in the Eastbourne Parish Register of 1600: "James Wykker that was slain by a fall from the cliff." Since 1965, more than 500 people have died at Beachy Head, some 13 a year, the majority of them suicides. In 2004 alone, a record 34 people died at Beachy Head, the equivalent of one death every eleven days. About twice a week, a bartender, cabdriver, or walker alerts police to potential jumpers, while other would-be suicides go undetected. Distraught over unflattering press coverage during her last years, Princess Diana allegedly drove to Beachy Head, intending to jump, only to be drawn back by thoughts of her two sons.

Beachy Head, then, has a well-earned reputation. It is the deadliest cliff in the world and the third most popular suicide spot after Japan's Aokigahara Woods and San Francisco's Golden Gate Bridge. The former is an ancient forest of three-hundred-year-old trees, cool hollows, and narrow volcanic rock paths at the base of Mount Fuji, where police found so many bodies during the peak years of the late 1990s—many of them disgraced businessmen hanging from trees or, having overdosed, lying on the forest floor—that nearby villages ran out of space to store the remains. The bridge is a fabled span above shark-infested waters and the site of some thirteen hundred suicides since its opening in 1937.

But I'm not thinking of Beachy Head's notoriety as I lie on my belly. I'm thinking of my wife and daughter, mother and father, who, if they saw me now, would be horrified. Enough of this foolishness. Slowly, I retreat to terra firma. It's time to meet the Higgses, my hosts in the farmhouse.

WHEN I BOOKED MY STAY at Black Robin Farm, I envisioned an inn-like place where guests were taken in. Yes, I'd be lodging in my own bungalow, but in the evenings, I and the other guests would leave our converted chicken coops to gather in the main farmhouse, where Bob and Jane Higgs would ply us with hot toddies and inquire about our travels. In a few short days, I'd become as familiar to my hosts as a pair of old Wellingtons, someone whose lap might even be entrusted with a junior Higgs during story time.

In fact, the Higgses are as accessible as jungle warlords. A short ways past the farmhouse front door, I step off the driveway and pass through an ivy-covered archway into a damp, lattice-roofed patio filled with monstrous potted plants and cages of anxious parrots. I slip past them as quietly as I can and come to a door that yields with a firm push, releasing warm air and the pulpy smell of lint. I step inside. A washing machine swishes and gurgles alongside the tumble and hum of a dryer. I knock on a door marked PRIVATE. Seconds later, the barn-wood floor tremors. The burgundy curtain covering the door's glass window parts and closes, briefly exposing an unsmiling face. The door swings open.

"Yes?"

Jane Higgs stands back from the doorway. Her cheeks are flushed, her mouth shut tight. I buck myself up and tell her who I am and when I arrived, the words pushed along by the air of her impatience. She briskly walks away and returns with a key. "Is that all, then?"

"How do I turn on the heat in my bungalow?"

"There's a timer on the kitchen wall. You set the tabs around the time you want the heat on."

I nod, it seems to me, unconvincingly. I have the mechanical aptitude of a tree stump. If left to my own devices, I'll spend a few mindless minutes moving around the different-colored tabs until I break one of them in frustration. I consider asking Jane Higgs if she can show me how to set the timer, but, noticing the choke hold she has on her dishrag, I absurdly thank her and slink off to my bungalow, fearing the worst.

Surprisingly, the timer gives up its secrets without a fight, and soon I'm planted in front of the television, leftover airport sandwich in hand, wallowing in heat.

That evening I return to the farmhouse. The gale is now a whisper. I pad across the concrete patio into a haze of light, the parrots eyeing me distrustfully through the bars of their chilly cells. I glance at the brightly lit window opposite the cages and stop. Jane Higgs stands over the kitchen sink, sleeves rolled, arms working furiously. Her face is still flushed, as though years of cold winds and blood-boiling annoyances have permanently left their mark. She looks lonely and unknowable, like a character in an Edward Hopper painting.

I continue on to the laundry. Inside, cracks of light fringe the burgundy curtain drawn across the door to the Higgses' living quarters. I flick on the light switch and step toward the pay phone, another hurdle in the Black Robin Farm obstacle course, and one I had better clear: my wife is expecting a call in two minutes. But the phone won't cooperate. I forget America's country code. I get the wrong operator. And then beepings, clicks, and silence. I place the receiver back in its cradle and stare at the burgundy curtain. I have no choice. I step up to the Higgses' door and, with a few irretrievable knocks on the glass, cross the Maginot Line. Seconds later, the barn-wood floor trembles, the curtain parts, and Jane Higgs peers through the window, her Old Testament gaze piercing my trespassing self.

She stands impatiently in the doorway, a stone-colored apron wrapped tightly around her ample hips. "Yes?"

"I'm sorry for bothering you, but I'm having trouble making an international call."

Her mouth tightens a notch. She steps into the laundry and takes the matter into her own hands. "Collect?"

"Yes."

"Number?"

IN BED THAT NIGHT, I replay my encounters with Jane Higgs until I'm able to assimilate them. My vision of Black Robin Farm was a delusion compounded of the materials of my experience and literary imagination. From a distance of three thousand miles, I saw the alien term "self-catering" through the lens of "bed-and-breakfast," that quintessentially New England institution where lodgers are treated like houseguests. Sometimes I envisioned a quaint country inn on a Hardyesque heath, a refuge for a tired and hungry traveler. Had I given the designation some thought, I might have guessed that underlying a specific material *arrangement,* whereby guests provide their own bath towels and cook their own meals, was a fend-for-yourself *mentality.* The advertisement for Black Robin Farm—Beachy Head's only self-catering establishment, offering "self-contained bungalows in peaceful position on working farm"—was a thinly veiled declaration of independence. The Higgses would ride their horses, muck their stalls, and feed their sheep, and if their lodgers had any niggling requests, well, good luck.

And that's how it is. With rooms and machinery to maintain, two children to raise, and sheep to husband, the Higgses are, like a rare bird, caught only in glimpses. They zoom from chore to chore in a motorized cart, bouncing and careening like characters in a cartoon chase. On the one occasion I catch Bob footing it, we have a conversation. He says that shortly after becoming the farm's tenants in 1987, they converted two chicken coops into the four bungalows and began filling them with humans, while continuing to sell mutton to French restaurants. He says, too, that lambing season is about to begin, which explains why he tells me all this in front of a pen crammed with baa-ing sheep. When I mention the cliffs, Higgs's eyes shift beneath the brim of his wool beret. "Don't pay much attention to what goes on over there," he says, throwing a bag of feed over his shoulder. He unlatches the gate and parts the milling throng.

The solitary life of the single self-caterer turns out to be not so bad. I spend cocktail hour on the back stoop of the bungalow, watching rabbits scamper across the fields and crows forage on freshly tilled furrows. On clear days, the sinking sun charges the entire landscape, fringing the backlit farmhouses in an orange glow, turning the sea to diamonds and the grazing sheep to clusters of radiant dots. Never far away is the thought that if the Eastbourne Borough Council hadn't purchased the land some seventy-five years ago, I might be gazing across forty-one hundred acres of condominiums and parking lots.

One evening I imagine the Downs' different historical faces: a dense forest filled with bears, wolves, and wild boars hunted by nomadic tribesmen; a lightly wooded land of luxurious Roman villas and vineyards; an open land of French abbeys and castles; a scarred land dotted with radar trucks and downed fighter planes; and now a pristine land framing Jane Higgs and her daughter on horseback. As I watch, I begin to see Jane Higgs as the inhabitant of a place rather than as the owner of a business, and I reconsider her chilliness in this light. Is it the wariness of the provincial? Or a more unsettling thought—suppose she was in my bungalow and saw the suicide books piled on the kitchen table.

Another evening I watch a tractor crawl across a plowed field just beyond the hill that separates Black Robin Farm from Bullock Down Farm, the home of Beachy Head's oldest family, the Williamses. It was the senior Williams who, during a lull in German bombing in 1942, unloaded two cart horses, forty dairy shorthorns, and numerous calves off boxcars at the train station—the last complete farm stock to arrive at Eastbourne by train—then shepherded them down the streets of the town, his wife leading the procession in an old pickup loaded with milking churns and buckets, toward their farm in Beachy Head. Their son, Edgar, eventually took over the farm, then took on a sideline: recovering the bodies of Beachy Head suicides. Now retired from the coast guard's cliff team, Edgar, I was sure, had stories to tell.

On a warm spring evening, I pay Edgar Williams a visit, not knowing at the time what I subsequently learned from a former coast guard colleague: he's "a very private man who doesn't suffer fools gladly." A light knock on the screen door of his farmhouse triggers vague stirrings and muffled footfalls. The main door opens, and the fatty smell of cooked meat drifts across the threshold. A short, bald man stands on the other side of the screen door, eyeing me suspiciously.

I introduce myself and explain that I'm investigating the Beachy Head suicides. I ask if he'd be willing to talk about his experiences as a member of the coast guard's cliff team.

If my sudden appearance at his door has made him uncomfortable, my intentions make him even more so. Saying I was "investigating" the suicides probably didn't help matters; Williams has the look of a man who's about to take the Fifth. His gaze is disarmingly timid—and steady. "I've seen some pretty bad things on the cliff face that I'd rather not talk about." He pauses. "Can't, really. There's the Official Secrets Act. So let's just forget it."

And I do. Under that mossy voice lies stone. He will never budge. I thank him for his time and head off into the dusk, looking back once to see Williams still standing behind the screen door, his figure dark and motionless in a spray of porch light.

———

BY THE END OF MY FIRST WEEK in Beachy Head, I begin to feel thwarted by a conspiracy of silence. Bob Higgs says he doesn't pay attention to the suicides. Edgar Williams wants to forget them. Publican Steve can't talk about them. What should I have expected? Suicide is anathema and wariness the natural inheritance of a people long isolated, embattled, and policed. Long ago Sussex was cut off from the rest of England by the Weald, a stretch of forest just north of the South Downs, penetrable only by a few clay roads that were often so mucky that it could take upward of two years to transport a load of pig iron from the Beachy Head foundries to London. To the south lay the Channel, long a passageway for foreign invaders as well as for shady smugglers, whose pursuers were often thwarted by the willful ignorance of Beachy Headers who regarded "the trade" not as dishonest work but as a reasonable response to unreasonable taxation. So the local gentry left their stable doors unfastened at night and returned in the morning to find several spent horses and a keg of spirits or some other token of the smugglers' appreciation. Children were brought up to see and hear as little as possible, lest they inadvertantly pass along useful information to the Preventive Man. The rule of thumb, according to Kipling, was to "watch the wall, my darling, while the gentlemen go by."

So this is what I'm up against: a native leeriness. My response is to hole up in my bungalow for two days and binge on reality shows and packaged doughnuts, when I'm not scavenging the local newspapers for the latest Beachy Head news. One item catches my attention: the imminent move inland of Belle Tout, one of Beachy Head's two lighthouses. A massive cliff fall left the centuries-old lighthouse feet from the edge, and engineers are working around the clock to save it. What makes the story even more compelling is that Belle Tout is someone's home, the only lighthouse in England in private residence.

I EMERGE FROM MY BRICK HOLE on a cloudy Friday morning and head for the coast road. It's a half mile to Edgar Williams's farm and a half mile more to the pub, where I stop for a cup of coffee before heading west across the cliff top to Belle Tout.

About a mile past the pub, I pass a cluster of charming cottages situated on the other side of the coast road. Surrounded by farms on three sides, the modest estate is the black sheep of the neighborhood, the home, I later learn, of Roger Charlwood, a jeweler, bird-watcher, and man of independent means. On this morning, sitting with his wife and grown children in lawn chairs, watching the grandkids romp around the front yard, he seems to be just another patriarch enjoying the company of his progeny.

But I know after reading numerous police reports of Beachy Head suicides that mornings at Hodcombe, as Charlwood's estate is known, have not always been so pleasant. Sixteen months earlier, Charlwood was puttering around his garden on a sunny July morning when something on the cliff top caught his eye: a young man crouched behind a clump of gorse. When Charlwood looked again ten minutes later and saw that the man was still there, he took more notice. The man kept getting up, walking around a bit, and sitting down again. Charlwood didn't know that marital difficulties had driven the man to overdose on pills five years before, or that he'd had two stays in a psychiatric hospital after his divorce a year earlier. All Charlwood knew was what he saw: a young man in dark trousers and a pale-colored shirt acting strangely.

Having lived in Beachy Head for nearly thirty years, Roger Charlwood was well aware of the cliff's allure. He told Deputy Downland Ranger Don Ellis, who was mowing grass nearby, that a man was acting suspiciously on the cliff top across from Hodcombe. Ellis instructed Charlwood to call the police while he kept an eye out. As Ellis continued mowing, he saw a person walking toward the cliff edge about a quarter mile away. Because the sun was in his eyes, he couldn't tell if it was a man or a woman. He watched the person look over the cliff edge, turn away, and sit down on the grass. As he called the police on his cell phone, he looked up and saw the person disappear over the cliff. Minutes later, Ellis joined the police at the edge. They all assumed that the person who had jumped was the man reported by Roger Charlwood.

But that man was still alive, sitting on a hill two hundred yards west and being watched closely from far below by Charlwood, as his wife headed toward the cliffs to set the police straight. She pointed out the man's location. The police proceeded down a steep slope and up another. Charlwood, from his front-lawn perspective, saw the man get up as the police approached, walk east over the brow of the hill, and disappear from view. The police, from their hilltop view, saw the man striding toward the cliffs, sit down, and push himself over the edge.

Both bodies were recovered later that day. The person Don Ellis observed jumping was sixty-six-year-old Doris Haffenden, who just happened to choose the same time and place of death as twenty-five-year-old Allen Talbot, the man in the bushes.

Charlwood has other stories, I'm sure, but I'm not about to crash the family gathering of a man who's been known to give the Downs rangers an earful when they park their vehicles on his property. And Edgar Williams's rebuff is still fresh in my mind. The closest I ever get to Charlwood is at his jewelry store in downtown Eastbourne, where I watch a silver-haired man of proprietary air standing behind a glass display, explaining the virtues of a ring held primly between his thumb and forefinger.

I keep walking. Only half a mile to go, but the voluptuous terrain will make it seem twice that. I disappear into a deep fold, braking all the way down, panting all the way up, and when I emerge onto the crest of the next swell, I do it again, emerging this time on a brief but blessed stretch of flatland. An Asian family approaches as I stand with my hands on my hips, trying to affect a leisurely air, when I would like nothing better than to double over and suck wind. The father smiles broadly at me. Is he being friendly, or is he laughing? Whatever, the smile is enough to get me moving again—until I come to a bend of road at the base of a mountainous hill. Here the coast road swerves dangerously close to the cliff edge. A dirt embankment hems the curve, blocking the path of suicidal drivers.

A narrow access road branches off the bend, running up the steep slope and parallel to the cliff edge thirty feet away. Here I go again. I step onto the rutted asphalt drive and trudge up it, uttering labored greetings to passing tourists and pondering how best to approach the owner of Belle Tout, if he's even there. Do I tell him I'm a teacher? A journalist? A writer? Or do I just explain what I'm doing and let him assume the rest?

Soon I hear the distant clatter of jackhammers and the chug of compressors. Then a structure resembling a large cinder block abutting a runty, cork-shaped tower comes into view. This is what all the fuss is about? From the kitchen window of my bungalow, Belle Tout has a hazy mystique, but up close it's plain ugly. At the top of the hill, clumps of camera-toting tourists wander outside a work site encircled by bright orange perimeter fencing.

I find a spot by the fence and watch men in yellow hard hats and chalk-coated coveralls taking measurements around the excavated foundation, as burly men in T-shirts cart away wheelbarrows of rubble. A man carrying a clipboard scurries down the steps of a construction trailer. The sense of urgency that permeates the site is understandable. In just five days, thousands of tourists and hundreds of reporters and photographers from all over the world hope to watch the lighthouse glide down an aisle of greased tracks onto a massive concrete slab fifty-five feet away, where it will begin the next stage of its curious life.

BELLE TOUT WAS BORN of the largesse of "Mad" Jack Fuller, a local squire dubbed "the Hippopotamus" for his Falstaffian girth. But he was best known as a "creator of follies," one of which was the Sugarloaf, a thirty-five-foot-tall conical stone structure erected in a meadow near Fuller's home. Legend has it that Mad Jack made a bet with his mates that he could see a certain church spire from his home a mile away. When he discovered that he couldn't, he had workmen construct the Sugarloaf, hoping his cronies would mistake it for the church's steeple. They didn't, but 190 years later, the Sugarloaf still stands.

Then there was Belle Tout. Derived from "Bel," the name of an early pagan deity, and "Toot," Saxon for "lookout," Belle Tout was Fuller's answer to centuries of Beachy Head shipwrecks. But after its maiden lighting in the fall of 1834, the granite lighthouse failed as a lookout; the cliff edge cut off the beam as ships entered the danger zone, the result of Belle Tout's stubby size and ill-conceived placement one hundred feet inland.

Belle Tout lay fallow until a distinguished neurologist bought it in 1923. Assured by a geologist that the lighthouse wouldn't topple into the sea during his lifetime, the doctor proceded to renovate his new home, adding terraced gardens and a sun lounge, among other amenities. Twenty years later, the army requisitioned the lighthouse, and Canadian troops stationed on the Downs used Belle Tout for target practice, reducing the lookout to a pitted hulk for which the doctor was modestly compensated.

After the war, the locals weren't sure what to do with Belle Tout. Some proposed demolishing it; others suggested converting it into a youth hostel. They never could agree, so the lighthouse lay derelict and forgotten, its crumbling exterior and bombshell-littered garden sealed off from the public.

It was finally purchased and restored in 1955 by a couple from London, and it changed hands twice more over the next forty-one years. An author bought it in 1980 and sold it six years later to the BBC, who thought it the perfect place to film a popular sit-com. Set builders transformed the lighthouse into a timber-boarded "lighthouse love nest," complete with new lantern and swimming pool.

In the fall of 1996, Belle Tout was again for sale, and Mark and Louise Roberts were eager to buy it. Mark, a native Australian, had been so taken by England during a visit ten years earlier that he moved to London, finding a job as a food and beverage manager for a catering establishment. There he fell in love with a comely chef named Louise; after buying their own pub in Eastbourne, they fell in love with Beachy Head. So when they saw the real estate advertisement for a lighthouse in Beachy Head with "four double bedrooms, open-plan living area with olive wood floor, two garages, and walled garden," they jumped on it. The listing didn't mention that the lighthouse was fifteen feet from the edge of a crumbling 345-foot chalk cliff.

Some of their friends thought they were daft to buy Belle Tout. Their first few weeks in the lighthouse weren't reassuring. As winter storms battered the coast, Mark and Louise began each morning by anxiously checking for signs of cliff erosion outside their living room window. As nerve-racking as those initial weeks were, living on the edge was, for Mark at least, part of Belle Tout's attraction. "Beachy Head is so dramatic," he said, "and I think probably living so close to the cliff in a way summarizes the whole of Beachy Head and the community that lives here."

Still, they knew they'd have to move the lighthouse inland, a process that was already under way when, lying in bed on a clear January morning, they heard a terrifying rumbling and felt Belle Tout shake.

Three miles away, Eastbourne lifeboat crew members saw a section of cliff face the length of two football fields topple into the sea. The massive cliff fall, one of the largest losses of British coastline in living memory, spilled upward of a hundred thousand tons of rock smack down onto the stoop of Beachy Head's other lighthouse, two hundred feet out to sea, and left Belle Tout a mere six feet from the cliff edge.

Louise and Mark didn't know this at the time; they were too frantic to look outside the living room window. Louise, eight months pregnant, gathered their young daughter, and the three of them drove to the town hall. There, a shaken Mark tried turning in their house keys to an Eastbourne council member. He had had enough of Belle Tout and its drama. But Louise stopped him.

AFTER THE CLIFF FALL, Roberts asked the workers to go "just that little bit faster." They appear to be doing just that. The hard hats continue to confer, measure, dump, and hammer as if their lives are on the line, which, in a sense, they are. The man with the clipboard struts toward the construction trailer, his eyes scanning the onlookers as if coolly calculating our numbers.

I call across the perimeter fence, "Is Mark Roberts here?"

The man with the clipboard turns. His unshaven face looks ghostly in the gathering mist. He walks over to the fence. I explain that I'm a writer from America and would like to talk to Roberts about the move. As I speak, I study his bookishly handsome face, looking for signs of skepticism, but there are none. "Let me see if I can ring him." He retreats into the trailer, and when he emerges minutes later, he tells me that Roberts will be here shortly.

Some thirty minutes later, a red sports car comes to an abrupt halt just outside the construction site. Out springs a prematurely balding man in a brightly colored sweater, holding a cell phone to his ear. He leans back against the car and speaks with his eyes to the ground, his free hand covering his free ear when it isn't wiping his nose with a handkerchief. His words, muffled by machinery and mist, are indecipherable, but their cadence and tone exude jaunty self-assurance.

When he's done talking, I walk over and introduce myself. He apologizes for not arriving sooner; he says he's been in bed the last two days with the flu. His watery pool-blue eyes turn toward the work site. He shakes his head. "Don't ever buy a lighthouse."

I hadn't planned to. And if I did, I would never move it. I know all about Roberts's two-and-half-year quest to save his home: the bureaucratic red tape and failed funding bids; the cliff fall that has them living out of a suitcase; the race against time. A wet winter has destabilized the cliff even further: the lighthouse could fall at any moment. And scores of dignitaries have planned to attend the move. Wednesday is Eastbourne's day to shine. If Belle Tout isn't ready to walk, it will be a public embarrassment.

Roberts asks if I'd like to take a tour of the work site, and we're off. He leads me toward the excavated foundation, nimbly navigating the ruts and rubble. He's greeted by the man with the clipboard, who assures him that they will be ready by Wednesday. Roberts nods approvingly.

He hikes up his slacks and crouches and peers under the lighthouse, which is elevated about three feet by objects that resemble giant salt shakers. Roberts points at one of them. "Eighteen jacks support the lighthouse. They'll raise it onto four greased steel tracks, and then those hydraulic rams over there will push it one meter at a time to the new foundation down there." He turns and gestures inland to a huge concrete platform. "It is, of course, a very delicate operation. Six hydraulic rams exerting sixty tons of force moving in two different directions is a cliff fall waiting to happen."

The work site energizes Roberts. He abruptly raises himself and glances around at the men and machines that his money and vision have brought together. There's something surreal about the scene, as if the mist were scrim, the workers scurrying stagehands, and Roberts the proud producer. He explains that Belle Tout sits on the remains of a Roman hill fort and that archaeologists love to sniff around here. One dig yielded a trove of prehistoric earthenware. A few years back, a cliff fall exposed a four-thousand-year-old well shaft. And just a few days ago, excavators found old bullet shells under the subflooring.

I listen intently, and Roberts seems to feed off my interest. He wants to show me more. He assumes, no doubt, that I'm another foreign journalist reporting on the move, and as we head toward the new foundation, I feel like an imposter. Soon I'm standing on the concrete floor of what will be the Robertses' new bedroom, beneath a concrete slab thick enough to support the second floor of an 850-ton lighthouse, not to mention heavy enough to reduce Roberts and me to human sandwich spread should the cliff top give way and the pillars around us collapse. Roberts's imagination takes a different flight. He describes the thrill of reading in the lantern room during a sunset or storm. He points to a rectangular opening in the wall that will give them a "brilliant" view of the Downs from their bed, and describes their plan for a bed-and-breakfast.

It seems like a perfectly realized vision—assuming all goes well on Wednesday—and one that's elicited as much head scratching among the locals as excitement, because they aren't quite sure what to think of Roberts. He's an urbane Aussie living among Sussex farmers (one local derisively referred to him as "a self-proclaimed lord of the manor, one of our Australian colonial chappies"). Some believe he's angling to become mayor and resent that he tried to secure public monies and appeal to local pride to save a personal investment.

But in four days, some of the same people who impugn Roberts will toast the fruits of his labor. He seems to know this. Looking out the rectangular opening at the distant fields of Cornish Farm, the lush green broken by a rambling flint wall built by French prisoners of war in the time of Napoleon, he exudes the calmness of one deeply in his element. An unabashed romantic, he finds himself on a dreary Friday morning in a room with a view, near the edge of an historic cliff, on top of the world.

I, on the other hand, am a practical man grounded in reality. I'm a teacher trying to adopt the bulldog posture of an investigative journalist and failing miserably. But no more. I feel a twinge of pity, listening to Roberts describe the floor plan of his new home, because I know I'm about to sucker punch my unsuspecting host. There is no way to segue from interior design to suicide, no tone or look I could muster to soften the blow. I ask if he's ever seen any suspicious people hanging around the lighthouse.

Roberts turns from his future bedroom window. His narrowing eyes bore into mine, as if I were some new person, some sudden harsh light he's trying to adjust to. "What do you mean?"

"People who may be suicidal."

"That's just not part of our life here. It's not what Beachy Head is about." He swipes his nose with his handkerchief and turns the conversation back to the renovations and the toll the move has taken on him and his family, but the damage has been done.

In the construction trailer, Roberts hangs our hard hats near a desk strewn with blueprints. A filmy window overlooks Belle Tout, and Roberts blocks most of it. "What brings you to Beachy Head?"

It's the question I've been waiting for but still feel unprepared to answer. Roberts crosses his arms as a jackhammer outside resumes its chatter. I explain that I'm interested in how the various groups in and around Beachy Head—the residents of Beachy Head, the cabdrivers, the Beachy Head pub employees, the local Samaritans, the coast guard and police—work together to deal with a community problem.

"I think you're wrong there. There's no such 'community.' The police and coast guard aren't part of the community up here. They like to talk up the suicides, which makes it seem worse than it really is, but the people up here don't talk about them. Have you seen Brian Johnson? I'd be surprised if he talked to you. Mr. Charlwood isn't going to talk to you, Edgar Williams isn't going to talk to you, the Higgses aren't going to talk to you, because there's nothing to talk about. Millions of people visit here every year, and how many kill themselves? Ten? Twenty? More people are killed in New York City in a day. Go to New York."

"But New York City isn't a beautiful place. Beachy Head is interesting because it's tragic *and* beautiful." Then, as if to apologize for my ardor, I offer a more humble explanation. I'm flying by the seat of my pants toward some unknown destination, I say, because it's just something I have to do.

That he seems to understand. His face relaxes. "It *is* a beautiful place. There are orchids here that you won't find too many other places." Burnt tip, fly, frog, early purple, bee: he recites them with a tenderness usually reserved for the names of one's children. "The orchids, the sunsets, the Downs—that's what Beachy Head's about."

I nod out of respect for Roberts, whose view of Beachy Head seems nobler than mine. He offers me a lift into town. Minutes later, we're zooming along the coast road, and I'm asking Roberts about the orchids and the history of Belle Tout and when they expect to open their bed-and-breakfast. And all the way to Eastbourne, he doesn't stop talking.

On Wednesday I join thousands of camera-happy locals and tourists to watch the lighthouse slide to its new location. The move is not without incident. Five hours after the first push, operations are briefly suspended as bomb disposal experts blow up a World War II bombshell found near the cliff edge. Later, a security person assigned to guard BBC satellite dishes on the cliff top is found dead in a camper van, the victim of an apparent gas leak.

WEST OF BELLE TOUT, the cliff top slopes three quarters of a mile to near sea level before rising again. Nestled in the fold, marking the western end of Beachy Head, lies the ramshackle hamlet of Birling Gap.

Venetian sailors called Beachy Head Caput Doble, the Devil's Headland, because its rocky foreshore ripped the hulls of vessels caught in the pull of its unpredictable currents. More than seventy shipwrecks are recorded at Beachy Head, and most of them occurred near Birling Gap, whose relatively modest cliff face made her a favorite landing place. Few of them were as calamitous as the demise of a Spanish galleon in 1747. In the mad grab for exquisite velvets, gold laces, quicksilver, "spiritous liquors," and other cargo, thirty Spanish sailors allegedly drowned. Others drank themselves to death. One was shot.

More often than not, the local police or militia were dispatched to the scene of a wreck before looters could stuff their pockets, but even they were known to help themselves. When a homeward-bound Swedish galliot loaded with Bordeaux came to grief in 1796, Eastbourne soldiers caught the wine in their hats and shoes as they unloaded the seeping barrels.

The morning after the move of Belle Tout, a cold rain falls across the dawn-dark cliff top, loosening my imagination. Wisps of fog resolve into ghostly smugglers. Magwitches lurk behind every gorse bush. From the nearest hilltop, Birling Gap is downright creepy. The hamlet's lone hotel, a gloomy ranch, brings to mind Norman Bates's infamous establishment; the coast guard cottage complex, a blocky monolith with multiple chimneys and closely spaced windows, looks disturbingly institutional, like an old French prison or asylum. The parking lot between is empty except for a red sedan parked alongside a fenced-off section of cliff top. Brian Johnson? I'm convinced it is when I finally reach the parking lot and see what's beyond the fence: stacks of lobster pots, plastic buckets filled with ropes and buoys, a rusted winch, its taut cable running toward the cliff edge.

An elderly man sits inside the idling Renault, staring at the sea. As I approach the passenger-side window, Mark Roberts's prediction that Brian Johnson won't talk to me is very much on my mind. He was right about the other locals, and I expect him to be right about this one. I also expect Johnson to be startled by the presence of an unshaven, insensibly dressed (no raincoat) stranger knocking on his car window while the rest of the world is sleeping. But his face turns slowly and shows no concern. He leans over and rolls down his window. He says he'd be glad to talk about Beachy Head and invites me into the car.

He wears a tight-fitting sweatjacket with rips along the arms and an auto-racing insignia on the chest. The brim of his wool cap hides the tangled white nets of his eyebrows until he lifts his head and casts his crinkled eyes on my face. "So what do you want to know about Beachy Head?"

For the next twenty minutes, Johnson tells his story while staring at the whitecapped sea through a rain-streaked windshield. He comes from a long line of boaters on his mother's side: seven Erridges worked for the Eastbourne Lifeboat at one point, and his great-grandfather and grandfather were part of one of the most famous ship rescues in Eastbourne's history.

"I suppose you've heard about the *New Brunswick*."

I had. Over a century ago, a 480-ton Norwegian barque, its sails torn by a southwesterly gale, its anchor dragging, was about to run aground near Belle Tout. Crew members at the Eastbourne Lifeboat station saw the distress signals but couldn't launch the lifeboat into the storm. So they decided to launch from Birling Gap and ride with the wind. It didn't matter that Birling Gap didn't have its own lifeboat. Two hundred volunteers pulled the Eastbourne lifeboat on a wheeled carriage for half a mile over roads and fields before a hastily assembled team of horses took over, towing it the remaining five miles to Birling Gap. There, the crew rigged a slipway from timber and launched the lifeboat near Johnson's present base of operations. An hour later, the lifeboat pulled alongside the *New Brunswick* and took the crew aboard.

Johnson nods at the memory. "My great-grandfather and grandfather were on the tug that brought the *New Brunswick* to port."

He recalls fishing these waters with his grandfather, who owned a net shop in Eastbourne. After marrying a native of Birling Gap, Johnson continued to fish here for thirty-four years while working for the Eastbourne Water Company. Now retired, he can fish two or three hours a day—lobster, primarily, along with some crab, Dover sole, and sea bass, all of which he sells to an Eastbourne wholesaler. "Looks like I won't be going out this morning, though."

Johnson has learned not to test the waters, ever since an angry wave flipped his boat and trapped him beneath it. The sea has taken six of his boat ramps, and soon it will take his storage area. Despite townspeople's petitions for a seawall, Johnson doubts it will ever be erected. A British newspaper recently named Birling Gap one of the ten most beautiful areas of vanishing countryside in the world, but its proprietor, the National Trust, is apparently content to let nature take its course.

"It's really a job for a younger person," Johnson says, turning to me. "You can make a living at it, but only if you're fit enough to put in long hours." It's the sort of thing one would not expect a proud man to tell a stranger. He shifts in his seat, then turns back to the sea. His eyes wander the surface as if casting for an answer. "You know, I have five grandchildren, and none are interested in fishing."

There's an awkward silence. I'm reluctant to turn the conversation from his grandchildren to suicide, but I do anyway. "I've heard about Beachy Head's reputation for suicides. Have you ever seen a suicidal person on the cliff top or discovered a body?"

He shakes his head, seemingly unfazed by the question. "No, but in the seventies, I was an auxiliary coast guard. Saw my first helicopter rescue. Tide come in, trapped two people against the cliff face." He pauses. "No, I was involved in two or three rescues, but none were suicides."

And that is that. I'm sure that Johnson would answer other questions about the suicides, but I can't bring myself to ask. I'm tired of dishonest conversations—of showing interest in a man's home or livelihood before ambushing him with self-serving questions. Perhaps, too, I'm choosing to forget the reputation of a place I'm growing to love. When you fall for a woman with a history, you don't ask questions.

———

LATER ON, after I've spent more time traipsing around Beachy Head, a grieving husband of a woman who recently jumped off the cliffs tells me, "There's a sort of leprosy that goes with suicide that is added to death. I'm not saying people cross the road when they see you coming, but there is that added element." I know the feeling. I'm the carrier of a potentially harmful curiosity. I could earn a well-intentioned pub employee a reprimand or put an innocent farmer in violation of the Official Secrets Act. So they watch what they say.

For Bob Higgs and Mark Roberts, discussing the suicides is perhaps more unpleasant than unwise. They disapprove of suicide or resent the shadow it casts upon their home. Or maybe, for the native Beachy Headers, at least, suicide touches a national sore spot, as the Holocaust does for Germans. Self-destruction, after all, was once considered a British propensity. "It is a melancholy consideration," wrote the eighteenth-century Methodist preacher John Wesley, "that there is no country in Europe, or perhaps in the habitable world, where the horrid crime of self-murder is so common as it is in England." French political philosopher Baron de Montesquieu attributed the English yen for self-destruction to "a distemper," which some blamed on England's gloomy weather.

Maybe the reluctance to talk about the suicides is more than a matter of practical concern, moral censure, local pride, or national shame. The added element may be fear. "There is," wrote psychoanalyst Karl Menninger, "a little murder and a little suicide dwelling in everybody's heart."

Maybe the residents of Beachy Head are running not so much from me but from themselves.

3

Uncharted Territory

The lobby of the Eastbourne police station is empty and the front desk vacant. Through the dimpled glass of his office door, Eastbourne's coroner's officer is a blur, his voice a smudge of sound. Then there is silence. I knock on the door, which bears in small black letters the disquieting title ALIENS CLERK, and the blur moves slowly toward it, gradually sharpening into a silhouette, then becoming a grand-fatherly man framed by the open doorway. He wears a white dress shirt open at the collar and pulling at the stomach. His thinning silver hair bears the fresh tracks of a comb, his kindly face the markings of a too-close shave. He looks at me inquiringly, his eyebrows slightly raised, as if waiting for me to intro-duce myself. When I do, he smiles warmly and extends a hand. "Mick Davey." He motions me into a room the size of a walk-in closet. An outdated computer sits on a metal cart in front of a window covered by a closed blind. A bulletin board filled with scribbled messages takes up part of one wall; underneath lies an open appointment book on a barren desktop. As offices go, it's about as unassuming as one can get.

"Here they are," Davey says, dispensing with the pleasantries and pointing to a foot-tall stack of documents on the corner of a wooden table. "Hope you find what you're looking for." He reaches for the blue blazer on the back of his desk chair and drapes it over his forearm. "I'll be in court most of the day. Be back 'round four or so and will be happy to answer any questions then."

As Davey consults his appointment book, I sit down at the table and consider the paper heap, which is divided at intervals by black metal fasteners. After having seen Davey quoted in several articles about Beachy Head, I figured he might be willing to meet with me. When, a few months before my visit, I wrote to him asking to read the reports, I didn't expect him to say yes. Then I wondered if he'd follow through. Now I can't quite believe they're here and that I'm about to read them. I've always been drawn to darkness—to Dostoyevsky, Hopper, desolate landscapes, and the double lives of crooked CEOs, pedophiliac priests, and treasonous CIA agents. I gawk at disturbing movie scenes while others hide their eyes, and I prefer truthful endings to happy ones. For the most part, I've indulged these appetites without apology. My dark side is like a hyperactive child whose behavior has always fallen within the acceptable range of "boys will be boys." But here in Davey's office, I can't help feeling that I'm about to cross into territory that is harder to defend.

There's a light tap at the door. Davey quickly closes his appointment book and heads for the door. A hunched, silver-haired woman propped up by a cane shuffles in. Her heavy fur overcoat contradicts her shriveled face; coatless, she's as scrawny as a shaved Persian cat. Her rheumy eyes bore into Davey.

"I'm a friend of Emily's," she says curtly, news that Davey greets with a pronounced swallow. He asks if she'd like to sit. She refuses. Her cane wavers in her shaky hand.

"Is it true," she says, "that the police were in Emily's flat several days before her death?"

"Yes," Davey says. "A neighbor called to complain about the smell."

"And you saw her?"

"Yes."

"How did she seem?"

"She didn't look well. She'd been drinking."

"Did it *occur* to you that she may have needed help?"

Davey shakes his head. He can barely contain his impatience. "She didn't *want* help. If she wanted help, she would have asked for it. She was going to do what she was going to do."

For several minutes more, Davey and the woman go back and forth, getting nowhere. In the heat of emotion, they seem to forget I'm there. I try to get started on the reports, but concentrating is impossible.

After the woman leaves, Davey shakes his head and apologizes. He explains that the old woman's friend drank herself to death. "Her flat was absolutely wretched: cat urine, feces, rotting food, decomposing flesh." He shivers and scrunches up his nose. Then, abruptly, he says he really must be going, wishes me luck, and rushes out the door.

Finally, I'm alone with the sudden-death reports. I take one from the top of the stack and scan the cover page all the way down to the scrawled verdict: "Killed himself." I remove the metal fastener and begin to read the quarter-inch-thick document, chronicling the death of a thirty-one-year-old nursing home assistant who'd been deeply depressed for twenty years and had attempted suicide on a number of previous occasions.

Over the next eight hours, I read a year's worth of Beachy Head deaths, twenty-six in all, all but one a suicide. I read witness statements from loved ones, coast guard officers, police constables, cabdrivers, bartenders, and tourists; I read pathologists' reports, suicide notes, psychiatric evaluations, and police radio logs; I stare at the police photograph of a young man lying on the beach, his head flattened, his forehead bulging grotesquely. I turn the pages rapaciously, feasting on the misery of strangers. When all the reports are picked clean, I slump in my chair, glutted and blurry-eyed.

The door opens. It's Davey. He drapes his sport coat over the back of his desk chair and lets out a long sigh, as if he's momentarily forgotten I'm there. He asks if I found everything I needed. Yes, I say, though I'm not exactly sure what it is I needed.

"Good." He turns his chair to face me. His voice is soft and soothing. "Why don't we have a talk, then."

He says he's been a coroner's officer for the last twenty-four years and, by his estimate, investigates 820 deaths a year (and responds to God knows how many complaints like the old lady's). He discusses his various duties: visiting the scene of death to collect personal effects and arrange for the removal of the body; delivering the bad news to family members; witnessing the identification of the body at the morgue; taking depositions and preparing sudden-death reports; officiating at the inquest.

"How have you lasted?"

He laughs, looking away, briefly. "It's horrible to say, but you get used to it after a while." He pauses. "Except the death of a child. I *am* still affected by the death of a child."

He says he plans to retire in three years and do nothing,

which is what I'm thinking I'd like to do at this moment. We've both had enough of the Eastbourne police station for one day. It's getting late, and we agree to continue our conversation another day. As Davey escorts me to the door, he remembers that two Beachy Head inquests are scheduled for next Monday and invites me to attend.

AMONG GABLED VICTORIAN TOWNHOUSES in downtown Eastbourne loom the Law Courts, a postwar block of concrete hollowed into hearing and waiting rooms. In Hearing Room No. 3, three newspaper reporters, a police constable, a thin man with neatly parted hair, and two somber blond women in smart business suits rise as Coroner's Officer Michael Davey announces Eastbourne's coroner.

I await David Wadman's entrance with groupie-like anticipation. I read some of Wadman's closing statements in the newspaper reports of the inquests and was struck by their grandiloquence. Unlike the dry summations of his colleagues, Wadman's tended toward the melodramatic or meditative. A man didn't drive to Beachy Head and jump off the cliffs; he "deliberately drove to Beachy Head and then launched himself into the void onto the rocks below." An heiress didn't simply drive her car over the edge; she "left the road, went down a steep slope over something like three hundred yards, and went straight over the cliff." The picture painted is not of a depressed man but of "an unhappy man who found difficulty facing up to life and the problems it presents."

Wadman's verdicts are different in another way as well. In the absence of a suicide note, oral threat, or eyewitness, most coroners are reluctant to deliver a verdict of suicide, in part because English law requires that a clear expression of intent be proved beyond a reasonable doubt—a demand that can lead to some incredulous verdicts. In one case, a twenty-one-year-old Yorkshire-man threw himself out of a third-story window, cut his wrist so deeply that he needed a blood transfusion, and threatened to drink poison and jump off a roof before friends intervened, all in the space of three days. On the fourth day, he traveled to Beachy Head and bolted for the edge. When his companion grabbed his coat, he said, "If you don't let go, I will take you with me." After a brief struggle, he fell to his death. At the inquest, the coroner commented, "At no time on the cliff did he say he was going to take his life," and delivered an open verdict.

Such preposterous rulings are delivered not only in accordance with the law but out of consideration for the victim's family. Historically, this Episcopalian land of stiff upper lips has had little tolerance for suicides and their kin. In medieval England, "self-murder" was considered *felo de se*, "a felon of himself." The suicide was tried posthumously by a coroner's jury, and if he was found guilty, the Crown seized his assets, often reducing his family to poverty. Punishment also extended to the corpse, which was denied a Christian burial and desecrated, in some cases buried naked at a crossroads with a wooden stake through the chest and a stone placed over the face; in other cases, "drawn by a horse to the place of punishment and shame, where he is hanged on a gibbet and none may take the body down but by authority of a magistrate." To avoid such unpleasantness, coroners often took advantage of a loophole in the law that exonerated those who were declared non compos mentis, or not of sound mind. They also declared obvious suicides "accidents," a practice passed down through the centuries, as I discovered while reading a late-nineteenth century Eastbourne memoir.

The author recounts the death of a coast guard officer who shot himself in the mouth while stationed at Beachy Head. After reviewing the evidence—the victim's mouth was blackened by gunpowder, his false teeth were blown clear across the room, and the ball went "through his brain and thence through the roof of the building"—the inquest concluded that the deceased had been examining the pistol and, while looking down the barrel, accidentally pulled the trigger. "This, to myself and two or three others appeared very improbable," recalled one skeptical jury member, "but in deference to the opinion of the majority we gave way and a verdict of 'accidental death' was duly returned." As a result, the widow received an annuity that would have been forfeited had a verdict been returned "more in accordance with the facts."

Wadman isn't a literalist or a sentimentalist but a sensible man. In the case of an eighty-one-year-old man who left no note, had no psychiatric history, and had not been seen jumping but *had* placed a pile of his clothes near the cliff edge, Wadman concluded, "One must take a practical view . . . he would not have made this journey for a scenic outing." Before delivering a verdict of suicide at the inquest of a thirty-eight-year-old man who had jumped off Beachy Head, he explained, "It is true he did not leave a note and never indicated that he was minded to take his own life, but one has to take a realistic view."

When the back door to the courtroom opens, a jowly, hunched man in a black robe lumbers to the bench and slowly seats himself beneath the magistrate's seal. I look and listen for signs of the maverick I imagine Wadman to be—an odd mannerism, a loose remark—but all I see and hear is a bespectacled bulldog of a man clutching a gavel and rapping it, signaling the start of the inquest into the death of forty-nine-year-old David Evans.

Michael Davey, sitting at a long table perpendicular to the bench, calls the pathologist. The man with the neatly parted hair rises, walks to the lectern, and, with clinical detachment, testifies that the victim died from "multiple fractures to the trunk with damage to internal organs and hemorrhage, injuries which would have been fatal instantly."

The coroner listens impassively and asks no questions. Davey puts down his pen and calls a Ms. Iris Forbes. One of the blond women rises and heads to the front of the courtroom, heels clicking against the floor. Slim, fortyish, and immaculately coiffed, she resembles a flight attendant without the smile. At the lectern, she stands stiffly as she waits for the coroner to look up from the document in his hand. Is the power of his concentration such that he's forgotten us, or is he making a show of his judiciousness? Distracted, I find myself focusing on the silver bracelet that encircles the witness's slender wrist.

Finally, Wadman puts down the paper and slowly removes his bifocals. He greets the witness and asks her what her relationship is to the deceased. "I'm his sister," she replies. She haltingly reveals that she and her brother had had a falling-out seven months before, that he'd suffered from depression and their mother from bipolar illness, and that he'd been a postman for seventeen years but had quit seven years ago to take adult education classes in English and computer programming. She says that the day before he died, he'd taken a temp job as a data entry clerk.

The reporters scribble away on their notepads as the sister returns to her seat, teary-eyed. Her companion gently pats her on the back, then rises after she's called. When she reaches the lectern, the coroner utters a word of greeting, then begins the questioning. Her relationship to the deceased? She was a mutual friend of David and his sister. When did she last speak to the deceased? Last week, she says softly. He asked her for a job reference. Not long before that, he'd told her he wanted to kill himself but didn't have the courage to do it. She doesn't explain what she did with this information, and the coroner doesn't ask. So she skips ahead to the day itself—how she had a terrible feeling when David's new employer called, wondering why he hadn't shown up for work. The sister starts sobbing, and the friend briefly turns her head away from the coroner, as if torn between her instinct to comfort and her duty to testify.

The coroner decides he's heard enough, and Davey calls the constable to the stand. Gripping the sides of the lectern with his strong-looking hands, the young officer speaks earnestly and efficiently, as if responding to orders instead of questions. He says he saw the victim's body winched to the cliff's edge, and recovered the personal effects: seven pounds, a bankbook, a blood donor card, and a handwritten list of "particulars." I glance at the sister. Particulars—bequests? Burial requests?

Shortly after the constable has returned to his seat, the coroner delivers the verdict. "The deceased suffered from medical depression for some years," he says in a gruff monotone. "The written document that was found on him was a list of his personal particulars. It contains no explanation, but it is not the sort of document you carry about unless you have suicide in mind. A verdict of suicide is hereby recorded."

As the witnesses file out, I look up at the sister, who's wiping her eyes with a tissue. I turn away. What does she think about the end of her brother's life being torn open before strangers? Part of me wants and expects her to say to me, "What are you doing here?" And what would I reply? That I'm here because my brother-in-law killed himself? That I have some idea of the road she's been traveling down, the wondering why, the second-guessing? Or, instead of trying to justify my presence by appealing to our common experience, would I simply tell the truth: I'm curious.

But she doesn't care about me; her mind is elsewhere, and then she is gone. Minutes later a new set of principals files in for the inquest into the death of nineteen-year-old Robin Carter. A conveyor belt of grief. The drill is the same. The pathologist says the victim suffered "severe head and chest injuries with multiple rib fractures."

The father, looking deflated with his sagging cheeks, slumping shoulders, and rumpled sport coat, says that his son had been living at home while taking journalism classes at a local college. He noticed that Robin had been sleeping more in the weeks before his death, but that was the only thing out of the ordinary. His son's death, he says, was "out of the blue."

A stocky, ruddy-faced man explains that he was on his way home from work when he pulled off the coast road to talk to his brother on his cell phone. He heard a knock on the passenger-side window, looked up, and saw a young man holding a backpack. The man asked where the sea and cliffs were, and the man in the car told him. Then he called the police.

A constable testifies that at 0030 hours, he saw a helicopter land at Eastbourne District General Hospital and unload the body of a male with short, mousy hair, a black jacket, black jeans, and a black nylon backpack.

The coroner reads a letter from Carter's journalism professor, who isn't present. Robin, she writes, was quite intense and didn't seem to fit in: the other students called him "rat boy" because he was from the village of Ratby and always wore black. "I never felt Robin was totally happy," she writes, "and on some occasions, I saw that he had a fiery temper. . . . After the Christmas recess, he didn't return to school."

The father places a slack arm around the shoulders of his whimpering wife. It occurs to me that the compactness of the inquest is a mixed blessing. A neatly packaged summary of a suicide can bring closure, but it can also invite regret. Signs once scattered across time and viewed through a lens of denial are brought together at the inquest and seen in the context of the outcome. What at first blush seemed "out of the blue" now seems so obvious that you wonder if you'll ever forgive yourself. The sleeping, the dropping out of school, the penchant for black—why didn't we put them together?

The coroner picks up another piece of paper. He says he'll read a portion of a note that leaves no doubt as to the deceased's intentions. " 'The pain inside me is too much. There is no real reason for me doing this, but there is no real reason for me not to.' "

The mother's whimpers turn to heartrending sobs. The coroner puts down the note and removes his glasses. Looking at no one in particular, he summarizes the findings and delivers the verdict that Robin Carter killed himself. Twenty-five minutes after the first one began, the inquests are over.

A FEW DAYS LATER, I check out of Black Robin Farm. There isn't a wet eye in the house as Jane Higgs calculates my heating bill and takes my credit card. When she returns, we exchange a few syllables, and I'm off to the Hollies Holiday Flats, a gabled four-story house in the genteel Eastbourne borough of Meads, and one of the few self-catering establishments open in March. But that's not all. The Hollies is roughly equidistant between Beachy Head and Eastbourne center (no more two-mile walks to the grocery store), and the name has a cheerful, Christmasy ring that offers a bright contrast to the Gothic-sounding Black Robin Farm. It augurs sunnier hosts, and on this last score, it doesn't disappoint. Pauline Knowles greets me with a robust smile as her brawny, rosy-cheeked husband, Brian, offers to carry a duffel bag.

I spend the evening settling into my attic flat, a one-room spread with dormers overlooking tidy backyards. The next morning I consult the tide times in the local paper, then head out to

Beachy Head for a walk along the base of the cliffs, a venture I'd long put off because of the well-known hazards: falling rock, slippery shingle, rapidly rising tides.

The sparkling, cool spring morning is wasted on the Beachy Head shoreline. Torn fishing nets, plastic containers, beer bottles, and an occasional rusty car part—the remnants, I presume, of a drive-over suicide—litter rocks and tidal pools. I keep an eye out for more perishable items. A former coast guard officer's son once discovered the body of a Russian concert pianist while delivering Christmas gifts to the Beachy Head lighthouse. A boy searching for his remote-control airplane stumbled upon a skeleton dressed in a plaid skirt and roll-neck sweater.

I don't see a body, but looking up, I see a person standing on the edge of the cliff. I train my camera on the figure. I imagine his every movement—his moving away from the edge and then back ("He's not sure he wants to jump"); the turning of his head ("He wants to make sure no one's looking")—to be full of portent. I imagine him falling through the air and getting the plunge on film. A retired member of the cliff rescue team told me that "people come by coach or carload, train or taxi, to see where it's all happened, and if they're up there and somebody jumps off, then that's the cream of the cake for them." I don't get the cream—the figure withdraws from view—and suddenly I'm disappointed in myself for wanting it.

The sudden-death reports, the inquests, and my flirtation with tabloid photography have offered, by virtue of their immediacy, titillation of the highest order. But their guilty pleasure raises some troubling questions. How can something so tragic be of such prurient interest? Is it right to invade the privacy of the dead and their families? Is it right even to think about writing a book that might be perceived as selling suicide? How is this all going to play out? I'm desperate for answers.

Veronica Bennet's services are advertised on a storefront window in downtown Eastbourne. I take down the number before I know what my hand has done. A few days later, I get up the nerve to call and make an appointment. The next morning I'm in a cab headed for the seafront.

The cabdriver is an elderly man with bright silver hair and crow's-feet that spread attractively across his temples when he smiles. He asks if I'm on holiday. It's a question I'm beginning to answer without hesitation. "I'm researching the Beachy Head suicides."

The cabbie glances in the rearview mirror. "I drove a man up there once, 'spect he was in his thirties, something like that. Said he was meeting a friend. He seemed a bit suspicious. Well, it's one of those things. I wasn't happy about it. But there's not a lot you can do. You can't arrest them or anything. So I dropped him off and watched him for a while as he walked toward the lighthouse. Then I went down to the police station and told them I wasn't happy."

We pass the leafy grounds of a boys' school in Meads. Up ahead, the two-lane road morphs into a four-lane, four-mile straightaway bordered by massive Victorian hotels inland and sweeping lawns seaward.

"Well, they sent a car up, they had a chat with him. They were a hundred yards, I s'pose, from the edge. They'd driven on the grass off the road to talk to him. All of a sudden he just pushed one of the police and ran and jumped over the edge. Of course, it made them feel rotten, and it made *me* feel rotten because, you know, should I have tried to grab him or not let him out of the car or something like that? It stays with you for a while, but life goes on, doesn't it?"

I barely hear the question. I'm thinking of my meeting with

Veronica Bennet. I can't believe what I'm doing. I've always lumped fortune-tellers with TV evangelists, promoters of rapid-weight-loss programs, pitchers of pyramid schemes, and any others who trade on people's hopes and fears.

The cabbie glances down at the dashboard and reaches for his radio. I see now why the cab is so eerily quiet: the dispatches are read off a small onboard computer. He tells the dispatcher he can pick up the Bolton Road fare, and gently places the radio back in its holster.

"Well," he goes on, "you have that inner feeling that something's not quite right. But, as I say, what can you *do*? I could've hung on to him. He could've given me a black eye. He could have done anything if he was—you know—did have those intentions. That wouldn't have mattered, because he was just trying to do a job."

Just trying to do a job. Attaching the hose, fashioning the noose, positioning the gun, dashing for the cliff edge. Punching in, punching out. Just trying to do a job.

On the seaward side, we pass a marshmallow-shaped fortification built in anticipation of a Napoleonic invasion that never happened, and a bronze statue of a former mayor overlooking hedge-lined paths and immaculate flower beds.

"It's usually marriage problems, health problems, or even money problems. People that get made redundant, they get depressed, and there we are. They brood over it, they think to their self, 'Well, what's the point of going on?' They've read in the papers about people coming to Eastbourne, all about Beachy Head, so they come up here in their car. They leave it in the car park, they go in the pub, have a few drinks, give 'em a bit o' courage, and walk to the edge."

The cab slows as we approach the Carpet Gardens, a seemingly endless strip of gaudy perennials, water fountains, and floral sculptures that runs along the seafront's main walkway, the promenade.

The driver pulls over. "That'll be three pound twenty."

I hand him a five-pound note and tell him to keep the change.

"Thanks, mate. Ride the cabs, and you'll have enough Beachy Head stories to fill a book. Cheers."

"Cheers," I say, as if toasting a brilliant idea. I step onto the promenade, into the bright light of an unseasonably warm spring day. A man chattering in German tries to assemble his brood for a picture in front of a row of daffodils, as two jacketless businessmen watch with amusement from a park bench. Across the broad thoroughfare known as Grande Parade, a bus idles alongside a sunwashed hotel. In the middle of a side street stands an imposing statue of the seventh duke of Devonshire, the founder of modern Eastbourne, "a town conceived by a gentleman for gentlemen at a period when most development was being conducted by speculators for their own pockets," and "a graceful dame, whose beauty is enhanced by every kind of becoming ornament." Though exhaust-spewing buses and cars hardly qualify as ornaments, the seafront has retained much of its Victorian splendor. It's not hard to imagine Edwardian ladies parading across the lawns with their parasols, or horse-drawn carriages clopping down Grande Parade, or men in top hats smoking after-dinner cigars on the iron-railed balconies of the Burlington Hotel. The tacky souvenir shops, greasy fast-food restaurants, pulsing arcades, and other eyesores common to tourist-town seafronts are all crammed onto the pier, leaving the surrounding area pretty much as the duke had envisioned it.

From a distance, the thousand-foot-long pier looks like a middle finger flipping off the stuffy hotels across the street. Up close, it feels like an isolated colony of kitschy consumers and bored teenagers whose unique adaptations—the abilities to use a joystick with surgical precision; to tolerate a cacophony of bells, buzzes, and booms; and to digest several Whoppers at a sitting—allow them to flourish in this environment.

I stroll along the pier's railed, blustery edge, past signs forbidding jumping, digressing occasionally to peek into a gift shop, restaurant, or arcade, turning often to glance westward at the luminous cliffs of Beachy Head. The smells of fried food and cotton candy waft through the briny air as the sea laps against the pilings below. After walking the equivalent of three football fields out to sea, I come to a forlorn booth at the end of the pier. Ruby curtains cover bay windows plastered with promotional literature. An old bicycle leans against a set of stairs near the booth's entrance. A box of faded magazines and a plain wooden chair sit just outside the door. Veronica Bennet's credo is taped to the door:

> Fairies at the bottom of the garden? Unlikely. A palmist at the end of Eastbourne Pier? Definitely. Veronica Bennet interprets, not just the lines, but the size and shape of the hands, variations in color, texture and temperature, and the way you hold your hands.
>
> Passersby are often heard to mutter that "they'd rather not know what the future has in store." Apart from implying a lack of hope in what it may bring this is a bit like stepping out into the middle of the road with one's eyes shut. Nothing is so negative that it can't be changed. We *always* have a choice. There may well be an element of "fate" involved but the way we respond to life's slings and arrows is entirely up to us. As a palmist, I can look at your hands and ad-

vise you of the choices available to you, but the
decision is yours alone.

This should be interesting. I bend my ear to the door. I hear
nothing. I knock.

The door opens, and a fiftyish woman with a beatific, gap-
toothed smile welcomes me in. A heavy sweater covers her broad
shoulders. Her hair is gray with black streaks and gathered into a
bun. Stray strands fall attractively around her temples. In a lulling
voice, she tells me to have a seat, pointing to a table not much
larger than a TV tray. The room is womblike: cozy, dark, and
bathed in the sound of the lapping sea. Posters of a blue dolphin
and a wistful Native American fill one wall; a palmistry map of
two hands and a small shelf lined with crystals, polished stones,
ceramic angels, and half-burned candles take up another wall; a
bookcase packed with palm-reading tomes, a third. It's the type of
room I could easily fall asleep in if there were space to lie down.

The session will consist, I am told, of the usual fare: nu-
merology, palmistry, tarot cards. She asks for my birthday, and
we're off.

"We've taken your date of birth, May thirteenth, 1960, and
find that you're a number seven, which makes you probably a bit
of an introvert, somebody who is quite analytical, might be interested in the so-called occult, but I think perhaps you are somebody who doesn't take things on face value at all, who likes to
look under the surface. If it's intriguing enough to cause you to
ask questions, then you want to take it further, yah?"

Analytical, yes. Introverted? More than a bit. But if you think
my presence here betrays a fledgling interest in the occult,
you're mistaken. I'm here on a whim. "That sounds about right."

She expounds on nine-year cycles, but none of it rings true.
Then she turns to my palms. "A lot of Taureans have hands that

have got very fleshy phalanges here. Yours aren't. So I would probably say you like things of quality but don't go overboard for quantity. Would that be appropriate?"

"Yes, it would." Who's going to say no to such a question?

"Yah?"

I turn my hands over.

"Palms up, please. Good." She leans over my hands. "There's a sort of squareness about these palms, but they are slightly longer than they are broad, so we have somebody who can plan ahead. Independent-minded from a very early age: there's a slight gap between the head line and the life line. If you put those fingers together, can you see how there's gaps between them?" She pauses. "Now, there's an imagery here. If somebody fills your hands with something, then it's going to come out through the holes. It could be money. Money comes into your hands and goes out again quite quickly. You're not a parsimonious sort of person."

"I would say that's true—not that I have much money to spend."

She laughs. "No, right. But when it comes in, it's got somewhere to go to. You don't sort of hang on to it or stuff it under the mattress or whatever."

Stuff it under the mattress? "That's right."

She picks up my hands and holds them lightly. Her hands are tuned to mine; she probably feels every tremor. She asks if I'm tense. I am. It's not that I fear being exposed, of confirming things I don't like about myself. It's the physical intimacy. We're close to each other in a small, dark room, and she is studying a part of my body about which I've always felt self-conscious. She sees the calluses and asks if I make a living with these puny appendages. It's a flattering question. I feel like a homely girl who's just been told she's pretty.

"No. The calluses are from playing tennis."

She nods and releases her hold. "What about music? Do you enjoy music? Do you have a hobby that involves music? Because"—she traces an arcing line with her finger—"you've got this deeply curved area here, at this angle of time here, so if you were to find the right instrument, I would think that you would have found quite the talent."

The world is full of people who suspect they have a hidden talent for music, and it is teeming with introverts, lovers of quality, and profligate spenders. Did she quickly size me up as a romantic and deduce the particulars from there? Is that how the fortune-teller's art works? Or are the details truly in the palm of my hand? And how specific, really, are they? Half the human race shares most of the traits ascribed to me. What am I doing here? "Yes, that's my biggest regret. I've always wondered if I started when I was younger—"

"You don't have to start when you're younger," she interrupts in her singsongy way. "You can start now."

"I might do that."

"The potential is there. When you get this deep area at the base of Mount Venus," she says, pointing to an area that looks nothing like a mountain, "quite often it could be drumming or something with a very strong beat, rather than a flute or a piccolo or a wind instrument."

I'll take the wind instrument. I'm growing impatient. I want her to tell me about my research, about the consequences of my choices. What will happen if I continue to indulge my morbid curiousity without restraint? If I decide to write about my experiences? How many people will I hurt? Can't you see my questions in my hands?

She points to a tangle of lines on my left palm. "The swirly-whirly patterns that are here say, 'I do my own thing. I do it in my own unique, individual way. My belief systems are my own, and I don't owe very much to what I've learned.' They come from the heart, and your god could be a composite of all the religious stuff that you've ever heard. Or it could be that you have your own, very deeply personal relationship with God or the great spirit or whatever."

I am the son of a minister who never got religion, a former Sunday-school misfit who believes in kindness, kindness, kindness. "That's accurate."

She doesn't seem to hear my response. "This is exceptionally long, the last phalange on your thumb. Whatever you set out to do, you will accomplish. That's where stubbornness can be manifest as well." She pauses to study my fingers, which are curled. "If you'll put those down for me for a sec. That's it. Lovely. The fingertip patterns—there's no horizontal or vertical lines on these fingertips, so I would say whatever you are doing, you are feeling unobstructed. There don't seem to be any blockages in your way at all at the moment."

Interesting.

She points to something on my finger that I can't see and stares at it with a furrowed brow. "What that on there means, I really don't know, because it's a closed bird's-eye loop, and I've only ever encountered it before on *that* finger or *that* finger. It gives protection. I suppose we could hazard a guess that you'd be protected from libel suits. Are you a writer?"

I'm stunned. With one question, Veronica Bennet has flown the coop of quackery I'd unfairly caged her in. "I'm a teacher, but I write as well."

"What sort of writing is it that you do? Is it imaginative stuff or practical stuff?"

"I'm doing research for a possible book about Beachy Head, but I'm beginning to question if I'm doing the right thing."

She smiles sweetly and again offers a singsongy reassurance. "But I would *think*, with your methodical way of approaching things, that you would make absolutely sure there was nothing that could cause any problems."

I feel a great weight lifting. Of course I would. I just needed to hear someone else say it.

She returns to my fingers. "Just noticed something else which is exceptional, and I didn't even look for it because it's very seldom there. And that's a light loop in the skin ridge patterns. Can you see there's a curve there, similar to the one you've got there and there?" She points to lines I pretend to see. "Well, between those two fingers, it happens once in, say, ten thousand cases, and usually, that's just on one hand. You've got it on both hands. It looks to me as if you've got royalty somewhere way back there." I glance at my fingers as if I'm seeing them for the first time. "It's called a Raja Loop. In Indian palmistry, it's a sure sign of somebody who has the ability to take control in any situation. There's a natural authority, usually, about somebody with that in their hands. Have you got any Scottish forebears? Celtic?"

"I'm part Scots-Irish, but I don't—"

"So there could be at the very least a laird or somebody like that." She looks for a response, but I have none. A laird? "Okay, I think that's all for the palmistry. Are there any specific questions you would like to ask?"

I have none, so we move on to the cards, which are clearly the weakest part of her game. No, I don't have a son; I didn't do something impetuous two or three years ago that I regret (is she hinting at an affair?); the grandfather I was closest to was not intimidating or stubborn; and my father isn't moody and doesn't drink.

"I think we'll call it a day, then, because there are no swords, and there's nothing at all to suggest that anything could go wrong. It's unusual."

Unusual, unbelievable, even, but I'll take it. Strolling down the pier, I feel as if I own it. I'm descended from a laird, whatever that is, relieved of writerly anxieties, and blessed with a hidden talent for music. I feel as I imagine many people do when they leave the booth at the end of the pier. Like a new man.

IT DOESN'T TAKE LONG for other doubts and fears to fill the vacuum created by Veronica Bennet's sunny forecast. I'm drinking a bottle of wine a night in my attic bungalow and an occasional half-pint of whiskey, a disturbing development for someone who was a weekend wine-and-beer drinker. Though I want to believe that my intemperance is a harmless aberration brought about by a convergence of unusual circumstances—I'm alone in a foreign land, investigating a disturbing subject, and rocking boats along the way—I fear that I'm beginning a slippery slide that will be difficult to halt even after my circumstances change. "In the end," writes psychoanalyst Karl Menninger, "each man kills himself in his own selected way, fast or slow, soon or late." Will drinking be my way? Staring bleary-eyed one evening at the startling accumulation of empty bottles on the kitchen counter, I have the disturbing feeling that, in reading the sudden-death reports, I've absorbed the demons of the Beachy Head victims. The bottles are flash points for two of my deepest fears: losing my mind and messing up my life.

When I was twelve, my forty-three-year-old uncle was committed to a hospital for the criminally insane after being convicted of several murders (he was exonerated and released eighteen years later). My mother explained at the time that her brother's schizophrenia was probably something he was born with that didn't reveal itself until adolescence. I remember being terrified by the possibility that madness could leap out like a jack-in-the-box after years of sane living. It didn't help to learn that relatives of schizophrenics have only a 10 percent chance of developing the illness. I feared that I might be one of the unlucky few.

A year later, when I was in eighth grade, puberty hit, tripping a humming melancholy, which I acclimated to as one does a distant car alarm. But during my junior year of high school, the volume inexplicably intensified. My emotions were flat, my movements leaden. I coughed incessantly, had trouble concentrating, and withdrew from friends. I slept a lot. I wasn't suicidal, but I was scared. I thought I might never be my old self again. The depression lifted the summer before my senior year, but in its place grew the skittishness of the once-bitten. I spent the rest of my adolescence looking over my shoulder, waiting for depression's return. The sensitive, introverted son of a melancholy father, I thought I was a good candidate for a lifelong acquaintanceship with mental illness.

Though these fears have not come to pass—I'm safely past the age when most relatives of schizophrenics claim their inheritance, and depression has never again been a major presence in my life—my outlook toward the future is still characterized by a strong sense of foreboding. I fear that, like Kafka's Gregor Samsa, I'll someday wake up and find myself utterly altered, the innocent victim of some biochemical upheaval. Or that I'll slowly grow weary of life, be broken by hardship, or do something really stupid and lose everything: my family, my home, my reputation, my self-regard. Add to these fears a tendency to drink or sleep through adversity, and I have an unstable compound of a life that needs to be handled with vigilance and care.

It's possible that these fears are no more rational than a child's fear of darkness; that they're the delusions of a dementophobe and catastrophobe rather than the reliable warnings of memory or intuition. It's possible, too, that I'm more resilient than I think I am; that I'm no more repressed or delicately balanced than the next guy, and to think otherwise is egocentric rubbish. I wouldn't be surprised if I die wondering why I didn't trust myself more. Nor would I be surprised if the manner of my death vindicated my distrust.

4

The Lure of Beachy Head

The cliff top is empty and covered in cloud shadow. I'm taking my usual Sunday-morning stroll along the cliff top, head down, lost in thought, when my gaze drifts to the edge fifteen feet away, and I feel a sudden urge to bolt toward it. For a moment I actually feel caught in a current that will sweep me over the edge if I keep looking. So I turn away and veer inland, where the feeling disappears as quickly as it came. "What was *that*?"

I'm not the only one who's experienced the siren-like pull of the cliff edge. In the newspaper article that introduced me to Beachy Head, a veteran of the East-bourne police force took the reporter for a walk along the cliff top. "Can you feel it?" he asked. "There's a funny feeling that the cliff draws you over the edge. I don't know why." Novelist Louis de Bernières writes that each time he approached the edge, he felt himself drawn over: "the vertical became the horizontal, and a terrifying sickness took me at the stomach and throat. I have never felt this anywhere else, even when mountaineering or when I was a tree surgeon, and I wondered how many people might have been hypnotized into committing suicide unintentionally. . . ."

THE FRENCH SOCIOLOGIST Emile Durkheim refers to sudden, unpremeditated acts of self-destruction as "automatic suicides" in which "the suicidal tendency appears and is effective in truly automatic fashion, not preceded by an intellectual antecedent. The sight of a knife, a walk by the edge of a precipice, engender the suicidal idea instantaneously and its execution follows so swiftly that patients often have no idea of what has taken place." This reminds me of Anna Karenina's impetuous lunge under the wheels of a train, a suicide that essayist Edward Hoagland thought particularly frightening "because it was unwilled, regretted at midpoint, and came as a complete surprise to Anna herself."

"To a lesser degree," Durkheim continues, "patients feel the impulse growing and manage to escape the fascination of the mortal instrument by fleeing from it immediately."

That was me. But why? Was I drawn to Beachy Head for the same reason that a mechanically gifted child is drawn to tools and gadgets? Did my interest in the cliffs betray a hidden aptitude for suicide that was content to express itself vicariously until that day when, standing on the edge, gazing at a sunset or watching a distant fishing boat, I would jump before I knew what I was doing? Are some wounds buried so deeply that we can't feel them? Is it possible to live a relatively happy life, unaware of the unresolved conflicts that roil beneath the surface, until one is ambushed by a suicidal impulse that is nothing short of a revelation? But what is my wound? I had an uneventful childhood, no major losses or betrayals. Anyhow, I'd know if I were damaged. I'd feel a vague and gnawing sadness. Wounds are always felt; we pick at them.

If my urge to jump off the cliff wasn't the sudden emergence of a long-repressed death wish, then what was it? What is the lure of Beachy Head? The question is all the more compelling because it's the last of the five W's still begging for an answer. Thanks to Dr. John Surtees, a retired Eastbourne pathologist who has studied the Beachy Head suicides extensively, I know *who* jumps off Beachy Head: mostly clerks, students, housewives, and psychiatric patients. Males outnumber females by a ratio of three to two. Most male suicides are between fifteen and forty-four years old, and female suicides between thirty-five and sixty-four. Just under half live within a ten-mile range of the cliffs. Three Americans have jumped, two of them from New York.

I know *where* most people jump—between the pub and the Beachy Head lighthouse, the highest half-mile stretch—and in *what* manner: of forty-three cliff falls witnessed in a thirty-year period, twenty-seven were "active" (jumping, diving, running, stepping over), and sixteen were "passive" (sliding, rolling, kneeling down and bending backward, sitting down and pushing off). Though the majority of passive attempts were made by women, the most passive attempt on record likely belongs to a twenty-four-year-old man who fell off the cliffs in his sleep. "I hadn't got the nerve to jump over," he explained to a newspaper reporter after being plucked off a ledge some two hundred feet down the cliff, "so I took sleeping tablets and sat on the edge in such a position that when I dosed off I would fall over. I think it was about half an hour before I fell."

I know *when* people jump off Beachy Head. The summer months are the busiest; female deaths double in June, July, and August. More people jump on Friday than any other day of the week. Most jump within minutes of reaching the cliff top.

But I don't know *why*. Several days later, I pose the question to Dr. Surtees in a hospital office. Mr. Beachy Head, as he's known in some quarters, leans back in his office chair. He strokes his salt-and-pepper beard and smiles. He suggests I speak to Kevin Carlyon, a local witch of some celebrity who specializes in paranormal phenomena. He hands me the phone number and says I should find the visit quite entertaining.

I SET OUT FROM MY ATTIC under a cloudless sky. The sidewalk streams with clusters of chattering boys in blue blazers en route to their morning classes at a nearby prep school. I join the babbling current with the confidence of an elderly driver entering highway traffic. At the corner, we go our separate ways, and some ten minutes later, I'm boarding an eastbound train, leaving behind the "Sunshine Capital of the Southeast" for Hastings, Eastbourne's coastal neighbor and unofficial "Murder Capital of the Southeast."

There are no cardiganed retirees treading the streets. Through the narrow lens of a cab window, Hastings appears to be a city of boarded-up storefronts and vacant-eyed stoop-sitters. If the self-proclaimed High Priest of British White Witches lives anywhere in the vicinity, business must not be good.

In a few minutes, the cab pulls over in front of a drab gabled duplex on a busy potholed road. The driver takes my money and quickly departs, leaving me standing alone on a cracked sidewalk, contemplating an Addams Family–like front porch. A plastic devil's fork leans against a railing; a black cat reposes on the doormat, next to a traffic cone spray-painted a fetching silver. A dark object the size of a softball rests on its point. The cat skitters away as I approach the front steps, but I hardly notice. My attention is drawn to the traffic cone: the object propped on its point is a shrunken plastic head. You've got to be kidding. I hesitate before knocking on one of the few patches of door unclaimed by black pentagrams and dangling plastic bats, and wait for it to creak open.

But the door opens quietly, and the person standing on the threshold isn't a Lurch look-alike but a chunky woman with splotchy cheeks and orange bangs parted into bobbing coils. She wears a black T-shirt under a baggy, unbuttoned denim shirt, its tails hanging over faded jeans that taper to black high-top Reeboks. She smiles shyly and introduces herself as Sandie. We head down a narrow hallway into a cramped, disheveled office reeking of incense. A teenager dressed in black with hair and makeup to match sits on a tag-sale couch in an attitude of bored waiting, acknowledging our presence with a "whatever" glance. Sandie smiles gamely at the girl, then turns to me and explains that Kevin is doing a tarot card reading and will be with me as soon as he's finished.

She leaves me alone with the cheerless Goth in the waiting room. Ceremonial robes, one red, one white, hang in a corner above boxes labeled VERVION and BENZOIN (magical herbs, I later discover). Pamphlets and order forms litter a desk overlooking a tiny backyard dominated by a curious powdery circle. Instead of dog-eared magazines piled on end tables, tabloid articles plaster a wall. In a feature titled "The Witches of Suburbia," Kevin Carlyon describes his many priestly duties: ministering to the needs of fellow pagans at a local hospital; exorcising evil spirits from cursed cars, cliffs, and homes; and sending crystals or sympathetic energy to the hundreds of hard-luck people who write to him each month. His ministry extends even into space. I'm stunned to read that, at NASA's request, Carlyon sent his blessings to the Mir space station crew.

It gets even better. An article titled "We Owe Our Baby to Jolly White Giant" shows a beaming couple holding an infant whom Carlyon and his coven apparently helped conceive on the twenty-one-foot penis of the Cerne Abbas Giant, a two-thousand-year-old, 180-foot Goliath carved into a Dorset hillside. "They are 100 percent certain it was us who helped them," Carlyon told the reporter. "We invoked the forces of nature and sent positive thoughts to the couple to try to rejuvenate their naughty bits. It was quite a warm night so we didn't have too many problems. We just did the ceremony and let them get on with it." In another article, Carlyon describes how, during a tarot card reading for Sandie when her previous marriage was falling apart, he discovered that their future union was literally in the cards.

As I begin to question my presence here, a thin, timid-eyed woman walks in—the teenager's mother, it appears—followed by Carlyon, who ushers me into a large room with a half-dozen or so black cats sprawled on the carpet and sofa. "We have ten," he says. He is a sturdy, handsome man with shoulder-length golden hair tucked behind his ears. His high cheekbones and strong chin suggest a face once sculpted, before the valleys started filling in with flesh. He wears a black warm-up jacket unzipped to the top of his belly; a silver pentagram pendant hangs down his hairy chest. Black high-water sweatpants, white socks, and hiking boots complete the ensemble. He looks more like a middle-aged jock than a witch.

He tells me to make myself comfortable and excuses himself with apologies to take his client to the circle in the backyard. Meanwhile, I familiarize myself with the trappings of a modern-day witch's den. Horror movies and glossy, paganish hardcovers—*Stonehenge; The Complete Book of Herbs, Oils and*

Brews; The Lord of the Rings—pack a wall-mounted bookcase. A large cast-iron kettle and a space heater topped with crystals, candles, mortars, and pestles sit in front of the fireplace; dried flowers, melted candles, an antique sword, and a human skull adorn the mantel above. I'm hardly spooked, if that's Carlyon's intention. In the sense that a space reflects the tastes and interests of the people who live and work in it, all this weird stuff seems rather normal, no stranger than the trophies, autographed baseballs, and sports posters that decorated my boyhood bedroom.

When Carlyon returns from the circle, we exchange pleasantries at a long wooden table by a wall festooned with ivy. Then, behind a façade of earnestness, I ask him how he became a witch. Though skeptical, I'm genuinely curious. Doctors go to med school, ballplayers start in the minor leagues, blacksmiths have apprenticeships. What's the witch track?

Carlyon smiles, then turns serious. He says that when he was five, he started having prophetic dreams. He correctly predicted that a schoolmate would fall out of a tree and break his arm. When the headmistress heard of his impressive call, she summoned him into her office and told him he was possessed by the devil. "Mum wasn't too happy about that," he recalls with a smile. "She went storming up to school and performed an excellent explosion at the morning's assembly, to the amusement of all assembled."

As Carlyon grew older, he learned to use his "gift" more intentionally. Once he saw his father in the house with a female stranger. Angry and tearful, he later asked his mother why Daddy was doing "press-ups" on another woman. The next day his father suffered minor burns when his shirt caught fire on the gas stove, an incident Carlyon suggests was not a coincidence but a sign of his growing powers.

He was sixteen when he went to his first coven meeting. At twenty-one, he formed his own coven. He left the printing trade in his mid-thirties to become a full-time witch. Today he claims to preside over the largest coven in Europe. His *Covenant of Earth Magic* boasts sixteen hundred broom-carrying members, a figure that brings a small, proud smile to Carlyon's face. He asks if I'd like to see a copy of his newsletter and goes in search of one, quickly returning with a cassette tape and a green booklet, which he hands to me. *Beltane Fire* blares in large, bold letters above a crude drawing of a woman sitting inside a ring, staring at distant Stonehenge. I flip through a few of the articles ("Voices from the Void," "The Lure of Doom at Beachy Head") and tell Carlyon I look forward to reading it, though, in truth, there's only one article I'm interested in.

When I've finished inking up my fingers, I decide to buy the booklet, even though £1.25 seems a bit steep for eight pieces of computer paper held together by two staples and filled with typos and blotchy advertisements. He won't have it and proffers a complimentary copy of the obviously homemade cassette titled *Earth Magic,* the cover of which features a grainy xeroxed image of Carlyon standing in front of a stone ruin, gazing mystically into the distance. I notice that, in the picture, he's wearing the same jacket he has on now, and wonder if he owns several or just the one. It occurs to me that Carlyon is a poor man's Hugh Hefner, a self-proclaimed empire builder who spends his days lolling about in casual attire when he's not engaged in psychic congress with predominately female clients. I don't doubt that he is a true believer in Earth magic, but I also don't doubt that witchcraft allows him a lifestyle he finds much to his liking. I wonder to what extent Sandie's full-time bank job subsidizes his practice.

Carlyon sits down, and a white cat, the aptly named Dr.

Fluffy, jumps into his lap. He explains that the *Earth Magic* tape contains a series of cleansing, healing, and exorcising rituals that rely heavily on visualization. "Earth magic," he says gently, stroking the cat's nape, "is a science of the mind, not a superstition. It's the power of positive thought through ritual to bring about an end result." He pauses. "I guess it's similar to the *Star Wars* idea, in that there is a latent Force that can be tapped into, either for good or evil. But I stress that we never get involved in the dark side."

He recites his good works: performing absent healing for people all over the world in the center circle of Stonehenge; cleansing a post office built on a Gypsy site; ghostbusting on board a pirate radio station; and, as if he has abruptly remembered the reason for my visit, exorcising curses and evil spirits at Beachy Head.

"It's a dangerous place," he says in a voice both sober and eager, as if Beachy Head's perilousness is a secret pleasure to him. He recalls standing close to the edge during a spot for a morning news show eight or nine years ago, when he suddenly had a premonition that the cliff was about to fall. Seconds later, he heard a loud *crrrrrkkkk* and, jumping inland, watched the section of cliff where he'd been standing collapse into the sea. "Now I feel very spooky when I go up there. I can stand on the edge of any cliff, but Beachy Head has a very strange pull." I nod knowingly, and Carlyon smiles. "You've felt it, too, have you?"

"I had a pretty strange experience up there. I felt the urge to run off the cliffs." Carlyon listens intently. I ask him the question that's been preoccupying me for days. "What do you think causes the pulling sensation?"

"My personal belief is that ley lines run through various sacred sites like Stonehenge to the west and a prehistoric burial chamber called Kits Coty to the northeast, and that they crisscross at Beachy Head, creating negative energy that lures vulnerable people to the edge."

Vulnerable people. I feel my face flush. "What are ley lines?"

"They're like the national grid. It's like electricity cables, with positive and negative flows to them, but you can't see them. When they interlink, like at Beachy Head, it's like a short-circuit. Everything seems to go lally. My personal theory is that, because Beachy Head was actually used for sacrificial purposes going back many, many years, it's like a magnet to those who are in an insecure frame of mind, shall we say."

Listening to Carlyon, I don't feel as if I'm in the presence of a fanatic. He speaks confidently but calmly and prefaces his remarks with humble qualifiers ("My personal belief . . ." "My personal theory . . .").

He casts a paternal glance at a dozing Dr. Fluffy. "I s'pose you've heard of the black-robed monk."

"The black-robed monk?"

Carlyon tells the story of a monk who escaped Henry VIII's soldiers after the king fell out with the Church, shut down the monastaries and nunneries, churches and cathedrals, and ordered the slaughter of abbots and monks. The monk took refuge in a manor house, where he was soon betrayed, chained, and taken to Beachy Head. Before he was thrown over the cliffs, he put a curse on the lord of the manor, and within two weeks of his death, a mysterious fire ravaged the snitch's estate. Some believe the aggrieved ghost of the monk lingers on the cliff top, tempting others to suffer the same miserable death. "There was a chap I interviewed—he wasn't a crackpot, he was a cobbler in Eastbourne—who was walking up there one day, and he was convinced he saw a strange figure in a black robe. He said it looked him straight in the eye and pointed toward the edge."

I'm incredulous. "Have you ever seen the monk?"

He smiles. "We do have regular vigils to see if we can see ghosts, if you like, but to be honest, we've never seen anything." He hikes up his jacket sleeves; one of his forearms bears a pentagram tattoo. "It's a very strange place. We've carried out a couple of exorcisms up there to try to cleanse the place, as have Christian priests, but it still draws people to, you know, die, basically. Sometimes some of the people have gone off the top; there's no reason for them to do it, they're not depressed, they haven't got financial problems or anything like that." His pale blue eyes linger on my face, as if he's waiting for a response, but I keep what I'm thinking—that he's presuming more than he can possibly know—to myself. "We get people phoning us sometimes, and they say, 'It's either you or the Samaritans.' They actually tell us that they feel drawn there." He recalls one woman who called and said she was having relationship problems and was thinking of killing herself. She could see Beachy Head from her house and felt drawn there. He told her to come around, and when she arrived, he gave her the "short, sharp shock" treatment, showing her close-up pictures of the cliffs. He chuckles. "It scared her out of it."

As our conversation comes to a close, I ask Carlyon about the powdery white ring in the backyard.

"That's the circle. The circle contains energy. It's a ritualistic site where nothing negative can be transmitted."

"What happens if a person brings negative energy into the circle?"

"Then it will stay there until we cleanse it. It's like copying over a tape, basically. If something's not right, then you copy over it. If somebody goes in there with selfish motives, we can pick up on it and erase it."

Part of me would like to give the circle a try. The thought of having one's selfishness washed away like a layer of dirt is appealing. "What's the circle made of?" Fairy dust? Essence of something-or-other?

"Flour. 'Bout twenty bags' worth."

I HAVE GOOD FEELINGS about Kevin Carlyon when I leave his den. He seems, as advertised, a good witch: amiable, peace-loving, and genuinely committed to helping people. If his calling has also become a thriving business, I don't hold that against him. As for his art, I find it fundamentally sound, a rich, easily digestible brew of transcendentalism and cognitive psychology with a few spoonfuls of placebo thrown in. Yes, there are some hokey paranormal elements, but they're no more dubious than some Christian beliefs and rituals: virulent ley lines no less fantastic than the devil; cleansing oneself in a powdered circle no stranger than dunking one's head in a silty lake; tarot cards no less credible than the Book of Revelation. They're all, to my mind, harmless dashes of spice.

But a search of the Internet reveals a darker side to Carlyon. He's quoted as saying that "Hitler had the right idea to get rid of all the rubbish." He's accused of consorting with a Satanist who spent five years in prison for vandalizing tombs, performing black magic over coffins, and threatening police witnesses. Carlyon is purported to command upward of fifty dollars per spell, though he claims not to charge a fee, and his coven may have as few as five members instead of the alleged sixteen hundred. One fellow pagan called Carlyon a "self-promoting media whore who gives us all a bad name."

But all this I discover later. When I leave Carlyon's apartment, I'm more suspicious of his theories than of his character. Nothing he said added to my understanding of Beachy Head's weird magnetism. Ley lines? If they do exist and crisscross at

Beachy Head, as Carlyon claims, they also crisscross in areas that aren't popular suicide spots. A black-robed monk? The cobbler was probably drunk. Still, a part of me wants to believe in ley lines and ghosts in the same way that a skeptical ten-year-old wants to believe there really is a man with a white beard and red suit who circumnavigates the globe in one night in a little sleigh pulled by flying reindeer and crammed with presents for several million "good" Christians. My need to embrace a Beachy Head mythology, which for me is part of the cliff's allure, has made me susceptible to any theory or story that contributes to it.

Carlyon's theories might explain why people on the cliff top are drawn over the edge, but they can't explain why suicidal people come to Beachy Head, often from great distances. During my conversation with Carlyon, I asked if he ever worried that his articles about Beachy Head might draw vulnerable people to the cliffs. "If someone wants to kill themselves," he said, "they're going to do it. We don't think we're helping them by publishing this stuff. If somebody has that inside themselves, they'll do it, whether it's by gun, whether it's by electricity, whether it's by Beachy Head. My explanation is that it's kind of a paranormal thing, not so much the publicity. I mean, I had a Beachy Head piece in the *Sunday Mirror*, and about seven people jumped off the top after that, but they would have done it anyway." It was reassuring to hear him say that, but in my heart I couldn't agree.

IN AN ESSAY ABOUT BEACHY HEAD, Dr. Surtees tells the story of a fifty-year-old man who, while recovering in the hospital from an overdose, read an article about a Beachy Head suicide in the local newspaper and remarked, "Fancy putting that for people like me to see." A fortnight later, he jumped. According to Surtees, Beachy Head was quiet the first four months of 1988. Then the star of a popular British soap opera leaped to his death, rating banner headlines nationwide. During the next four months, ten people made their way to the cliffs and jumped.

"When the mind is beginning to aberrate," writes George Man Burrows, a nineteenth-century English physician, "it is very essential to prevent persons affected by moral causes or inclined to suicide, from reading newspapers, lest the disposition and the mode be suggested by something similar."

This is especially true, I imagine, when the coverage is sensationalized, as is often the case in the Eastbourne newspapers. Notorious Beachy Head suicides and dramatic rescues dominate the front page ("Wife Killer's Beachy Head Death Plunge," "Family Cliff Horror Suicide Riddle"). Lurid pictures usually accompany the text: a lumpy body bag dangling on a recovery line; the mangled wreckage of a family car at the bottom of the cliffs; a man in a windbreaker sitting on the cliff edge, his left hand bracing for a push-off as two police negotiators watch anxiously from the cliff top. Though reports of more mundane Beachy Head suicides are brief and relegated to the inside pages, the headlines are often disproportionately large. One, "Spurned Lover's Cliff Death Leap," spans nearly the width of the page, while the article below is smaller than a playing card.

Reading the accounts, I can imagine how different kinds of suicidal readers might be affected. A recently divorced and unemployed man might read the inquest report of someone who suffered the same hardships, and decide to follow in the suicide's footsteps. Romantics might be seduced by breathtaking photographs of Beachy Head, and flamboyant types by the idea of leaping off "the world-famous 600 foot cliffs." One fifty-one-year-old woman wrote in her suicide note, "I dramatically say goodbye. . . . The old days were terrific. . . . No more lovers for me. . . . For me the clean, courageous high jump in July. It's beautiful here and dangerous."

The sensible solution, it seems to me, is not to shield unstable readers from suggestive accounts of suicides but to exercise restraint in reporting. With that thought in mind, I arrange a meeting with a local newspaper editor.

TUCKED BEHIND the Eastbourne train station is a long, drab building housing the offices of the city's two tabloids, the *Gazette* and the *Herald*. Inside, a receptionist whose cheerfulness I can't possibly return rings Assistant Editor Spencer Rolfe and informs him of my arrival. Seconds later, a pale man with rolled-up sleeves and a preoccupied air emerges from glass doors. He utters a curt hello, forgoing the usual handshake.

He leads me to a small office with a large desk at its center. A single window overlooks run-down storefronts. Rolfe points to a swivel chair, says, "Please," and retreats behind his desk. He picks up a pen and leans back in his chair. "So you have some questions about our reporting of Beachy Head."

I explain the context of my visit—my brother-in-law's death and my interest in the Beachy Head suicides—lest he wonder what a relatively young American is doing at a fogyish English seaside resort town in the off-season. Then I get down to business. "I was wondering if you have a policy regarding coverage of the suicides?"

"We don't have a policy for covering the suicides," he says, repeating my words with such calm assurance that it sounds almost like a boast. "Generally, if the victim is someone famous, we put the story on the front page, and if the chap was from outside the area, we wouldn't do as long a report of the inquest."

I nod politely. Rolfe's statement hides more than it reveals.

The *Gazette* and the *Herald* also devote front-page space to infamous victims, such as the mother who drove off the cliffs with her two young daughters; or accidental victims, such as the two German high school students, a boy and a girl, who slipped and fell to their deaths sixteen months apart; or anomalous victims like the A-level student found dead at the base of the cliffs. The inquest reports of nonlocal victims are relatively short but often topped with sensationalist headlines such as "Directions to Death" or "Beachy Head Death Drive."

I ask Rolfe about the preponderance of stock phrases such as "Death Leap," "Death Plunge," and "Death Fall Drama." Is such sensationalism really necessary?

He nods sympathetically. "If you read 'Death Plunge' or 'Death Leap,' you say, 'How tasteless.' But you don't have many words to play with. And you have to try to make it different every time, but how do you do that without offending someone?"

That's a good one: time-crunched tabloid editors agonizing over headlines to avoid offending a crass readership. I look at Rolfe, who looks at me while pressing the top of his pen against his temple. The question, I realize, isn't rhetorical; he's waiting for an answer. "You can't," I answer, even though Rolfe's explanation strikes me as sophistic.

I ask him what would happen if the newspapers didn't cover Beachy Head. I tell him about an oft-cited study of suicides in the Viennese subway system. Researchers found that the number of subway suicides fell dramatically after the local media agreed to stop printing stories of the suicides for a full year. Could the same thing happen in Eastbourne?

A flicker of annoyance crosses Rolfe's face. He leans forward. "The duty of a local paper is to report what happens locally, nice or not nice, especially if the victim is local. Fact is, people would still do it even if we didn't report it. People who reach that state of mind aren't bothered by what newspaper articles say." The phone rings, and Rolfe snaps it up.

I gaze at nothing outside Rolfe's window as Carlyon's words come back to me. *If someone wants to kill themselves, they're going to do it. We don't think we're helping them by publishing this stuff.* It's wishful thinking. Thoughts of suicide are usually transient and marked by strong ambivalence. A study of 515 people restrained by Golden Gate Bridge police or bystanders found that 94 percent were still alive many years after their only suicide attempt. How many Beachy Head suicides would still be alive if they hadn't read about the cliffs in their darkest hour? But I can't bring myself to challenge Rolfe. The truth is, I need my fix of sensationalized Beachy Head stories as much as the next guy. This is about me, isn't it? I'm upset by the Eastbourne papers' tawdry treatment of the suicides because I'm feeling a bit sluttish myself. So when Rolfe gets off the phone, I don't bring up the next items on my agenda: the banner headlines and sensationalist front-page photos. I abruptly get up and tell him I must be going, weakly extending a hand.

WHAT HOLDS TRUE for blockbuster movies and thrill-filled amusement parks also applies to world-famous cliffs: hype it, and they will come. I came to Beachy Head because I read a newspaper article about a cliffside pub frequented by "suspicious ones," who in turn were drawn to Beachy Head (as opposed to, say, the White Cliffs of Dover) because of its well-publicized, often sensationalized reputation as a notorious suicide spot. But the media isn't responsible for what happened to me on the cliff top that Sunday morning. My urge to run off the cliffs didn't bubble up from the hundreds of suicide stories I'd digested. Crisscrossing ley lines didn't cause it. I wasn't suicidal. So why did I feel, for a brief, disquieting moment, an overwhelming compulsion to bolt for the edge?

The imp of the perverse. The phrase leaps across decades and arrives unbidden as I lie in bed one night, trying to fall asleep. I can hear the fascinated voice of my college roommate, trying to explain, but I remember only fragments: *the pull of a skyscraper window . . . Edgar Allan Poe . . .*

The next morning I take a trip to the Eastbourne library. In the musty pages of *The Complete Stories and Poems of Edgar Allan Poe,* I find what I'm looking for: "The Imp of the Perverse," a compact short story that abstrusely begins, "In the consideration of the faculties and impulses—of the *prima mobilia* of the human soul, the phrenologists have failed to make room for a propensity which, although obviously existing as a radical, primitive, irreducible sentiment, has been equally overlooked by all the moralists who have preceded them." Right. Undaunted, I slog on until I come to a passage that catches my attention.

It is merely the idea of what would be our sensations during the sweeping precipitancy of a fall from such a height. And this fall—this rushing annihilation—for the very reason that it involves that one most ghastly and loathsome of all the most ghastly and loathsome images of death and suffering which have ever presented themselves to our imagination—for this very cause do we now the most vividly desire it. And because our reason violently deters us from the brink, therefore do we the most impetuously approach it. There is no passion in nature so demonically impatient, as that of him who, shuddering upon the edge of a precipice, thus meditates a plunge. To indulge, for a moment, in any attempt at thought, is to be inevitably lost; for reflection but urges us to forbear, and therefore it is, I say, that we cannot. If there be no friendly arm to check us, or if we fail in a sudden effort to prostrate ourselves backward from the abyss, we plunge, and are destroyed.

Such actions, claims the narrator, result "solely from the spirit of the Perverse. We perpetrate them because we feel we should not." Consigned "to the hangman and to hell" after blurting out a murder confession on a crowded street, the narrator considers himself "one of the many uncounted victims of the Imp of the Perverse."

That's it. I look up from the book and recall my own brushes with the Imp: my compulsion to swerve into the path of an oncoming car, to filch an item from a briefly unattended store, and, here at Beachy Head, to inch my prostrate body over, or make a dash for, the unobstructed cliff edge. You do not need to be vulnerable, as Carlyon said, to feel the lure of Beachy Head. A mentally stable person can find himself "shuddering upon the edge of a precipice," contemplating a plunge, just as a moral person can find himself hovering over a bargain bin, contemplating a petty theft. The Imp doesn't strike the wretched, but the repressed, which means everybody, at one time or another, and it feeds on easy opportunity.

At Beachy Head, the easiness of suicide strongly suggests the idea, whether you're a foot from the edge or fifteen. How easy it would be to fall onto the rocks below—just a little lean. How easy to run over the edge of Beachy Head. No foot patrols to dodge. No barriers to negotiate, except for a few brief stretches of spindly wire fencing. Just a few strides will do it. As one failed suicide later explained, "All you have to do is keep walking."

Those who do are drawn to the edge not by an irresistible

compulsion but by the promise of relief from unbearable pain. I would like to think that I was blindsided by the Imp on that Sunday morning, but I still fear I may have more in common with those who actually go over the edge than I realize, that I am repressing some private, unknowable pain. Rather than "keep walking," I keep drinking.

5

Rescue and Recovery

On a warm May evening, a taxi driver finds a suicide note in the backseat of his cab, minutes after dropping off a Beachy Head fare. Hearing the details on her patrol car radio, Police Constable Julia Clasby flicks on the siren and steps on the gas. She pushes fifty through the narrow streets of Meads, the siren and radio retreating to the margins of her awareness. Tense, her partner stares straight ahead. Since graduating from the academy eight months before, Clasby has broken up Friday-night fights in crowded barrooms and served as an identification officer at the morgue, where she gathered the personal effects from a Beachy Head body with half a head and arms scraped to the bone. But nothing unnerves her like a call to Beachy Head, because you never know what's going to happen. "You don't know if the person's going back with you or if they're going to jump in front of you or if they've already jumped or if they're there at all."

She turns off the siren as she swerves onto the coast road. She passes Black Robin and Bullock Down farms, forlorn in the twilight, then the pub and Hodcombe, scanning seaward for a figure that fits the dispatcher's description. Nothing. She pulls into the car park near Belle Tout. Ordinarily, she and her partner would check the license plates of the six parked cars and peer through the windows for suicide notes and half-empty whiskey bottles. If a car is suspect, they'd walk a direct line to the cliff edge, where, looking down, they'd likely see a body. But the vehicle check isn't necessary this time. The person they're looking for can't drive. She's thirteen years old, a year younger than Clasby's own sister.

Crossing the cliff top, Clasby scans the edge, hoping to find a girl standing or sitting near it. Except for a couple watching the sunset, the edge is a clean line unmarked by people or possessions suspiciously abandoned: a backpack, a coat, a bicycle. Drawing closer to the edge, the officers split off, Clasby heading east, her partner west. She feels her heart quicken the way it did when she was a child watching the police on TV probe dark alleyways and bust open doors; now she's participating in a real-life drama. Hard-boiled coast guard officers or constables dread, above all, "pickin' up a kid." Clasby steels herself for that possibility.

She peers over the edge and scans the cliff face. Her eyes widen to absorb the sight of a girl in blue jeans and T-shirt, sitting on a narrow ledge six feet below the cliff top, twenty feet away. Silently, Clasby signals her partner to get the patrol car.

At Beachy Head, the police and coast guard adhere, in theory, to a strict division of labor dictated by training and resources. The police rule the top and bottom of the cliffs because only they have negotiators trained to lure potential jumpers away from the edge, and a helicopter near enough to recover bodies quickly and relatively inexpensively from the beach. The coast guard has the run of the cliff face because only they have a cliff team that specializes in rescuing and recovering casualties from slopes and ledges, and a rescue helicopter that can winch up the seriously injured. There are exceptions. If there's a body on the beach and the tide is high, the inshore lifeboat—a small inflatable with an outboard motor and a crew of four that dispatches from the Eastbourne marina seven miles east—will go in place of the helicopter. And if a rookie cop finds a girl who reminds her of her sister, sitting on a ledge a ladder's length down the cliff face, she may decide to bypass the coast guard and perform the rescue herself.

Clasby straps on a harness as her partner secures the rope to the bumper of the patrol car. She walks to the edge and peers down. The girl seems unaware of her presence. Clasby asks her name, even though she already knows it; she doesn't imagine there are too many thirteen-year-olds alone on the cliffs tonight. The girl turns slowly and looks up. Her scraggly hair swings to the side, revealing a pale, blank face. She says nothing and turns back to the Channel. Clasby asks if she can come down and talk but is again met with silence. "Well, I'm going to talk to you."

Her partner stakes a rope ladder to the cliff and drapes it over the edge. Clasby climbs down. Seconds later, she's sitting on a four-foot-wide shelf, her back against the chalk cliff face. The girl sits forward, her legs dangling over the edge of a three-hundred-foot sheer drop. If she pushes off, Clasby won't be able to grab her in time. But she's willing to take the risk; by giving the girl a little space, she hopes to earn her trust.

They quietly watch the sunset together, and gradually, the girl opens up. She tells Clasby her name (Emma) and talks about problems at home and school. They discuss whether there's a

God and a heaven and a hell. Emma says she isn't afraid to die; she tried to kill herself before. Then she starts to cry. Her delicate shoulders shake, and the sleeves of her T-shirt flutter in the evening breeze. Her grip on the ledge remains firm. Clasby assures her that the police will try to help her with her problems by getting social services a lot more involved. After forty-five minutes on the ledge, Clasby asks if she can help her back to the cliff top. Emma nods.

Six constables, all men, greet them on the cliff top. Clasby sits next to Emma in the backseat of the cruiser. The ride is quiet. At the station, Clasby sits with the girl for another five hours while administrators arrange for foster care. Later, she discovers that Emma has been a psychiatric patient at a local hospital and that she has indeed tried to kill herself several times before.

THE LOCAL NEWSPAPER ARCHIVES are filled with accounts of intrepid constables talking and dragging people away from the cliff edge or tackling and restraining them. I read about two police negotiators who spent seven hours of a stormy night trying to persuade a forty-seven-year-old man not to jump—the same man the same negotiators had rescued from the same spot once before. He finally accepted the offer of a hot drink after the officers agreed to withdraw to their vehicles. When he finished his tea, he headed back to the cliffs. But four feet from the edge, he slipped into a ditch, and the negotiators seized their chance. One dived across the five-foot-wide crevice before the man could scramble out, grabbed him, and, with the help of other officers, hauled the struggling man to safety, whereupon he was handcuffed and taken to the hospital.

In another incident, an unharnessed constable climbed twenty-two feet down a crumbly cliff face in a frigid February gale to rescue a man on the verge of slipping off a ledge. The man was so confused—high on glue, it turned out—that the constable had to force him back up the cliff face.

Julia Clasby's rescue also made the newspapers, but I learn much more about it from Clasby. I'm drawn to her for a couple of reasons: I'm intrigued by the rescue of a girl about the age of my daughter, and by Clasby herself, one of only a handful of women in a predominantly male police force.

I wait for P.C. Clasby early one morning in the lobby of the Eastbourne police station, a high-ceilinged, vinyl-floored space with pewlike benches set against chestnut walls, and presently reverberating with the unholy shouts of a ponytailed man in camouflage trousers standing menacingly in front of the receiving desk. On the other side of the counter, a grandfatherly, pencil-necked officer wearing wire-rimmed spectacles listens to the tantrum with heroic patience. I'm sitting on a bench against the back wall, a lone spectator, telling myself it will all blow over and that there's really no need to intervene and risk getting pummeled. Then, to my relief, the door opens, spilling voices, footsteps, and, finally, a pair of constables into the lobby. Amazingly, they only watch and shake their heads before disappearing through a buzzing door.

"You detain me for something I didn't do, now you won't give me back my watch and money? That's boolshit. Give me my fuckin' money!"

The officer calmly repeats that the property will be returned to its "rightful owner" after the investigation is completed.

The wiry man tautens. His fists clench tightly against his sides. His snug ponytail trembles against the hood of his sweat-jacket. For the first time, I see fear flit across the constable's face. The silver-haired receptionist would be no match for this coil of rage. He glances at me over the man's shoulder, and all I can muster in response is a lame "you poor bastard" shake of the head. Then the ponytailed man turns. He's leaving. At last. He exits with a prideful bounce, his mouth as tight as a vise until he uncranks it—"Fuck you!"—before disappearing into the vestibule and out the door.

The constable shakes his head and turns to me. "We get some quite irate, nasty people come in here." His gentle voice carries in the suddenly quiet lobby. I get up and walk to the counter. The officer's name—Ian Tubb—is pinned to the breast pocket of his police-issue shirt. "We have to put up with it, try to calm things down the best we can." He removes his glasses and wipes the lenses with a handkerchief. "A few days ago, we had half a dozen youngsters in the lobby, kicking up in the front office, making a thorough nuisance of themselves because they wanted one of their friends released from custody. Finally, when he did come out, they all plodded off. We were glad to see the backs of them."

He says that two years ago, a crazed woman grabbed a female constable by the shirt and tried to yank the officer across the receiving desk before a member of the public intervened. "After that," he says, carefully putting his glasses back on, "there were calls for a Plexiglas barrier, as banks have, but the chief constable rejected the idea because he feels the police should be accessible to the public."

I shake my head. It seems to me that a Plexiglas barrier might be a good idea in a town where delinquent behavior is clearly on the rise. The local newspapers regularly run stories of angry residents determined to take back the "yob"-ridden streets of Eastbourne. I read about a seventy-two-year-old woman who chased two teenagers in her "electric invalid carriage" after one spit in her face. After cornering one of the boys in a supermarket foyer and giving him "a good ticking off," she returned home and suffered a fatal aneurysm, which the coroner attributed to her stressful encounter with the hoodlums, or "yobs." Another story quoted a former Eastbourne councillor who was so fed up with "anti-social louts" urinating and vandalizing around his home that he considered spearheading a vigilante group. "We're not just talking about students mooning or putting a cone on the top of the statue of the Duke of Devonshire," he said. "We're talking about kicking in front doors and smashing windows. When I go to other places and tell people this is going on they say, 'Oh, I know. It's terrible.' But when I tell them it's Eastbourne I'm talking about, they say, 'What? It's full of old people.' "

Well, not really. Not anymore. God's waiting room, as the locals affectionately call Eastbourne, is no longer quite so crowded, since the city, out of economic necessity, caters increasingly to the young. The days when Eastbourne's commercial district shut down as soon as its aged residents retired to their terraced flats for dinner and cards, and the staid holidaymakers to their seafront hotels, are fading fast as hip pubs and cafés replace sedate gift shops and luncheonettes. Unfortunately, Eastbourne's fledgling nightlife attracts not only urbane tourists and young professionals flush with hard-earned cash, but also roving packs of thugs and brawling barflies—the very people who can make Ian Tubb's life hell.

He asks what I'm doing in Eastbourne, and I tell him. He listens with interest. "I was the Beachy Head patrol officer, oh, what was it, fifteen, twenty years ago. Back when there were patrols." He shakes his head. "You want stories."

"Did you ever rescue anybody?"

He pauses to consider the question. A door buzzes. Tubb turns to look over my shoulder, his eyes disappearing as his wire frames pick up the reflected ceiling light. He nods at a passing constable, then turns back to me. "Well, yes, it was right about 1980 when we had a call. A member of the armed forces had stolen a Land Rover from a base down in Kent, and he was coming through on the main road, on the A259." With the police giving chase, the Land Rover plowed through a bus blockade, then, speeding along the Eastbourne seafront, struck three other vehicles. At Beachy Head, the serviceman jumped out of the vehicle and ran to the cliff edge, where he threatened to jump. Tubb was the first police constable to arrive at the scene. He told the man to come to the station for a cup of tea, and he'd help him sort things out. Twenty minutes later, the man gave himself up.

"Once or twice," Tubb goes on, "I saw people there who were by themselves and not looking quite right. They weren't up there with anybody else. They weren't exercising dogs. There was something about them. You could tell by their demeanor and the way they were looking around, not going anywhere particular." He turns toward a beeping fax machine. Mick Davey steps out of his office and, passing behind Tubb, says a quick hello to me. "I brought back a number of people who I spoke to and found that they were distressed, missing from home, they'd had rows with their husbands, wives, whatever. And I brought them back under the—what we call Section 136 of the Mental Health Act, which gives the police powers to detain anybody we feel is a risk to themselves."

The street door opens and shuts.

"Did they—," I start.

Tubb turns toward the entryway, and I look, too. A stocky constable with alert eyes enters the lobby. She registers my presence with a quick glance, removes her cap, and strides over. Her eyes are chocolate-colored, her dark hair pulled back tightly around her round face. Her lips are full and slightly upturned at the corners. It is a pretty face that could be beautiful if the job required it. She asks if I'm Tom, in that dulcet tone that Englishwomen seem to specialize in.

"Yes."

"Julia Clasby," she says, extending a hand. I explain to Tubb the purpose of our meeting, and he suggests that we talk in the detention room off the lobby.

Clasby and I sit at the end of a table too heavy for the most enraged detainee to lift, within walls devoid of bulletin boards, framed pictures, and other potential projectiles, next to a barred window. Clasby plants her elbows on the table and interlaces her fingers, a pose that hunches her shoulders and conveys authority. She locks her eyes on my face, and we begin at the beginning.

She wanted to be a policewoman, she tells me, ever since she was a little girl, but she doubted she'd have the strength or courage to break up fights, bust down doors, or do any of the other things she saw police officers doing on TV. But a career day during her last year of university changed all that. A police recruiter invited her to go out on a few patrols with him. She did, and she was sold.

She describes the rescue of thirteen-year-old Emma. I ask how it felt to receive a prestigious Royal Humane Society Award for her heroics. She smiles uncomfortably. She says she feels a bit awkward about it in a way because, yes, she was the one who talked to the girl and built up a relationship with her, but she couldn't have done it without her colleagues. Besides, any of them would have done what she did.

I don't tell her that during an earlier conversation with two of her colleagues, one of them told me that though he knew it was his duty to try to save people, he was terrified of the cliff edge and wouldn't go near it. It occurs to me that I'm drawn to Clasby for the same reason people are attracted to movie stars and athletes. She possesses something I don't: physical courage.

"How did you feel sitting on a three-hundred-foot-high ledge?" I ask.

She looks away to consider the question. "I don't think I even thought about it. My concern was with her, and I'd worry about me later." She pauses. "I couldn't look down from where I was; all I could do was look across. It didn't occur to me how high up I was until I got back to the cliff top. Then I thought, 'My God.'" She laughs, then turns thoughtful. "With the thirteen-year-old, I actually liked the fact that I could be involved. I felt that I had played a part to help her in her life, and there is a sense of satisfaction in that. And if I can go do that for anybody up there and help them, then I will."

"What would you have done if she'd jumped?"

She looks at me as if it's a strange question. "Then," she says, "it would have been a job for the police helicopter. Or the coast guard."

IT IS A CRISP FALL EVENING. Colin Sillery slows his cab to pick up three men standing at the entrance of the Beachy Head Pub. He stops and rolls down his window. A skinny, well-weathered man wearing a black leather jacket tells him that they need a ride to Amberstone, a psychiatric hospital ten miles away. It'll cost thirteen pounds, Sillery says, which the men volunteer to pay before getting in. Though disheveled, they act quite normally, so Sillery has no worries about accepting them as passengers. He catches a strong whiff of alcohol as they pile in.

He has driven some four hundred yards when the man in the leather jacket says he's going to be sick and asks him to stop. Sillery pulls the cab over. The man gets out, walks behind the vehicle, and disappears into the darkness. Sillery asks the two men if they want him to wait for their buddy. He doesn't know that thirty-seven-year-old Adrian Rew attempted suicide ten years before and has been a long-term volunteer patient at Amberstone for the last five. Nor does Sillery know that two nights before,

Rew visited the site of a traffic accident that claimed his father's life a year ago, and that the following afternoon his mother drove her distraught and hungover son back to Amberstone, where she told the head nurse that she was gravely concerned about his mental state. The man's friends tell the cabdriver not to wait.

At midnight an Amberstone nurse calls Mrs. Rew to say that her son went out to dinner with a few friends and did not return.

The following day the police helicopter searches the cliffs but finds nothing. The next morning, it tries again. As the German-made Balkow flutters along the chalk coastline, the air observer scans the beach and cliff face through a pair of gyroscopically stabilized binoculars. Above a section of the cliffs known as Gun Gardens, he spies a sliver of black between two boulders some fifty feet above the beach. He zooms in as the chopper flies closer. It's a human torso. The air observer radios police headquarters, which contacts the Dover coast guard, which summons the cliff rescue and recovery team from their homes and workplaces.

Bob Jewson is talking on the phone in his government office when his pager beeps. He brings the conversation to a rapid close. Using the speed dial, he calls Dover coast guard and gets the skinny. Jewson grabs an apple off his desk and tells a colleague, "I'm off on a shout."

Jewson feels the ache of anticipation as he races through Eastbourne in his Jeep. Ten years ago he was a beardless, slightly thinner twenty-nine-year-old coming off a six-year volunteer stint with the local militia and looking for something to fill his spare time. A mate told him about the coast guard's volunteer cliff team, and he figured he'd give it a try. Some 125 rescued or recovered casualties later, Jewson still gets an adrenaline rush driving to the cliffs.

At the pub, Jewson turns off the coast road and onto the cliff top. The air observer and a police constable greet him beyond the wash of helicopter rotors. As Jewson listens to the air observer describe the location of the body, he glances over the P.C.'s shoulder at a small group of tourists peering over the cliff edge, searching for a body he knows they will not be able to see.

Leaving the air observer and constable to confer with each other, Jewson drives to a public parking lot near the pub. He parks next to an ice-cream truck and walks briskly toward a hut sprouting with antennae and packed with overalls, helmets, rain gear, a portable generator, a Land Rover with motorized capstan, and a small trailer holding two twelve-hundred-foot ropes and a collapsible aluminum tripod.

Chris Turner, already in his overalls, greets Jewson outside the hut's entrance. He's a short, perky young man with thinning sandy-blond hair and a penchant for pranks and off-color jokes. He's also Jewson's protégé, a cliff man in training when he's not producing car and erotic magazines.

"What do you have for us today, Bob?" Turner asks.

Jewson scratches his closely cropped beard. "Male casualty, Gun Gardens."

"Of course." Gun Gardens is the highest point of the cliffs; more suicides occur there than anywhere else along Beachy Head's four-mile length.

Jewson pulls a Clark Kent, disappearing through the doorway in a partially unbuttoned oxford and emerging minutes later in orange canvas overalls. He holds a scratched-up helmet in his left hand and gloves between his teeth.

Other cliff team members hurry in: a college tutor, a bricklayer, a retiree, a software engineer, all volunteers or auxiliary coast guard officers. As the auxiliary in charge, Bob Jewson is their leader, the one responsible for the day-to-day operation of the Eastbourne Coast Guard: for running training sessions, giving talks to local organizations, updating the vehicle log, recruiting, and keeping his eleven-man cliff team a happy and disciplined fraternity. Two men banter as they hitch the trailer to the Land Rover; two more check in with Jewson for assignments they never question; and Fat Freddy Sherwood, who, at 18 stone (250 pounds), is as round as he is tall, inspects the ropes in the trailer. When the trailer is hitched to the Land Rover, Sherwood drives his mates up the pub parking lot, slowing for another group of gawking lunchgoers.

The sky is clear, the air cold but not hand-numbing, the cliff top unusually calm: the perfect morning for a recovery. Sherwood parks fifty feet from the edge of Gun Gardens, a ledgy, sloping section of cliff face where, some two hundred years ago, locals reputedly planted a cannon after French privateers slaughtered the crew of an English brig on the shore below. Jewson hops out and searches for a level, compact, rabbit-hole-free patch of cliff top along the edge. After Sherwood aligns the Land Rover with the chosen site, the team unhitches the trailer, unloads the gear, and mucks in.

Fifteen feet from the cliff edge, Jewson pounds three wooden stakes deep into the turf and lashes them together with rope to form a triangular anchor point. Meanwhile, Turner and a mate erect the tripod on the cliff edge, spreading and staking the side legs, then running a rope from the base of each leg to the anchoring point inland. When the legs are secure, they fix the tripod at a forty-five-degree angle (allowing the top to clear the cliff edge by a good five feet) by running a steel cable from its apex to the middle anchoring stake. Then they hook the tripod's loose middle leg to the taut cable, so that it hangs horizontally suspended, where it will stay during most of the operation (functionally, the tripod is really a bipod). Finally, they unroll a rope ladder called a "Scotsman" over the cliff edge, staking its corners to the cliff top.

Inland, two cliff team members unspool the safety and main lines from the trailer bin. The safety line zigzags across the cliff top, wrapping once around a stake, then zigging to a pulley fixed to the front stake of the triangular anchor point and zagging to the pulley blocks on the tripod's apex. The main line takes a more direct route, winding twice around the capstan on the Land Rover's front bumper and running upward to the tripod's pulley blocks. Both will fasten to the cliff man's harness when it's time. Sherwood, meanwhile, sets the hand brake on the Land Rover, engages the four-wheel drive, locks the steering wheel, and loops one end of a steel cable around the tow-ball of the vehicle and the other end around a tall stake hammered into the cliff top and lashed to a second anchoring stake three feet behind. The men move quickly, and there is little talking.

Watching Sherwood is a growing throng of bystanders. At one time, onlookers would gather around the capstan during an operation and watch the affable veteran work the winch. Freddy Sherwood was all too happy to entertain them and answer their questions, which didn't sit well with his boss, Garry Russell, especially when the order came through to stop or hoist slow and nothing happened. Having anchored the Land Rover, Sherwood now raises a spindly rope fence around the perimeter of the site, chatting across it as he goes.

Meanwhile, Bob Jewson tightens the straps on his harness as he prepares to step off the cliff edge. Five members of the cliff team are missing, more than usual for a shout; he wonders if there'll be any late arrivals. Then, as if on cue, a hearty "Hello, boys!" rises above the murmur of the crowd, and Jewson knows immediately that in gaining the body he wished for, he's lost command.

Garry Russell, thick-chested, ruddy-cheeked, and bushy-browed, struts through the work site like an alpha leprechaun. Officially, he's the sector officer, overseeing several coast guard stations along the East Sussex coast. Metaphorically, he is superintendent to Jewson's principal, showing up for jobs when he happens to be on duty locally, as he is today. Colloquially, he's a "goddamn legend," rescuer of twenty persons and fourteen dogs, recoverer of more than a hundred Beachy Head bodies, survivor of two rock falls (one sidelining him for thirteen weeks), and recipient of the British Empire Medal for bravery. He once "thumped on the chin" a big bloke who threatened to jump off the cliffs, and his policy not to shout unless one of his cliff team mates stepped drastically out of line was honored more in the breach than in the observance, which may be why Turner quickly double-checks the lashings on the anchoring stakes.

Jewson greets the shorter, bulbous-nosed Russell with the deference accorded prickly bosses and local heroes. Rather than tell Russell what to do, he explains the situation, his voice muffled behind the face guard of his helmet; he figures that by the end of the briefing, Russell will assign himself a task. He does—he'll be the third legman on the tripod, a job that doesn't begin in earnest until the final stages of the recovery, allowing Russell to focus on his speciality: overseeing the operation.

Twenty minutes after the first stake is pounded into the ground, Jewson is ready to descend. A cliffmate grips a rope attached to his harness as Jewson works himself under the apex of the tripod. There his harness is hitched to the main and safety lines and the sling of a lightweight stretcher. When he's secure, he releases his grip on the tripod and unfastens the rope held by his cliffmate. Briefly, he's in swaying suspension, a radio and a pair of binoculars hanging from his neck, the lightweight stretcher swinging vertically beneath his seat. To stabilize the tripod, Turner and a cliffmate kneel and push against the legs of the apparatus with outstretched arms.

If Jewson fears the prospect of descending a cliff half the

height of the Empire State Building, he doesn't show it. The lines have a breaking strain of four and a half tons, and the harness is of the finest quality. Because the air is calm and there's daylight to spare, he doesn't have to worry about being blown against a cliff face flecked with razor-sharp flint, or pummeled by boulders tumbling down out of darkness. And it's not as if he's venturing into unknown territory. Beachy Head is a cliff of many faces, and Jewson knows each like the hairy back of his leathery hand—the ledges and headwalls, scarps and notches, bramble and scree that are largely invisible to all but the cliff men who clamber over and around them. He knows that Boulders Bank, which looks as smooth and white as a ski slope from above, is an obstacle course of well-deep holes and refrigerator-sized boulders, and that the seemingly compact scree slope at the Nudist Colony (once the site of a ledge just above the high-water mark where nudists sunbathed in privacy until a rock fall buried their driftwood-sheltered perch) is like a tilted tray of white marbles. He knows that the towering chalk obelisk known as Devil's Chimney is even more detached from the main cliffs than it appears, because he's rappelled down the frighteningly deep chasm. And he knows the relatively honest face of Gun Gardens. He knows but doesn't think about the softness and porousness of the rock in which his life is staked, how one sudden, massive cliff fall could cause five years' worth of erosion in thirty seconds, violently turning the stakes, ropes, harnesses, and trusted colleagues into a heap of good intentions, because why dwell on something so unlikely and beyond his control? Gloved hands clasping the line, he's eager to go.

Jewson radios Sherwood to "lower slow," the order spilling out of the loudspeaker mounted on the Land Rover's fender. Sherwood slowly feeds the main line around the winch as two of his cliffmates pay out the safety line.

Jewson backwalks over the rope ladder, dislodging chunks of chalk as he goes. When he's clear of the ladder, he radios, "Faster," and rappels down the sheer cliff face, toes pushing off the chalk every few yards. A hundred feet down, he radios to stop as he lands on a ledge the width and length of a tractor-trailer truck. A few years ago on this very ledge, he found a woman in a yellow sundress lying in a patch of bramble. Her back was broken. As Jewson and a paramedic tried to stabilize her, she begged them to push her off. Had she gotten her wish, she would have fallen another 50 feet onto a 250-foot-long scree slope that ends in a 120-foot drop to the beach. As it was, she was winched into a coast guard helicopter and never heard from again.

Jewson checks his harness to see that the lines are still securely fastened. He looks up and sees the tripod, a silver triangle framing cloud and blue sky. Turner, still pushing against the leg of the tripod, peers over the cliff edge. Jewson waves, then backwalks off the ledge and down its face, constantly looking up for falling rock. Turner has disappeared from view, as has the tripod, and the sound of its clinking pulleys has receded. All Jewson sees are a gull gliding across the sky, two cliff lines hanging over a crumbly ledge, and pieces of tumbling chalk; all he hears are the bump of the stretcher against the cliff face and the crunch of chalk beneath his boots.

When he reaches the scree slope, he radios, "Full speed." On the cliff top, Fat Freddy Sherwood, dripping sweat, feeds the line around the winch as if paying out the anchor of an iceberg-bound ship. With one hand on the line and the other lifting the stretcher to prevent it from dragging across the rocks, Jewson rappels down the steep incline with Spider-Man-like speed.

Pushing off the hard-packed scree, one leg after the other in a series of long, arcing backjumps, he constantly glances over his shoulder to survey the terrain below: the crumpled remains of a car in a hollow, patches of bramble and gorse, scatterings of chalk boulders that, in the sunlight, seem to glow with radiant energy. He passes them all, counting down on his radio as he goes ("Seventy-five feet . . . fifty feet . . . twenty-five feet . . .") until he finds himself standing near the heavily eroded edge of a drop-off overlooking the Channel. Sweat trickles down his rib cage; his calves burn. He radios for a bit of slack line and peers over the edge. The sight is no surprise: sixty feet of sheer cliff and another sixty of chalk boulders massed against the base of the cliffs, fall-out from the waves' ceaseless undercutting of the headland. More bodies hang up there than reach the beach, and this body will probably be no exception. It'll just be a matter of finding it.

It isn't hard. As he scans the boulder slope with his binoculars, Jewson's attention is drawn to a flashing light high up on the scarp, approximately twenty feet to the left. His eyes linger on two boulders, one oven-shaped, the other taller, their sunlit surfaces contrasting sharply with the flashing black bulk lying atop the smaller boulder. He's certain that's it. He asks for slack line again and sidesteps along the slope until he's in line with the body. He radios Sherwood to lower slow and rappels down the sheer drop. When he reaches the rock pile, he backwalks awkwardly down its forty-five-degree slope until he comes to the oven-sized boulder. He hops onto its flat surface, pivots, and gazes down at the corpse. It lies on its side. The torso and legs are wedged between the rocks (not deeply, Jewson is relieved to see), and the head and feet stick out like the ends of a hot dog. Below the hiked jacket sleeve of the corpse's right arm, a silver watch encircles a bony wrist. Jewson guesses the body hit the front of the taller, seaward boulder, then dropped into the space between the two.

Eight minutes after beginning his descent, Jewson radios the team that he's alongside the body, approximately fifty feet above the beach, and then he requests slack on both lines. He studies the two boulders. He'll pack the body on top of the shorter, landward one, he decides, which is flat and has just enough surface area to accommodate the stretcher. (The other option is to have the body winched to the scree slope and pack it there, a two-man job he would rather avoid.) But there's the problem of extraction. There's little room to maneuver on the boulder. Jewson would have to lift the body while standing on a wobbly stretcher, then roll the body onto the stretcher while shifting his feet, a project requiring the balance and nimbleness of a surfer, which Jewson isn't. He turns inland and considers the terrain he just came down—the rock he's standing on abuts a slope of basketball-sized rocks. Of course: use the slope as a ramp. He unhooks the sling of the stretcher from his harness and props the stretcher against the side of the boulder. Wearing rubber gloves now, he bends over the body and catches a whiff of urine. He grabs the right arm and leg and pulls the corpse free. The body is stiff (not surprising, since the man has been dead for over a day) and relatively light. Still, it is deadweight and a grunt. Shuffling backward, Jewson hauls it up on the surface of the boulder. He straightens and catches his breath. For the first time, he hears the lapping of the incoming tide before it's replaced by Russell's crackling voice: a progress check.

When Russell is satisfied that Jewson hasn't been carried out to sea, gobbled by a crevice, or knocked silly by delinquent boulders, Jewson lifts the body again by the right arm and leg, turns, and drops it on the slope above the boulder. He grabs the stretcher and places it on the boulder so that it lies parallel to the corpse. Then he unbuckles the canvas straps and the larger webbing straps and removes and unzips the body bag. He lays it across the stretcher, spreads the opening, and places chunks of chalk on one side to keep the bag from shifting. Crouched behind the stretcher and facing the slope, he pulls on the stiff body with outstretched arms until it yields to gravity and rolls into the bag. Only then does Jewson take stock of the injuries and indignities along its length.

He's seen some horrible things on the cliff face: maggot-infested orifices, strewn intestines, bent and shorn limbs, flattened heads and cracked skulls oozing yolklike brains. He's followed a trail of body fluids, organs, and stench to bodies. He's also seen some pretty strange things. He once discovered the body of a German woman screwed headfirst into the beach; nearby lay her daughter, wearing a swimmer's nose pinch and earplugs. He found one body with a handkerchief stuffed in its mouth, another with a rubber cord tied around its ankles.

This man's body, though, is remarkably intact and unremarkably accessorized. Maggots have yet to invade the ears and nostrils. There are no unusual protuberances beneath the chalk-dusted jeans and jacket to suggest broken bones. The limbs are all present and accounted for. Only the face hints at the massive destruction beneath the skin (a pathologist once compared a Beachy Head body to a slab of cellophane-wrapped peanut brittle dropped on concrete). The forehead is dented, the nose askew, and reddish-purple bruises mottle the cheeks and chin.

Jewson slides the watch off the wrist and wrests a silver ring from a finger. He removes a leather wallet from the dead man's urine-stained jeans pocket. He puts the items in his pocket and starts packing the body, which shouldn't take long. There's no prickly bramble to remove or organs to fetch. He doesn't have to worry about accidentally smearing blood on the stretcher or body bag, because there isn't much blood to speak of.

Jewson feels nothing for the man as he zips him up. The caved-in forehead doesn't repulse him. The violent repudiation of life doesn't anger him. He doesn't consider the man selfish or feckless. He doesn't ask why. That's the beauty of cliff work. Jewson is so focused on the job that there's no room for the judgments or feelings that may come later.

With the body strapped in, Jewson radios Sherwood and says he'll be ready in a few minutes, to prepare to hoist. On the cliff top, Sherwood starts the Land Rover, which powers the winch. Another cliff team member takes the safety line off the stake and feeds it through an anchored metal device with a serrated edge— a "clogger"—that grips and locks the rope as soon as the pull is taken off, as when Jewson orders stop hoist or if, by chance, he should fall.

Jewson puts away his rubber gloves and reattaches to the main cliff line. He fastens the safety line to the sling cradling the stretcher. When Russell radios that they're ready to hoist, Jewson gives the okay. Slowly, the winch takes up the slack, and the stretcher rises until it hangs horizontally below Jewson's chest. Ordinarily, he'd position the stretcher below his feet to avoid the drip of leaking body fluids, but not now. Because the cliff line runs at an angle down an undulating cliff face, more than 600 feet of line is required to recover a body 470 feet down the cliffs. The weight of so much rope, the weight of the cliff man at the end of it, and the tension created by the bend of the rope over the crumbly edge of the final drop will stretch the braided nylon rope twelve feet beyond its normal length once the slack is taken up and the winch begins to exert its pull—which is why Jewson keeps the casualty horizontally suspended just below his chest. Should he slingshot against the sheer cliff face, the dead man will bear the brunt of the impact.

As Jewson begins to feel the pull of the winch, he tries to control the ascent by leaning back as he's pulled forward, like someone on the losing end of a tug-of-war. But the tension soon overwhelms his resistance, and he's flung forward. He clings to the stretcher as his feet skim the boulder pile. Cliff team members call it a Nantucket sleigh ride, a charming if dubious comparison. Jewson crashes against the sheer cliff face, the stretcher cushioning the blow. Again and again Jewson bumps against the sixty-foot cliff wall, the corpse absorbing the impact and catching most of the falling scree, until he's up and over the wall, and the line's tension—most of it, anyway—has been released. On the scree slope, he radios to stop and repositions the stretcher so that it hangs below his seat.

With a bruised shin, he alternately walks, runs, and hops up the slope, occasionally stopping to catch his breath or lift the head of the stretcher when it snags on a boulder or bush. At the base of the ledge overlooking the scree slope, he stops before he's hoisted fifty feet to the ledge and then another hundred to the cliff top. For the remainder of the ascent, he'll have little foot contact with the vertical cliff face, nothing to check the spinning caused by the braided line's tendency to twist.

Ten feet from the cliff top, Jewson stops for the last time. He touches the cliff face with his feet to brake his twirling and untwists the lines so that they don't snag on the tripod's pulleys. He continues the ascent until the knots on the line lock against the pulleys, lifting the tripod's apex up and away from the edge. To keep the tripod grounded and slow its backward pivot, Turner and a cliffmate push lightly against the front legs as Russell holds the unhooked horizontal back leg. Slowly, the tripod swings back, the stretcher is unhitched, and with the aid of the rope ladder and a few helping hands, Jewson climbs over the edge and staggers onto the cliff top.

Watching it all is a crowd of fifty, the undertaker (whose unmarked van is parked on the cliff top), a police constable, and Coroner's Officer Michael Davey, who relieves Jewson of Adrian Rew's wristwatch, ring, and wallet. An hour later, Davey calls

Mrs. Rew to inform her that a body thought to be her son's has been recovered off the cliffs of Beachy Head.

TEN YEARS LATER, Bob Jewson and Chris Turner look back on their cliff team experience with understandable pride.

"We weren't glory seekers," Turner says. "We did it as a public service." He reclines his small frame against the back of a velvet love seat and stuffs his hands in his jeans pockets. The pendulum of a wall clock swings above his balding head. "Unlike in the States, most rescue services here are volunteers. Cave rescues, mountain rescues, cliff rescues—all volunteers. You had a very dedicated band of people, Herberts like us, who were doing it because they wanted to do it."

Bob Jewson, sitting plumb-line straight in a plush armchair, nods. "We were very much unsung heroes. The police got medals left, right, and center, but the attitude of coast guard management was no medals. That's what you're expected to do." Then, as if he's just remembered something, he places his teacup on the floor and excuses himself.

A couple of hours earlier, Jewson greeted me at the threshold of his Eastbourne flat, wearing a puffy warm-up suit and a smile that seemed contained by the neatly trimmed salt-and-pepper beard around it. He had bags under his eyes, and his short, thinning hair was slightly mussed, as if he'd just taken off a hat. He stood like a gunslinger—arms bent at the side, shoulders thrown back.

He led me into a formal sitting room with a modest fireplace. A framed picture of a beauty pageant contestant, his wife, presumably, sat on a lacquered hutch. In front of a shade-drawn window, a parrot watched me warily through the bars of his cell. Jewson introduced me to Chris Turner and then to Percy, a yellow-winged Amazon, he told me with a hint of pride. Then

Turner and Jewson described in tag-team fashion the satisfactions of cliff work, the logistics, and, finally, the dangers and difficulties: swinging like a pendulum in a gale four hundred feet above a rocky beach; bouncing against rock projections; stabilizing a casualty on a narrow ledge in freezing rain and darkness; playing dodgeball against tumbling boulders of neck-snapping force.

To me, someone who has difficulty braving the last rung of a household ladder, theirs is a gripping and vicariously fulfilling performance. Which is, I suppose, what I was hoping for when, after noticing Jewson's ubiquitous presence in the old newspaper accounts of Beachy Head suicides, I gave him a call. In fact, for anyone seeking to penetrate the arcane world of cliff rescue and recovery, it is hard to find a more qualified insider than Bob Jewson. He was, until his retirement not long before my visit, the most experienced cliff man on the most experienced cliff team in the United Kingdom, a veteran of twenty years and some 250 rescues and recoveries. Recently retired from his government job as well, he now fills his days with part-time jobs and volunteer work.

"I thought this might interest you," he says, returning with a thick, well-preserved scrapbook. I place the album on my lap and slowly crack open the binding. I flip through pages of photographs, most of them showing Jewson dangling on a cliff line or returning to the cliff top with a casualty suspended under his harness. I peruse cuttings that leave out far more than they tell:

> A woman gave her handbag to a pair of walkers on Beachy Head and moments later plunged to her death over the cliff top. The couple raised the alarm and auxilliary coastguard Bob Jewson was lowered 130ft to the ledge where the woman was seen to be moving.

A woman who became Beachy Head's 12th victim this year may have slipped over the edge by accident. Mrs. Jean Wood, 36, of Essex Place Brighton, fell to her death on Saturday afternoon after walking along the cliffs with her husband, Edward. The couple were sitting by the edge when civil servant Mrs. Wood stood up and fell backwards. Auxiliary coastguard, Mr. Bob Jewson, was lowered down the 400-foot drop to recover the body.

An inquest into the death of Mr. John Robertson, whose body was recovered from the foot of the cliffs west of Beachy Head, was opened and adjourned at Eastboune Law Courts. His body was discovered at the base of the 250ft cliffs at Falling Sands by a passerby walking on the beach. Auxiliary coastguards Mr. Bob Jewson and Mr. Ivor Pollard took four hours to recover the body, under the supervision of Mr. Garry Russell.

I close the album and the sounds of the room return: the ticking of the clock, Percy's annoying nutcracking. I ask Jewson and Turner to tell me about some of their more memorable jobs. They trade glances. Jewson takes a sip of tea. The cup looks like a child's toy in his hands.

"We once had three bodies reported in the space of twenty minutes," Jewson says. "Saturday morning, twenty-first of January, 1990." On foot patrol with another coast guard, Jewson spotted the first body on a ledge while performing a routine scan of the cliff face between Devil's Chimney and Gun Gardens. After he called in the cliff team, the Dover coast guard radioed him that the police were attending to a naked female body on the beach at Whitbread Hollow. Then a young woman with a dog approached him.

"You've come to pick the man up on the beach?" she asked.

"No, it's a female," Jewson replied.

"I know the difference between a male and female, and this is a male."

"Is there a policeman with him?"

"No."

"Has he got any clothes on?"

"Oh yes, fully dressed."

Jewson then knew he had a third body and a problem. "Because we had three bodies and two body bags, and knowing that each recovery would take about two hours, I asked the inshore lifeboat to come in and pick up the one at Falling Sands. In the meantime, we went and got the woman that the police were with, and then we went back about four and a half hours later to pick up the one I had spotted in the first place."

How strange. Clustered suicides usually occur in confined places with rigid social structures—prisons, colleges, army barracks, mental hospitals—and among teenagers living in the same community. And they're usually imitative. But the three Beachy Head suicides are different. It's unlikely that either of the last two to jump had witnessed, and therefore was influenced by, the person who jumped before. Were the suicides pure coincidence? Or were they an example of morphic resonance, a phenomenon by which animals of the same breed are able to communicate with one another without having had direct contact? A few years back, sheep in an English farming village were observed rolling across cattle grids meant to block them from greener pastures. Soon there were similar sightings across the United Kingdom. Maybe some Beachy Head suicides spread in the same way: one person jumps, and the information reaches others in the same psychic or "morphogenic" field.

"Sometimes we'd get four or five people who jump in almost exactly the same spot consecutively," Jewson goes on. "There's a place, there's bits of cliff that come down in slight little block steps right above Gun Gardens, the scree of Gun Gardens. We had four consecutive bodies exactly at the same spot. We used the same stake holes. And then it stopped there completely and moved to Boulders Bank. There were about four or five at Boulders Bank." He once found two bodies a week apart at a spot on Falling Sands—named for the millions of tiny chalk grains that continuously fall down this most unstable section of cliff face—that hadn't seen a body in twenty years. He pauses and shakes his head. "I can't explain it. You suddenly get a cluster of bodies, and then it will stop. And then you'll get a cluster somewhere else. And the people have totally no relationship with each other at all."

Morphic resonance again? But how do you explain clusters moving from spot to spot? Kevin Carlyon said that ley lines can move, creating shifting centers of negative energy. I'll be damned. Maybe he's on to something.

Jewson and Turner continue to reminisce like two blokes in a bar, punctuating each other's tales with nods and shakes of the head. Turner remembers the Devonshire farmer whose life Jewson probably saved. They'd just recovered a body from the beach and were packing up their gear when Jewson noticed a man sitting near the cliff edge. He walked over and sat between the man and the cliffs. "I got talkin' to him," Jewson recalls, "just chatting, making conversation, and I said, 'What do you do?' And he said, 'I'm a farmer from Devon.' I said, 'Well do you come here often?' He said, 'No, it's the first time I've ever come to Beachy Head.' We got around to talking about other things. He said he'd been treated for depression six years before. We talked about suicide. After half an hour, he got up, shook my hand, and said, 'Thank you very much,' and went off and got in his car and drove away."

Jewson remembers the driver of a silver Citroën who repeatedly rammed a gate that once barred access to the cliff top, and, once through, gunned his car down a slope and over a drop. The vehicle whizzed over the heads of two retirees sitting on a bench, then nose-dived onto the beach. There was the Volvo they found one morning sticking out of a crevice halfway up the cliff face. The passenger door was open and the hazard lights on. The driver, they later discovered, had climbed out and jumped to his death. Turner remembers recovering the body of a one-legged man who crawled under a fence, rolled off the cliffs, landed on some bushes, and, somewhere along the way, lost his head. "Bob says, 'Where's his head?' I said, 'You're standing on it.'" Turner chuckles, his deep-set eyes turning to black slits. "We used to treat it as a hoot, really, otherwise we'd be over the edge with them."

I force a smile.

"We had to," Jewson adds. "It was self-defense." He looks at me uncertainly. I wonder if I am, in my silence, communicating the suspicion that their gallows humor is not just a defense but also an expession of contempt. Jewson turns solemn. "The saddest moment was the woman who went over the cliff with her two kids. I still get a lump in my throat when I talk about it. I've been involved in hundreds up there, and that's the only one that hurts."

Turner nods. "It's the only one that ever upset the team."

I knew some of the details. A former airline stewardess, Elizabeth Kentish was the thirty-nine-year-old third wife of a millionaire racehorse owner and mother of a five-year-old and a two-year-old. A police inspector who interviewed acquaintances said, "She was quite an unassuming person, always very pleasant and polite." According to her mother, "she had enjoyed life and bringing up her two children to the full," though, in retrospect, she wondered if her daughter had suffered from postpartum depression.

During the last week of June 1990, Kentish was feeling put out. She had been planning a birthday party for her elder daughter, Kate, when she discovered that a mother of one of her daughter's friends had scheduled a birthday party for *her* daughter on the same day. The mother offered to postpone her daughter's party so that Kentish's could go ahead as planned, but Kentish declined, saying she'd already made other arrangements. According to Mr. Kentish, his wife was very upset by the whole episode; she thought she was being "persecuted" by the other mothers at Kate's private girls' school.

Several days after the party conflict, Kentish told her husband she was taking their daughters to the zoo. Before leaving, she left a note for her husband on the back of an old envelope. It read, "I loved you very much and Mum."

That afternoon an Eastbourne man walking along the beach came across the mangled wreckage of a car. Floating in the sea was a child's body. He called the police, putting into motion one of the most epic recoveries ever staged by Eastbourne's emergency services. Faced with a potential carload of bodies scattered across a churning foreshore, Garry Russell sent nine auxiliary coast guards onto the beach. They were joined by six members of the Eastbourne Fire Brigade, dropped by helicopter, and armed with cutting equipment. Several police officers were dispatched to the scene, as well as the inshore lifeboat. Russell ran the operation from the cliff top, three hundred feet above.

Strong winds flipped the inshore lifeboat, throwing four crewmen into the sea. A fireman recovered the elder daughter's body from the water and, crying, carried her to shore. Later, Jewson moved her closer to the cliffs. "You're almost trying to hide her away from what's going on," he explains to me, eyes moistening. "Hide her from all the other people that were around. You've got this lifeless little five-year-old with no superficial marks at all. And that's sad." He pauses. "We packed her first, then came back and took the others."

The bodies of Elizabeth Kentish and her two-year-old daughter were still strapped inside the silver Ford Orion. The car was upside down, and the rescue workers couldn't get to it because the tide was in. Jewson suggested that when the tide went out, they push the car back on its wheels. Twenty minutes later, that's what they did. "Many of us pushed it over," he recalls. "The door came open, and you could actually see the woman's foot. It was about the only thing you could see, because the car was so compacted. You could see the little baby seat." He shakes his head at the memory. His voice grows husky. "We put the mother and baby in the same body bag, and we put a teddy in the bag as well. Emotionally, that's the only job that's ever affected me."

I feel as if I'm in a different dimension. Percy is silent. The clock ticks louder. Jewson turns pointillist behind slants of sunlight and floating dust. Of course. Two innocent children were killed. "That's the only job that affected you?" I ask.

Turner leans forward. His steady gaze hardens his boyish face. "We didn't have sympathy for the victims. There's a lot easier ways to do it if they want to do away with themselves and jump from a great height. They could do it in a multistory car park. It doesn't put anybody at risk—provided they don't jump on somebody."

This I expect. Turner and Jewson are no different from the other rescue workers I spoke to or read about. They thrived on the camaraderie and excitement of cliff work but disdained the miserable people who made it possible. "Sorry to say, you get a bit hard after a while," Garry Russell said to me in an earlier conversation. "I always looked at it that they were over there of their own accord, and they were puttin' other people's lives at risk. I'm afraid I had no sort of feelings for them." It reminded me of a *Wall Street Journal* article I'd read about the Golden Gate Bridge's suicide squad, which is manned entirely by ironworkers. A veteran rescuer was quoted, grousing, "I don't like these people. My job is to get them off the bridge. Beyond that, it's up to someone else."

Julia Clasby was different. She spoke about her work as if it were a ministry. Is she more sympathetic because she rescues suicidal people rather than recovering their bodies? Because she's a woman? Or are the differences the result of an age divide, the men of the "suck it up and deal" postwar generation, Clasby of the "I feel your pain" *Oprah* generation? Or are they merely separated by experience? Will Clasby harden after so many cliff top encounters?

There's a lot easier ways to do it—as if suicide were a stroll in the park. It's getting harder to maintain the pose of the objective journalist. "Do you think it takes courage to jump off Beachy Head?"

"I would think the opposite," Jewson says. "I think in a way it's almost the coward's way out. It would take far more courage to actually face up to life, to face up to the problems, depression or whatever it is, that's bringing them to that point than to actually take, in a way, the easy option."

If he only knew. My brother-in-law, Conrad, wasn't a healthy man who'd hit a bad patch; he was a sick man beset by imagined terrors with no end in sight. The last years of his life were a living hell. What kept him alive, I think, wasn't a belief that his life was still worth living but a fear of dying. Months before his death, he told his father he wanted to kill himself but couldn't do it. If he was weak for not facing up indefinitely to his problems, to his terrifying delusions and diminished prospects, his loneliness and self-hatred, then I'm dumb for not understanding quantum mechanics. When one wants to neither live nor die, it takes courage to do both. Death wasn't an easy option for Conrad. It was, in his mind, the *only* option.

I keep probing. "Do you think people who kill themselves are insane?"

Turner considers the question for about a second. "I've always said, at the time they step off the cliff into oblivion, they're mad. At the time they step off, doing that final leap off, or step off or roll off, or however they do it—that split second their mind has gone, they're mad, crackers, 'round the bend, whatever you like to call it."

A common view, this. Clinicians, tiptoeing around words like "insane" or "mad," often describe suicide as an irrational or coerced choice. Harvard psychiatrists Harvey Schein and Alan Stone call it "a maladaptive action, irreversibly counter to the patient's sane interests and goals." Renowned suicidologist Edwin Shneidman writes that "in every case of suicide the person is getting bad advice from a part of that mind, the inner chamber of councilors, who are temporarily in a panicked state and in no position to serve the person's long-range interests."

But that can't be true in every case. There can't be only one kind of suicidal mind. Suicide is too complex for absolutes. A physically handicapped man who attempted suicide at Beachy Head told a reporter, "When it takes four hours to get dressed of a morning, an hour to eat anything and two hours to go to the lavatory, when your parents are getting on and when even the Ministry recognises your situation with an Invalidity Allowance, you come to the decision that you have to think of something." An elderly man wrote to the editor of the *Eastbourne Herald*,

"Over the past several years I have really wanted to do this but because of my children I've coped somehow, sometimes I don't know how. . . . I feel we all have different reasons which give us this feeling of wanting to commit suicide. . . . A lot of you who read this will probably think I'm a 'mental case.' I can assure you I'm not." A chronically depressed woman who drove over the cliffs wrote in a note addressed to the coroner, "I fully intend to take my life. My mind is in perfect balance and I know what I'm doing." These are sober voices, not panicked ones. I can imagine these people reaching the precipice rationally, after years of suffering and failed remedies, and jumping off it lucidly, fully aware of the consequences for themselves and those they leave behind. Maybe more people would believe that there's such a thing as a sane suicide if the English language had a name for it. In an interview months before he took his life, psychoanalyst Bruno Bettelheim noted that German has another word for suicide, *freitod,* which means a free, willed death. "And there are tribal societies in which at a certain moment one goes up in the mountains and lies down and dies," he wrote. "Theirs is certainly a more civilized way."

Turner is still waiting for my response. I keep pressing the point. "What about people who've been in and out of psychiatric institutions their entire lives? If you can see it from their perspective—"

"But then," Turner says, suppressing a smile, "if they've been in and out of institutions, they've *got* to be mental."

But "mental" people don't always think or act that way. Those grubby, muttering street people can have moments of heartbreaking clarity. The schizophrenic who mistakes a BBC news anchor for a Russian spy might have no illusions about his own prospects. It's an unsettling possibility for some. Maybe for Turner. A local police constable told me, "It's easy to rationalize everyone who kills themselves as being insane, because that makes everyone feel better. Because if they're insane, then it's not you. If they weren't insane, any person can do it."

Jewson, perhaps noticing my discomfort, cuts in. "I don't know if our perception is different from other people's because we've been touched by it so much," he says. "We're involved in probably the worst part of the suicide, which is actually recovering the casualty. We're the first people to actually be there and handle the body after they've made the decision to commit suicide. Whether that actually tarnishes our perception of them, I don't know."

"All of our perceptions are probably tarnished in some way," I say. We see suicide through the lens of our experience, training, values, and temperament, and there's no way around that. To people in the business of saving lives, suicide must seem a disturbingly subversive act. "Something about acute self-destruction is so puzzling to the vibrant mind of a man or woman whose life is devoted to fighting disease," writes surgeon and author Sherwin B. Nuland, "that it tends to diminish or even obliterate sympathy. Medical bystanders, whether bewildered and frustrated by such an act, or angered by its futility, seem not to be much grieved at the corpse of a suicide."

The same could be said of emergency workers such as Bob Jewson and Chris Turner. Their hard-heartedness toward the suicides, it occurs to me, is not unlike the xenophobia that greets the "wetbacks," "spics," and other illegal aliens who come to America. In the mental landscape of the cliff man, the suicide is the smelly, graceless stranger from a dark and distant continent, the coward or nutcase who speaks a language of despair that few of the natives understand.

Turner shakes his head as if trying to loosen a knot in his brain. "I can't understand what goes through their mind. I *can't*. I can't get in their mind."

6

The Morgue

My sleep-blurred eyes scan brick walls painted bright yellow and dotted with charming framed pictures of lighthouses, before landing on a solitary window, which, for the first time since I arrived at Belle Tout two days ago, isn't shrouded in fog. I haul my jet-lagged body out of bed and pad across the cold stone floor to the window. The cliff top is empty save for the distant figure of a man walking his dog; nearer the lighthouse, a massive chalk promontory juts into the sea. I look down. Gone are the camera crews and tourists who milled about Belle Tout a year ago. Gone the sounds of jackhammers and compressors.

I slap on some clothes, finger-comb my hair, and head upstairs for breakfast. The opportunity to participate in the Robertses' "experiment," as Mark called it, is one reason I left my home and family for another English spring. The idea of staying at the only bed-and-breakfast lighthouse in England was irresistible. But the experiment doesn't seem to be working. The living room appears to be undergoing a painful face-lift. Boxes are piled on boxes. Chairs and sofas are shrouded in drop cloths covered with plaster dust. Electrical cords dangle from scabrous walls. The kitchen is a scene of domestic unbliss: Mark kneels on the kitchen floor, his head and shoulders thrust inside the opening of a bottom cabinet, unhappily attending to a heating problem. It's the first time I've seen him since my arrival, though I've heard him plenty—the crackling modem, the TV voices, the kitchen rummagings: the nocturnal sounds of a dot-com entrepreneur relaxing at the end of a sixteen-hour day. Louise, meanwhile, joylessly slices fruit into a glass bowl, her wispy bangs dangling attractively over her forehead. She's already set out the boxes of cold cereal. In a few minutes, this former chemistry major with a fondness for Faulkner and writing aspirations of her own will take orders from a small assembly of well-heeled gluttons. Then she'll spend an hour or so cooking while making small talk. After the gourmands waddle out, she'll scrub their dishes. Little wonder she greets me with a feeble smile. When it's time to chow, I can't bring myself to order anything that requires cooking. While my tablemates feast on a traditional English breakfast of sausages, bacon, eggs, toast, grilled tomatoes, mushrooms, pancakes, kippers, smoked salmon, and hot downland porridge, I eat cereal and fruit.

That afternoon I leave Belle Tout for cheaper, guilt-free lodging. Mark and Louise drive me to Meads. The car ride is filled with long silences. Mark doesn't ask about my research—a considered decision, I would like to think, for which I'm grateful.

Five minutes later, we're trading brisk goodbyes in front of the Hollies. Pauline Knowles greets me at the threshold of the family quarters just beyond the entryway. She asks how I've been and hands me the key to the attic bungalow without issuing a set of instructions, a gratifying recognition that I am no longer a rookie in this country, in this place.

The next morning I head out for Eastbourne center, passing glistening, dew-covered lawns and driblets of blue-blazered students wearing Monday on their faces. Cloud wisps marble a pale blue sky. In the center of town, the squad cars are already lined up outside the police station, and a bookstore owner is unlocking the plywood doors on the bookcases in the alleyway alongside his shop.

The chance to sleep in a cliffside lighthouse is just one of the reasons I decided to return to Beachy Head. Julie the Mortician was another. Chris Turner had mentioned her during my conversation with him and Bob Jewson. I don't recall the context, but I do remember feeling bewitched by the oxymoronic sound of "Julie the Mortician." If she had been "Barbara the Mortician" or "Margaret the Mortician," I probably wouldn't have given her a second thought, but Julie is a pretty name conjuring a pretty face. "Julie the Mortician" was, like Beachy Head, an alluring combination of beauty and death. I pictured a comely, pale-faced woman wearing hospital scrubs, with pulled-back hair the color and sheen of a hearse. When Turner told me that Julie's husband was an undertaker, my imagination went into overdrive. Did their eyes meet over someone's dead body? Did they enjoy a little dark reading before turning in for the night? Were embalming and dissection topics of spirited discussion at the dinner table? I had to meet her.

I also had to see the bodies she cared for, especially the

Beachy Head ones: the bodies behind the sudden-death reports, the bodies spirited away in dusky helicopters, the bodies whose injuries I'd heard about but not seen.

I call Eastbourne District General Hospital from a pay phone outside McDonald's and ask for the mortuary. A woman with a perky voice says that Julie doesn't work there anymore. She whispers away from the receiver, "It's a man with an American accent." A woman giggles in the background. Composing herself, Ms. Perky turns her attention back to me. "I'm Sharon Debenham, the senior mortuary technician. May I help you?"

I'm at a loss for words. I can't ask where Julie went, because that's none of my business, and I can't bring myself to arrange to see a Beachy Head body, because it sounds so vulgar. Stories. She can tell me stories about Beachy Head bodies, and in the telling, I'll find out how she feels about them. "I'm researching the Beachy Head suicides, and I was wondering—"

"It's funny you should mention that. A Beachy Head body just came in yesterday. It's on the dissection table now. Would you like to see it?"

FIRST I SEE the transfixed faces. Then I hear shouts. In the lobby of the hospital, twenty-five feet to my right, a man is having a heart attack. His shirt is hiked over his ample belly. Physicians in blue scrubs hover around his supine body like flies around a beached whale. Then a curtain closes over the scene, and I feel a flash of indignation, as if someone has abruptly turned off the television in the middle of *ER*.

With difficulty, I turn my attention to the reception desk, which is manned by a serene, blue-haired lady. I tell her I'm here to see Sharon Debenham. Minutes later, a compact blond woman in a white lab coat marches toward the receptionist's desk. She extends her arm and, smiling sunnily, says that I must be Tom.

She shepherds me across the lobby and down a flight of stairs. The phone is ringing when we arrive at her office. "Go away!" she says. She strides over to her desk in a mock huff and picks up the receiver while directing me to take a seat on the other side. The windowless, surprisingly odorless room feels compressed, as if it bears the weight of the entire hospital, which in a sense it does. Videos and black binders with eye-glazing titles—*Mortuary Standard Operating Procedures, Coroner's Rules,* and *Safety Committee Minutes*—fill a wall-mounted bookcase. Below it sit two glowing monitors, one displaying what I recognize to be the sobering image of a sudden-death report; on the other are split-screened security shots of the morgue. Behind Debenham's desk sits a small table with an arsenal of tea-making supplies and a copy of *Cosmopolitan.* Debenham leans over her desk, the receiver wedged between her cocked head and shoulder, and rifles through the pages of a black leather notebook. "Ah, yes, it's an await." She flips a page. "Yeah, it's an await. All right." Pause. "Ah, three this morning. Okay, bye, Mick."

She puts down the receiver and says, "That was Mick Davey, the coroner's officer, inquiring about a body." She closes her notebook. "So what would you like to know?"

I ask her how she became a mortician.

Debenham smiles wistfully, as if recalling her first kiss. She was seventeen and working in a pharmacy, she explains, when a coworker encouraged her to apply for a job in Eastbourne District General Hospital's morgue. Though she didn't get the job, the tour piqued her interest in mortuary work. She quit her job at the pharmacy and worked part-time for a local undertaker. Months later, a mortuary in Brighton hired her as a trainee, and in another two years, she reapplied for a position at Eastbourne Hospital's mortuary. After ten years, she's the hospital's senior mortuary technician.

"We prepare the bodies for postmortem, which means we do all the cutting. We remove all the body organs, so what you're left with is a shell. Then we put them on a dissecting table next to the body so that the pathologist can try to determine the cause of the death." Debenham speaks briskly and earnestly. She describes how she weighs each organ after the pathologist dissects it, then places it in a bucket lined with a black bag; and how, when the body is completely gutted, she ties the bag, places it in the cadaver, and stitches up the opening. "The brain also goes in the black bag," she quickly adds, "because it's too soft to put back in the head. You'd never get it back in. So the head is packed with paper to stop leakage." They usually do twenty postmortems a week, she says, each one taking about an hour: twenty minutes for prep, forty minutes for the examination.

Somehow Sharon Debenham manages to make a job that combines the skills of a butcher, garbage collector, and seamstress sound like a higher calling. She plants her elbows on the uncluttered desktop and looks at me with a hint of a smile, as if reading my mind. "Most people think that we in mortuaries are weird. They think that we wear built-up shoes and have a hump on our backs." She pauses. "There *are* some people in mortuaries that are a bit odd, but I do the job for the medical interest."

There's a knock on the door. A slender man in a white dress shirt and dark slacks steps into the office. Debenham introduces him in an ominous tone as "the undertaker" and me as the journalist from America who's researching Beachy Head.

The undertaker looks at me curiously. "Really? Interesting place, Beachy Head. We get called up there occasionally."

"We're going to push you off there one of these days, aren't we?" Debenham says to the man with a straight face.

"Please do," he says, handing Debenham a manila folder.

When the undertaker leaves, Debenham tells me that she and

her crew have good relationships with everybody—the undertakers, the doctors, the hospital. "We're a very happy ship here."

She reaches for a blue binder and opens it gently. She flips through pages filled with lists of names under different section headings ("Cardiac Arrest," "Motor Vehicle Accident"), then stops at a section labeled "Beachy Head" and turns the binder around. "I thought you might be interested in this. It has all the Beachy Head bodies that have come through since I started working here."

I lean over the logbook and scan the columns. Each victim's name, birth date, age, date of death, and examining pathologist are recorded in tiny, meticulous cursive. I flip ahead to the last three years. Many of the names are familiar to me from the sudden-death reports. I spoke to the husband of Doris Haffenden and witnessed the recovery of John Meacock, a London artist. I learned of Ram Doll's mysterious death from the Internet. Police suspected that his two brothers, one of whom had been sleeping with Doll's wife, pushed him off the cliff, but they were acquitted. The name of the victim I'm about to view hasn't been entered. Like an anxious child traveling to an unfamiliar destination, I need to know more about where we're going. I close the binder and push it back toward Debenham. "What kinds of injuries do you see in a Beachy Head body?"

"Oh God. Smashed heads. Smashed arms. It's . . . it's something that you'll never see anywhere else. It's horrendous, horrible. Just, sometimes you can't recognize them, sometimes their head . . . their head's that . . . *smashed*. There's no brain there. The head's like a paper bag flapping in the wind on top of the shoulders." She pauses. "Does this disturb you?"

"No," I say. But it does.

She continues, "Sometimes if they hit a jagged cliff with their front, that cliff will rip them to pieces, it will rip them open.

Quite often they come in and they got bits hangin' out. Those are the ones that send the police to the toilet. We've got one policewoman, she's so sweet, who just hates it here. When she comes through the door, I always open the door to the toilet. I remember one day we brought a Beachy Head body in, and in my opinion, it was relatively clean—from the point of view it wasn't smashed up to smithereens. And, uh, she came in, and she was only here for fifteen minutes, and she was sick seven times." Debenham breaks into cackles of laughter. "I just found that amusing."

I laugh weakly. Listening to Debenham is exhausting. She's an introvert's nightmare. Every quip and colorful phrase, every laugh and exclamation, deserves a more animated response than I can give, and my face is tired of trying. "That's probably what I'll do when you take me in there."

Her eyes soften as she smiles. Her game face, I imagine. The face that grieving family members see. "Have you ever seen any bodies?"

I shake my head. "No."

She nods and leans forward. "My one and only thing that I say to everybody and really mean is that you got nothin' to fear from the dead. It's the *living* you've got to be afraid of, if you look at what a living person can do to you compared to what a dead person can do to you."

Maybe some people are drawn to mortuary work for that very reason, I think.

"Would you like to see the body now?"

My heart quickens. "I suppose so."

WE TAKE THE SCENIC ROUTE. Debenham directs me into the waiting room. With the heightened sense of a skittish animal, my eyes dart from three wooden chairs with tightly upholstered seats and glossy oak arms, to the vacuum marks on a plush carpet, to Debenham herself, who walks over to a large window with drawn blinds that stir in our wake. "This looks into the viewing room. Some people prefer to look at the body from a distance."

She flicks on a light switch, and my reflection vanishes. I step closer and peer through the glass into a small room. A painting of a secluded mountain hut hangs on one wall. Floral curtains cover the wall opposite the window. An empty coffin sits against another wall.

We enter the viewing room through a slender doorway. Debenham stops in front of the coffin. I stand next to her and peer into the bier's pillowed, quilted interior. The room is quiet except for the faint hum of a fluorescent light. "When we lay the body out," she says, turning to me, "we have a cover over it, and we put the head on the pillow and dress it around that so it looks like it's laying in bed."

For a moment I see my brother-in-law lying in his casket: the fluffy black beard, the splotchy, reemergent birthmark on his forehead, the bullet hole in his right temple, touched up to a charcoally smudge.

"I talk to a lot of relatives in here and see them at what I call their critical point," she says, reaching down to smooth the wrinkles on a pillow. "I have one policy: always tell the truth. Don't try and cover relatives in cotton wool because they're grieving. Because they don't want it. They want to know the truth: 'Did he suffer? What were the injuries?' That sort of thing."

I turn to Debenham. Though she's standing nearly shoulder to shoulder with a stranger, in an underground space surrounded on all sides by unoccupied rooms, she shows no sign of discomfort. Her head tilts intelligently; her gaze is steady, unselfconscious. "What kind of reactions do you get?" I ask.

"The general reaction is crying," she says without hesitation. "Always. And then you've got different categories of crying. You've got your screamers and wailers. Sometimes you can hear them at the other end of the building."

"Do you get silence?"

She nods. "Silence, yeah, definitely. You've got anger. I've seen laughter." She pauses. "Somebody once tried to steal their relative—to wheel them out of here. And I'm like, 'Bring that back! You haven't paid for it!' " I laugh as Debenham breaks into a loud cackle. "If it's a young person," she says, turning serious, "I find it distressing. If it's a baby or child, as a result of an accident, it's horrible. I've cried with relatives. I want them to feel that it's a visit that's been beneficial to them. When they're crying and saying, 'I can't live without him,' I can understand that. The feeling of such utter pain is horrible. You think, 'I might die as well because it's never going to get any better.' And I try to say to them, 'It *will* feel better,' and I want them to believe me when I say it."

It's a side of the job I never considered. I now understand why Debenham said to me during our conversation in her office, "Where you've got women in mortuaries, you've got a good mortuary."

"People often place keepsakes into the bier," she goes on. "Flowers a lot, teeth—'Can you put his teeth in?'—pictures from the children—'To my daddy' or 'To my mommy, we will miss you.' Photos of children, clothes, teddy bears."

Were there mementos in Conrad's coffin? I don't remember. I remember the black suit he had borrowed from his father weeks before his death but nothing lying on top of it or tucked around it. Did it simply not occur to anyone? Were they never told they could? And what would he have wanted? A family picture?

Debenham heads toward the door beyond the head of the coffin. She flicks off the light and turns the door handle. Her silence puts me at ease. Surely she'd say something if we were about to enter the dissection room. The door opens into a bright, echoey room dominated by a wall of stainless steel refrigerators, their thick, square doors speckled with colorful plastic magnets. Opposite, a gurney stands beside a retractable aluminum door set into the wall.

"The fridge room," Debenham says, her voice bouncing off the stainless steel and linoleum. She walks to the center of the room and explains that when the hospital was built twenty years ago, the mortuary could hold only thirty-four bodies, which was sufficient because there were three or four other hospitals in the area. But as the years went by and the other hospitals closed down, more and more corpses came to Eastbourne. The mortuary was able to accommodate the growing numbers until Christmas of 1992, when Debenham's worst nightmare—"a flu epidemic in a community of old people"—filled the fridges and then some. At one point, twenty-two unrefrigerated corpses littered the morgue floor. The fiasco necessitated a refit, increasing the morgue's capacity to its present limit of sixty-five, which Debenham says is adequate on a day-to-day basis.

But it was far from adequate when another flu epidemic swept Eastbourne during the previous year's winter holidays. On Christmas Day, Debenham received a phone call at her parents' home. All sixty-five fridges were full, a worker covering the morgue frantically explained. "So I said start doubling them up: two on a tray, top and tail." Three nights later, she stopped by the morgue on her way home from holiday and was greeted with a "horrendous" sight: 30 corpses strewn across the floor, another 120 crammed inside the refrigerators. A hundred and fifty bodies in a morgue built for 65. "The reason that we had that backlog,"

Debenham explains, "is because we closed for four days and so did everybody else. The crematorium was closed, the undertakers were closed. So the bottom line is the crematorium is not burning, the undertakers are not collecting from here, so the mortuary is not getting rid of their bodies."

Over the next several days, Debenham performed the mortuary version of musical chairs, rotating corpses in and out of the fridges to keep them all reasonably fresh until she could arrange for a refrigerated truck. After midnight, under cover of darkness—"if the press found out, there'd be a scandal" (the press did, and there was)—she and several colleagues moved the extra bodies into the truck.

During the four days before New Year's, Debenham performed ninety postmortems—seventy more than her weekly average—starting at four in the morning and finishing at midnight. She shakes her head. "The mortuary didn't make it to any New Year's parties."

She walks toward the fridges, and I take a mincing first step, the image of unrefrigerated cadavers fresh in my mind. She stops in front of the column of gray doors with bank vault–like handles. "Fridge magnets." She points to Winnie-the-Pooh. "You'll not see them anywhere else," she says proudly.

I don't doubt it. What next? Magnetic business cards?

She says they're from the hospital staff and other "friends" of the mortuary who apparently have no qualms about adorning the temporary resting place of the newly dead with tacky souvenirs. "The relatives don't come in here," she quickly adds.

That's a good thing. What grieving widow would want to see LAS VEGAS emblazoned in hot-pink letters across her husband's fridge? It doesn't occur to me to ask who started this quirky tradition, but my guess is that Debenham did. She seems determined to make the morgue a cheerful place, a worthy, if somewhat risky, endeavor.

We walk down refrigerator row, stopping at the last fridge, which, curiously, has no magnets on the door and an ominous padlock under the handle. "Deep freezer. Locked at all times because it contains two murder victims."

"Why—"

"Because the press—the press are mongrels," she says, turning to me. "They'll do anything to get in here. And the other reason is if somebody brings in a body in the middle of the night, and they mistakenly put it in the freezer, it's like a frozen chicken in the morning. You *cannot* get a knife into that. We don't have a microwave big enough to defrost it."

She looks for a response, but I'm still stuck on the first reason. I knew about the British tabloids' well-earned reputation for sleaziness, but busting into a morgue freezer? "The press would really—"

She nods. One of the bodies, she says, is the first Beachy Head victim of the year, a thirty-two-year-old mother of a five-year-old and an eleven-year-old. She's been in deep freeze for over two months. Her husband told the police they had been discussing marital issues in their parked car before she jumped. But since discovering he'd been having an affair and had taken out a life insurance policy on his wife several months before, the police now suspect he pushed her off. The postmortem was, as it almost always is in such cases, inconclusive: whether someone has jumped or been pushed off Beachy Head, Debenham says, the injuries are the same. Unless, of course, the victim was killed before being pushed off. In the winter of 2004, police discovered the badly decomposed body of a black male at the base of the cliffs. His head was covered in a plastic bag, and he was bound and gagged with tape and nylon rope. A crumpled blue fifty-gallon plastic barrel lay beside the man. After the pathologist discovered multiple stab wounds from a knife and screwdriver across the victim's body, the coroner concluded that the known cocaine user and suspected gang member was killed elsewhere and then pushed over Beachy Head in the blue barrel.

Debenham says to me, "The second Beachy Head body of the year is the one you're about to see."

We walk across the room and stop in front of the retractable aluminum door. Debenham explains that the bodies pass from the refrigerator room to the dissection room through this opening.

And the chart on the wall? She glances over at the whiteboard filled with last names and numbers written neatly in black marker. "That's so we know which body is in which fridge. A Dewey decimal system for bodies."

It's an apt analogy. The quietness and relaxed pace of the morgue remind me of a library. The rubber-wheeled gurneys bring to mind the metal carts that librarians use to transport books to their proper shelves.

We walk toward the entrance of the dissection room. My heart thumps at the uncertainty of what lies on the other side of the wall. She looks at me when we reach the door. "I can cover the face if that would make it easier for you."

"No, I'll see the whole body." The words sound crass. I'm embarrassed by them.

She turns the handle and slowly opens the door. The scene is not what I'd expected. There are three corpses, not one: a fiftyish man with a big belly (a heart attack victim); an elderly man whose toothless mouth is open in an attitude of surprise (the victim of a stomach aneurysm); and, closest to me, the Beachy

Head body. They lie on metal trays atop gurneys some five feet apart. Debenham slips on a pair of latex gloves and stands beside the young suicide. I stand next to her. She says again that there's nothing to fear from the dead, but as she casually picks through the human wreckage before us, I feel an amorphous fear: a discomfiting recognition tinged with relief, a "but for the grace of God go I" kind of fear. It is as if I am looking at my own potential for self-destruction right in the battered eye.

She presses the cheeks and chin of the body's grotesquely flattened face: "Landed on his face and smashed all the bones." Pinches and pulls back the scalp of black hair and points to a convex of bone that resembles a cracked ostrich egg: "Fractured skull." Points to the bone poking through the skin of the right arm: "Broken humerus." Points to the crooked hip: "Cracked femur." Points to the exposed right shinbone: "Broken tibia." Flaps the right foot: "Broken ankle."

Debenham says the body hasn't been identified. Investigators took fingerprints and faxed them to constables at Scotland Yard, who compared them to the fingerprints of criminals on file. They didn't find a match. After the postmortem tomorrow, she'll arrange for the hospital dentists to do dental charts. In ten years, she recalls only three or four bodies that went to their graves unidentified.

"It's so sad, isn't it?" she says. "They're young people, as well, some in their twenties, thirties, and I think, 'They belong to somebody.' "

"I hope so." I'm barely listening. Looking, at the moment, monopolizes all of my senses.

Debenham peels off her gloves. "It's the end of the book, isn't it? You're really starting at the back of the book. 'Cause you've got the body, but you don't know anything about it. You know what the outcome is, but you don't know the circumstances leading to it. And I love that. *That* about this job is what I love. Everybody is a book, everybody has a story."

DURING THE CAB RIDE back to my flat, my own story undergoes revision as I reflect on my response to the Beachy Head body. The volunteer work at the mental hospital, the job at the residential treatment center for mentally ill children, the stint at the psychiatric boarding school—maybe I was drawn to those places out of a sincere desire to help people who are less fortunate, but there was another, deeper reason, which explains, too, why I devoured the sudden-death reports, attended the inquests, and stared at John Doe's shattered body: I wanted to take the measure of my greatest fear, to check out the territory I fear I might be heading toward. Did Conrad's suicide affect me so deeply not because I loved him while he was alive—we were never close— but because I identified with him after he was dead?

The storefronts are a blur outside the cab window, but my conscience begins to clear. My attraction to that body wasn't trivial. I wasn't gaping like a teenager bent over a centerfold. My senses weren't so much aroused as heightened, like the watchful eyes of a stock-still deer.

7

A Range of Reasons

To explain why so few suicidal people actually kill themselves, psychiatrist Robert Litman invokes the metaphor of a slot machine. "You can win a million dollars on a slot machine in Las Vegas," he says, "but to do that, six sevens have to line up on your machine. That happens once in a million times. In a sense it's the same with suicide. In order to commit suicide, a lot of things have to fall together at once, and a lot of other things have to *not* happen at once."

Ever since Conrad died, I wanted to know all the numbers on the slot machine—all the biological and existential variables that, when lined up just so for any one person, compel his or her self-destruction. By my second visit to Beachy Head, my interest in suicide has become an obsession. I spend evening after evening plowing through a duffel bag filled with suicide books. A few days after my visit to the morgue, I return to Mick Davey's office to read another year's worth of sudden-death reports, this time bringing a notebook and pen. The next day I travel thirty miles north of Eastbourne to the county seat of Lewes, where, in a quiet public records office situated between a castle and a medieval battleground, I read the brittle and faded sudden-death reports of Beachy Head victims who died during World War I. I read of minds racked by mental illness and bodies wasted by disease and age; of reputations destroyed and love and labor lost; of grief and loneliness, self-hatred and disillusionment, alcoholism and drug addiction. "No one," wrote Italian writer Cesare Pavese, "ever lacks a good reason for suicide."

MENTAL ILLNESS IS, predictably, a common theme running through the sudden-death reports. I read of one fifty-three-year-old psychiatric patient who had attempted suicide at Beachy Head once before and was so distressed by her ritualistic hand-washing and other compulsive behaviors that she expressed a wish to try again. A twenty-seven-year-old psychiatric patient had suffered from depression since the age of fifteen, cut himself off from his family, and, according to his social worker, "struggled with his internal world of anger and hate, yet wanting love." A twenty-seven-year-old auxiliary nurse had developed psychiatric problems three years before her death; during the year before her suicide, she'd taken some fifteen drug overdoses, one of them culminating in the death of an unborn child.

It's estimated that 90 to 95 percent of people who kill themselves have a diagnosable psychiatric disorder. Eastbourne pathologist and Beachy Head researcher Dr. John Surtees studied 115 Beachy Head suicides between 1965 and 1979 and found that 80 percent of the victims had a history of mental illness.

Of all the variations on this dismal theme—bipolar disorder, schizophrenia, borderline personality disorder, antisocial personality, to name a few—depression is the most common and, at its most virulent, the strongest predictor of suicide. Sufferers of severe depression are twenty times more likely to kill themselves than the general population; 15 percent of them actually do. The good news is that 85 percent don't. Between the feeling of despair and the idea of suicide is the barrier of self-preservation, scaleable only by the most hopeless. There'a no deadlier combination, suicide researchers say, than depression and hopelessness.

The book on depression's sibling, manic depression or bipolar disorder, is equally cheerless. Though less lethal than depression—manic depression increases the suicide risk only fifteenfold—the illness is in many ways more precarious. Manic depressives are more likely to *attempt* suicide than those who suffer from depression only, and they're more apt to abuse alcohol or drugs. They're especially vulnerable when caught between the alternating currents of mania and depression, a "mixed" state characterized by morbid thinking, paranoia, extreme agitation, and physical aggressiveness. I read of one thirty-one-year-old artist who had a history of substance abuse and was in the middle of divorce proceedings when she threw herself off Beachy Head. She was also in the throes of a "manic depressive psychosis"— very likely a mixed state.

Several years ago I witnessed its horrors while teaching at a small private school in Pennsylvania. A manic-depressive officemate stopped taking his lithium shortly after the birth of his first child, a risky experiment that threw his finely calibrated chemistry dangerously out of whack. He used up all his sick days and then some, waiting for his system to stabilize. Fearing that he might lose his job, he returned to work before he was ready. He accosted the headmistress outside her office over some perceived offense. I heard the shouting but didn't see the push that got him fired and barred from the building.

Days later, he sneaked into the school. It was late in the day in the dead of winter, and I was the only one there. He pulled me into a classroom, closed the door, and, alternating between rants and whispers, explained how the whole mess wouldn't have happened if the doctor hadn't screwed up and the headmistress had been more understanding. What was he going to do now, with a baby and a mortgage, he demanded. With each outburst, he stabbed his finger inches from my chest, as if I'd wronged him.

Weeks later, I visited him at his house and found him even more frenzied and delusional. He insisted that he'd been misdiagnosed fifteen years earlier and that he didn't really have manic depression. He opened a notebook and rifled through the pages until he came to two scribbled lists of names: the bad people at our school and the good people. With a chapped, shaking finger and blazing eyes, he went down the bad list, pausing at each name to enumerate the person's evils. Soon afterward he began having suicidal thoughts and was hospitalized.

There are no digressions, changes of scene, or additions to the central cast of characters in the sudden-death reports. The place is always Beachy Head; the main characters are always despondent victims, grieving family members, shocked eyewitnesses, and stoic police and coast guard officers; the reports always march to a foregone conclusion. Still, they are riveting.

A thirty-four-year-old musician heard a story on the radio about a woman who had been too busy to do her washing. She was convinced they were talking about her. Several days later, she jumped. A twenty-three-year-old shop assistant believed she was Satan and that the voices she was hearing were the devil's. During her parents' last visit to the hospital, she became angry when her mother told her that she wasn't Satan, and she accused her mother of not caring about her.

Both the musician and the shop assistant suffered from schizophrenia, a disease that afflicts 1 percent of the population, increases the suicide risk eightfold, and is utterly transforming. Demanding, reproachful voices, blunted emotions, fragmented thought and concentration, conspiracies, and apocalyptic fantasies are all part of the hellish and largely imagined world of the untreated paranoid schizophrenic. There's a one in ten chance the illness will end in suicide. My brother-in-law was one of the unlucky 10 percent.

HE WAS ELEVEN and I twenty-two when we first met in the summer of 1982. A freshly minted college grad, I was knocking around Europe while his sister, Gabriel, my classmate and crush, was visiting her grandmother in Switzerland. We met at the famous wooden bridge in Lucerne, as agreed, where I was introduced to Conrad, the youngest of her three brothers. He was beautiful: full lips, chestnut eyes, long, fluttering eyelashes.

We celebrated his eleventh birthday during a Fourth of July fireworks display on the shore of Lake Lucerne, and later hiked up a series of switchbacks on Mount Pilatus. Conrad walked apprehensively, hugging the inside of the trail.

Four years later, his sister and I took a trip to the altar, and over the next three years, I watched the baby of the family grow into a strapping, talented young man. He developed a bodybuilder's physique, read widely and deeply, rebuilt computers, taught himself to play the piano, composed music, and became a top-notch gymnast. He was quiet but vainglorious, always boasting about business schemes that would make him millions someday. It was easy to play along. We all thought him brilliant; his mind, we were sure, would take him places. At the very least, it would take him to college, where he'd become the first of the three brothers to earn a degree.

My wife and I helped him move into his dorm room. It was a sweltering August afternoon. Curious younger siblings and solicitous parents lugged stereo equipment, computers, and suitcases through the hallways while a clique of moved-in boys earnestly debated the evening's entertainment choices. It was their personal Independence Day, but Conrad wasn't celebrating. He walked stiffly down the hallway, arms close to his body, head still, as if he was trying to contain himself. He didn't speak to anyone. I thought he was just being his normal, socially skittish self. He'd grown up feeling different—they all had, his sister believes. They were never quite sure where they stood with strangers. It was an understandable reaction to the lifetime of stares they'd endured from people who disapproved of or admired or were simply curious about the mixed couple and their young coffee-colored children. So they mostly avoided venturing into unknown social territory—the very territory where Conrad found himself on that hot August afternoon. I wonder, though, if his leeriness wasn't just the ingrained suspiciousness of a biracial teenager but the first stirrings of the full-blown paranoia to come. The stress of moving day, the prospect of living away from home, may well have triggered his schizophrenia.

His college roommate, Matt, said Conrad was "quite high-functioning" during the two years they lived together. He studied quite a bit in his room, emerging from time to time, sometimes frustrated, sometimes happy. He worked out a lot. He dated on and off. He was intimate with at least one woman, a law student, who seemed, according to Matt, "a little in his thrall," judging by the phone messages she left. But Conrad eventually broke off the relationship, his roommate vaguely recalls, because he thought she was too fat.

He did sleep a lot, come to think of it, and they did argue about race and politics, Conrad at one point proclaiming himself a follower of the Nation of Islam; and he did tick off his roommate once or twice by accusing him of things he didn't do. But there was nothing that made Matt stop and go "Hmm," or anything that gave my wife and me pause when we visited him during his sophomore year. I just noticed he was a little heavier.

But inside, he was cracking up. Nobody knew, because he kept his delusions to himself. He didn't tell his roommate or his family about his ex-girlfriend's vendetta against him—the "more than twenty separate occasions" when individuals he believed to be associated with her removed air from his car tires. He didn't tell anyone about the time someone illegally accessed his Internet account "and used it to send electronic messages of an obscene and inflammatory nature to a number of school faculty and students." He didn't tell anyone that this "campaign," which he believed to be also his girlfriend's doing, resulted in his being picked up and questioned by campus security, who made it clear that they thought him guilty. We didn't know the true state of his mind until five years later, when my mother-in-law discovered a four-page "chronology of events" tucked inside the drawer of his nightstand. By then it was too late.

Everybody was surprised but not alarmed when Conrad decided to take time off from college after his sophomore year. He'll go back when he's ready, we said. When he started living the life of a recluse, sleeping during the day and surfing the Internet at night in the basement of my in-laws' house, we thought that he was in a rut.

During my wife's and my infrequent visits, he was a ghostly presence, more heard than seen. We went through a six-month stretch when we didn't see him at all. When we finally did, I was shocked. We pulled into my in-laws' driveway, our car loaded with Christmas presents, and I saw this pale, rotund man with a shaved head and a sloppy grin lumbering across the front lawn toward a bird feeder. "*Conrad?* My God, he's schizophrenic," I thought. It was the smile. He was smiling as if tickled by some private joke. My schizophrenic uncle had that grin. So did many of the patients at the mental hospital where I'd done volunteer work as a teenager.

During the next three years, the disease tightened its hold. In his chronology of events, he accused the police and a plain-clothes detective of trailing him and cutting him off while driving. He claimed his neighbors made harassing phone calls and used FM/ham radio equipment to jam his parents' television sets and to broadcast obscene and threatening voice messages such as "Die, nigger" and "You're a faggot." He accused them of burglarizing his car. "The passenger side front window was smashed in," he wrote, "and a toy pistol was stolen from the passenger seat. No other items were missing. I was able to follow a trail of disheveled bushes which seemed to lead to their house directly behind our residence." He wrote that friends of another aggrieved ex-girlfriend threw a party in his honor "at which slander and aspersions were cast over loud music using some type of microphone amplifier for everyone in a 200 meter radius to hear."

Other stories came to us, like dispatches from a distant country we were afraid to visit, my mother- and brother-in-law the usual correspondents. Conrad thought his bedroom ceiling was covered with bugs. He was sleeping in the furnace room. He bought a gun. He sat in the kitchen poised to shoot as weed-whacking lawn workers buzzed around the window.

We celebrated his last two birthdays without him. The family sat in the backyard around an umbrella table scattered with unopened presents and a cake but no Conrad to blow out the candles. Once I glanced at his bedroom window and saw a crack in the blinds quickly close. I was surprised that he'd been watching us; I foolishly assumed that his illness had rendered him as insentient as a mollusk, dulled of longing or mourning or any other human feeling. It hadn't occurred to me that he might have been participating in the family gathering the only way that he could: from the safe remove of his bedroom.

The last time I saw him was a year before his death, when he chauffeured my mother-in-law to our house for a brief visit. Sitting bolt upright on our living room couch, his hands tensely clutching his thighs, he spent most of the time pattering on about Halley's Comet and the end of the world. He prefaced one of his doomsday prophecies with "I know you probably think I'm crazy, but," a comment that seemed to reflect his own worst fears.

In the months before his death, he started talking more, often keeping his father up till well past midnight with paranoid fantasies and bizarre accusations. Once he broke down and cried and admitted he'd tried to kill himself but couldn't.

It doesn't surprise me that he eventually did. He lived his final years like a fugitive, always looking over his shoulder, suspicious of any prowling car or lingering stare. Suicide may have been his way of putting an end to the chase. There was no one to surrender to. He couldn't will away his imaginary pursuers. He wouldn't medicate them away. He wouldn't even entertain the idea of seeing a therapist, and being well past the age of legal consent, he couldn't be forced. So he destroyed the very thing that produced them.

ACCORDING TO DR. SURTEES, a fifth of the people who jump off the cliffs suffer not from mental illness but from "exogenous stress, varying from impending court proceedings to unrequited love."

I read of one thirty-three-year-old boarding school music teacher whose achievements, according to the headmaster, "were really quite extraordinary. It is difficult to imagine anyone could have done a better job. He was one of the most popular and respected members of the staff." But on a late summer morning, the beloved teacher's reputation imploded when police, acting on a tip, searched his campus apartment and found a trove of child pornography. He was arrested that day and released on bail. Two days later, as details of the investigation leaked to the press, the accused drove to Eastbourne and bought a bottle of aspirin at a pharmacy. He wore baggy trousers and an unzipped windbreaker and appeared, to the shop assistant, "disheveled and very nervous and shaky." The following morning, police found the teacher's green Volvo in a car park at Beachy Head. That afternoon, the Eastbourne lifeboat retrieved his body after boaters discovered it floating on the sea. At the inquest, the coroner concluded that the deceased "feared the result of the criminal procedures would bring about the end of his professional career even though there was no evidence he was interfering with young children. It leaves me with no doubt he killed himself."

No less absorbing was the story of the thirty-nine-year-old businessman who was fired after only five days on the job when his employer, a London business consultancy, discovered that their new hire had served prison time for stabbing his wife to death. (According to his brother, the deceased had been distraught over the state of his marriage, which began to deteriorate after his wife joined an evangelical Christian sect and pulled their children into the fold.) The evening he was fired, the businessman called his brother on his cell phone and said he'd lost his job and was about to take his life. He wouldn't say where he was. His brother tried to persuade him that there was another way, to try a different approach to easing back into life, but the businessman wouldn't listen. He told his brother to give his love to everyone and hung up.

Later that evening, a young couple were sitting in their car near the Beachy Head Pub when they noticed a man standing near the cliff edge and looking around nervously. Concerned, they left the car and walked toward the cliffs, but the man jumped before they could reach him. In the note he left behind, the deceased apologized for deserting his loved ones: "I just couldn't continue with this mountain of pain and torment and guilt."

According to suicidologist Edwin Shneidman, "when an individual commits suicide, that person is trying to blot out psychological pain that stems from thwarted psychological needs vital for that person." Some people, he says, have a vital need to achieve; others to affiliate, to dominate, to avoid harm, to be autonomous, to be loved, to understand what is going on, and so on. There are as many theories of suicide as there are cable TV channels, but Shneidman's rings most true. Suicide happens when we lose what we most need.

Which probably explains why I read the sudden-death reports of the music teacher and businessman with more than passing interest. We share the same vital need: to be respected, to be thought of as competent and good. I tend to my reputation and self-regard the way others do their relationships and health. I buff them with conference presentations, chairmanships, and self-serving acts of kindness, then stand back and admire the shine. The tiniest dent—a public speaking gaffe, an unwise decision, an insensitive remark—sends me into a ruminating funk. Shame and guilt are my slipperiest slopes to depression. For me, a major moral failure would be catastrophic.

I encounter surprisingly few tales of transgression in the sudden-death reports. There's a lesson here, I believe. Three lessons, really: most people can live with their bad behavior so long as they don't get caught; most people don't get caught; and many who do get caught have little to lose in the way of reputation or self-regard. As the German philosopher Immanuel Kant observed, "A man of inner worth does not shrink from death; he would rather die than live as an object of contempt, a member of a gang of scoundrels in the galleys; but the worthless man prefers the galleys, almost as if they were his proper place."

It's probably also true that for every good man or woman who would choose death over dishonor, there are scores who could bear a tarnished reputation more easily than a loveless life. I encounter far more disappointed lovers and spouses in the sudden-death reports than scoundrels. According to the Samaritans, "relationship problems are the most common, persistent problems of suicide attempters, both adolescent and adult." As one would expect, love tends to disappoint teenagers and grown-ups differently. Adolescents and young adults usually kill themselves over unrequited love. Typical is the nineteen-year-old department store manager who told a friend she'd jump off Beachy Head if her boyfriend ever left her—he did and she did—and the twenty-eight-year-old hotel waiter who, after his girlfriend said she wanted to cool off their relationship, stormed out of her apartment, shouting, "I'm going, I'm going, goodbye, world!" and leaped off Beachy Head the next morning.

There's no mention or suggestion of mental illness in the sudden-death reports of these scorned lovers, and the witness statements reveal surprisingly little about their character. But knowing what I know about the kinds of people prone to impetuous, lovelorn suicides, I have a feeling that the nineteen-year-old was a borderline personality: impulsive, moody, self-injuring, went through jobs and lovers like cigarettes, feared abandonment. And the twenty-eight-year-old? An antisocial personality:

volatile, manipulative, possessive, and intolerant of rejection, authority, and anything else that stirs up feelings of inadequacy—the type of guy daughters are warned about and borderline personalities are drawn to.

As one who is neither young nor passionate, I find it far easier to understand and sympathize with the other kind of relationship suicide: that of the long-suffering spouse. There are several in the sudden-death reports, one of them a middle-aged mother who, one November morning, bought new winter clothes for her two sons and asked her estranged husband to pick up the boys from school, since she'd be coming home late. She didn't say where she was going.

She didn't return home that day. Or the next. The following day, the husband received a letter telling him that he'd find the car at the top of Beachy Head. He phoned the police. In a parking lot near the cliffs, two investigators found an abandoned Subaru Legacy bearing the missing woman's plates. A note taped to the steering wheel indicated that the driver had jumped. It directed the police to contact her family.

The mother of two left behind four typewritten suicide notes. In one, addressed to her children, she expressed the hope that someday they would forgive her. In another, she apologized to her mother and brother, and mused that her children might be happier with one of the parents gone. In a bitter note to her husband, Sean, she accused him of wanting to "screw" her in their separation, leaving her nothing if he could. And in a note to the whole family, she wrote, "I'm sorry but I can't fight on anymore. I feel completely oppressed by my marriage, and I just never have the energy to push on and out. Sean has taken the lifeblood from me."

The notes are convincing, playing as they do on my prejudices (men are bad; women are good) and my own failures as a husband. I'm in the wife's corner, poor thing. Why did she marry the rotten bastard? But I remind myself that a separated, suicidal spouse isn't the most reliable narrator; authors of suicide notes seldom are. The only innocent victims are the children.

I TAKE A DEEP BREATH before reading the sudden-death report of forty-three-year-old John Chetwynd; it is an inch thick. His criminal file, Mick Davey told me, resides at Scotland Yard.

John Chetwynd was an accountant for a London bakery. One coworker described him "as 500 percent reliable, always there and hardworking. He never came across to me as anything other than his normal, happy-go-lucky self." A Vietnamese nurse who occasionally helped out at the bakery said that Chetwynd was "a very normal person, jovial and always very helpful." Her brother, a coworker at the bakery, also had nice things to say about Chetwynd. In fact, the brother and sister were so fond of Chetwynd that they encouraged him to strike up a pen-pal correspondence with their younger sister, Thi Bich Hien, who lived in Vietnam. Eventually, they arranged for Chetwynd to meet her, inviting him on a visit to their family home. The trip to Vietnam was a huge success. Chetwynd won over Thi Bich Hien's family and friends, then won Thi Bich Hien's hand in marriage.

They lived apart for four years while his wife waited to receive her British citizenship. Then, according to one of Chetwynd's neighbors, "she just appeared with a child" at Chetwynd's London flat. The child was fourteen-month-old Kevin, conceived during one of Chetwynd's visits to Vietnam. In ten months, brother Christopher was born. Not long after that, Chetwynd, who'd been working twelve-hour days to support his growing family and was suffering constant stomach pain from a hernia operation, stopped providing for his wife and children. A month before Christopher's first birthday, John Chetwynd assaulted Thi Bich Hien. The police issued a restraining order, barring Chetwynd from the home he had struggled so hard to maintain.

He spent the next three nights in a hotel before leaving for a one-week holiday in Scotland. When he returned, he didn't show up for work the next morning, unusual for someone who was, according to a co-worker, "as regular as clockwork"; he drove to his flat instead. On the way, he stopped at a gas station and filled his diesel Land Rover with gasoline, a strange lapse for such a deliberate man. It was about noon when he rang the doorbell of his apartment. Thi Bich Hien thought it was the postman. She opened the door, and Chetwynd barged in. At first nothing happened. The estranged husband played and cuddled with his sons. Then, as his wife leaned over to change a diaper, he picked up a baseball bat and struck her several times over the head. She screamed and tried to block his blows. She heard Kevin and Christopher scream. Then she lost consciousness. When she came to, Chetwynd hit her again on the head, shoulder, and chest, hissing, "I'll kill you." She again lost consciousness. When she awoke, Chetwynd was gone. She crawled to the sitting room, intending to call the police, but the phone line had been cut. Worse, there was no sign of the children anywhere. She crawled to the front door. She noticed that the key she'd left in the keyhole was gone. She reached for the knob and frantically turned it, but the door wouldn't open; it was locked from the outside. Then she remembered the spare key in her purse. She crawled to it, then to the front door, then across the landing to her neighbors, who answered the knock and saw Thi Bich Hien on her hands and knees, covered in blood. In the ambulance, she again lost consciousness. When she awoke, she found herself lying in a hospital bed, with a police constable and translator by her side. She dictated her witness statement, a five-page single-spaced horror story buried between pages of police radio transcripts in the sudden-death report.

As Thi Bich Hien lay in her hospital bed, Chetwynd, the subject of a nationwide alert with two kids in tow, somehow found the time and place to compose a farewell to his father. In a note bristling with exclamation marks, Chetwynd began, "By the time you read this I shall be dead." He wrote that he never loved his wife and that his marriage was just a ploy to get her out of Vietnam. He loved his children, though, and couldn't bear to be without them; if they were left with their mother, they'd have a bleak future. He wouldn't allow that to happen. "If I cannot have them, then she certainly will not!" He asked his father to forgive him and not to grieve.

The morning after the assault, a Tuesday, local farmer Edgar Williams was driving his Nissan pickup along the coast road when he noticed a red Land Rover in a car park near the Beachy Head Pub.

The following morning, just after dawn, a busboy was cleaning the doorway of the Beachy Head Pub when he noticed a man with glasses and short dark hair walking slowly and hesitantly across the parking lot.

Some ninety minutes later, Williams was again driving along the coast road when he noticed that the red Land Rover was still in the same place. Knowing Beachy Head's reputation, he decided he'd better stop and have a look. He peered though the driver's side window. A road map opened to Beachy Head lay on the passenger seat; a suitcase, magazines, and a half-filled bottle of cola were scattered across the backseat. Williams immediately alerted the police, who dispatched a helicopter.

An hour later, a police air observer located what he thought were the bodies on a ledge ninety feet below the edge of the cliffs. He radioed for the coast guard helicopter, which lowered a paramedic down onto the narrow ledge. He unhitched and took a look. A shoeless man in a black leather jacket and dark trousers lay on his side, legs bent, head turned toward the cliff face, hair matted with blood. A pair of shattered eyeglasses and a dark bunched-up jacket lay next to the man. Nearly touching his head were the bare feet of a baby clad in pajamas. It lay faceup and had no obvious injuries. There was no pulse.

The bodies of John Chetwynd and his eleven-month-old son were flown to Eastbourne Hospital's morgue, where Sharon Debenham would spend the remainder of her shift cutting them open, while police and lifeboat teams searched for two-year-old Kevin Chetwynd. His body was never found.

The Chetwynd sudden-death report includes a wallet-size photo album of the sort commonly used to hold family snapshots, but the baby pictures inside are unlike any I've ever seen. They're postmortem photographs, top views of a doll-sized head, the scalp peeled back to reveal the horribly fractured skull beneath, and body shots of scrapes and bruises.

I gape at the pictures, flipping back and forth. Then I put the album on the table and pull out two loose photographs. In one, Chetwynd smiles tightly as he stands by a pond with Kevin; in the other, he stands by Thi Bich Hien's hospital bed, the proud father of another son. I pick up the album again and open to a head shot of Christopher; my eyes go between it and the two family photographs as my brain wrestles with the incongruities of killing what is loved, and saving children from a bleak future by depriving them of it. I study Chetwynd's image closely, thinking that if I look long enough, I'll see intimations of the madness to come. But all I see is a dark-haired, bespectacled everyman of vanilla coloring and countenance striking the pose of the dutiful husband and father. Ridiculously, I turn over the picture as if looking for signs of decay behind the façade.

Slumped in my chair, I look at the Chetwynd tragedy from different angles. Was his suicide a preemptive strike of sorts, an example of the "You can't fire me, I quit" phenomenon known as counteraction? Did Chetwynd leave Thi Bich Hien before she could divorce him? Or was the suicide an act of rage turned inward? "No neurotic harbors thoughts of suicide," writes Sigmund Freud, "which he has not turned back upon himself from murderous impulses against others."

And what about the infanticide? Was he really trying to protect his children? British forensic psychologist Gerard Bailes says that men like Chetwynd "may be driven by delusions that make them think they're acting out of love, saving their children from intolerable or harmful circumstances." Chetwynd wrote in his suicide note that the children could not be left with their mother. "She's an awful dangerous mother with no sense of the dangers of simple everyday things."

Maybe he killed his children as a hedge against losing them. He loved his children "and cannot bear to be without them as has happened before." Or perhaps Chetwynd wanted his wife to pay the ultimate price for taking his home and children. "The overwhelming urge in these men is to hurt the mother as much as they can," says psychotherapist Adam Jukes, author of *Why Men Hate Women.* "They know that the cruelest thing they can do is to kill the children and leave her alive."

I give up. I gather together the photo album, the family pictures, the radio transcripts, and witness statements, and place the bulging folder on top of the growing pile. I close my notebook and put down my pencil and sit for ten minutes, images of a "good and lovely man" and the infant son he murdered flashing through my mind.

"LOVE AND WORK are the cornerstones of our humanness," writes Freud. If so, losing both at once can trigger a major collapse. In a local newspaper article, I read of a forty-nine-year-old American who visited Beachy Head while vacationing in England "to lick his wounds, after suffering financial, legal, and domestic problems." He was so enamored of the country that he returned fifteen months later to make a new life for himself. He ended up jumping off Beachy Head instead. "His business had failed some eighteen months ago in America," summarized Coroner David Wadman at the inquest, "and at about the same time his marriage had come to an end. Obviously these matters preyed on his mind, even though he came to England with the idea of making a fresh start." Wadman also recorded a verdict of suicide in the death of a sixty-one-year-old former German prisoner of war who was upset over both the breakup of a three-year relationship and his inability to find work.

Work problems alone are enough to trigger severe depression. In fact, according to the Samaritans, job woes are second only to relationship troubles as a source of external stress leading to suicide. Judging by the sudden-death reports, they're a close second. I read several accounts of workers who jumped off Beachy Head days after being "made redundant," a phrase with a chillingly sci-fi ring, as if British companies are constantly cloning new workers to replace old ones. The reality is that businesses are closing their doors, especially in the north, where the decline of heavy industry has caused massive unemployment in some areas, as well as a dead housing market, a spike in crime and drug use, and a reversal of traditional roles, as more husbands stay at home and more wives work in often low-paying part-time jobs—ideal conditions for what French sociologist Emile Durkheim calls anomic suicide, a class of self-destruction that recognizes the unmooring effects of an abrupt change in social position, good or bad. Think of the inner-city thug who, by virtue of a champion-felling right hook, suddenly finds himself in the spotlight, exploited by greedy handlers and hounded by racist reporters; or the wife of a disgraced mayor who moves out of the mansion into a two-bedroom ranch.

It's interesting to consider that the unemployed steelworker who fritters away his days channel-surfing at home, instead of looking for another job, may actually be employing an outmoded survival strategy. UCLA researchers found that serotonin levels in dominant male vervet monkeys fell some 40 percent when they were displaced in the social hierarchy, and that the levels of the feel-good neurotransmitter in the victorious monkeys rose by the same amount. Predictably, the downwardly mobile monkeys were reduced to a depressive, couch potato–like state that, researchers surmise, prevented them from wasting precious energy on futile challenges to the heirarchy. Perhaps what was an adaptive response for our hirsute ancestors has become, for humans, a maladaptive response to a loss of social rank by different means. Instead of losing fights, we lose our jobs, but the effect is the same: we stand less erect, we pick at our wounds in private, we lose our drive.

I don't come across any unemployed Yorkshire miners or Lancashire steelworkers in the sudden-death reports. Perhaps Beachy Head's beauty and fame don't have the same allure for practical provincial types. A more common figure in the reports is the white-collar southern Englishman reeling from job loss or, as in the case of a fifty-year-old college lecturer, wilting under job stress. On a drizzly February morning, the professor and his wife, a secretary at the same school, rode to work together in their Mercedes and kissed goodbye in the campus parking lot. She didn't notice anything different about her husband. She knew he'd been under a lot of pressure recently. His department was being restructured, and there was a possibility that he might be demoted. But he was the sort of person who kept things to himself. So he didn't tell her what he told his officemate ten minutes after kissing his wife goodbye: that he wasn't feeling well and was going home.

That afternoon a woman was walking along the cliff top, making her way toward the pub, when she stopped to take a photograph. Off to her right, she noticed a man perched on a ledge just below the cliff edge. He was leaning forward, as if looking for something. She stood and watched quietly, curious about what he might be doing. Some fifteen seconds later, he seemed to raise himself up slightly before leaping out toward the sea.

The wife took the bus home from work, as usual. She expected her husband to pull in half an hour later and, after a quick snack and change, leave for his weekly evening out with the guys. Then she listened to the phone messages. One was from her husband's officemate, calling to see how he was feeling. She thought it strange that he'd never said anything to her about being sick. And why wasn't he home? She assumed he must have left early for the pub. But why would he go if he wasn't feeling well?

When she heard the outside gate open later that evening, she figured it was her husband. But when she opened the door, she saw two grim-faced police constables standing on the stoop. They asked if her husband had lost his wallet recently. They asked questions about his clothing and car. Toward the end of the conversation, they told her that a body believed to be her husband's had been recovered at Beachy Head.

Reading the sudden-death reports of the mother of two, the accountant, and the college lecturer when I am in my early forties is like watching television replays of plane crashes in an airport lounge. I dread boarding middle age. It seems unsafe and utterly unromantic—not a time of innocence or rebellion or nest-building but of crisis, of things falling apart because the flabby center cannot hold: of invasive annual checkups and early-retirement incentives; of menopausal wives and declining parents; of empty nests and tired marriages; of disillusionment and regret.

I fear that I might add my own story to this horror collection, a piece about love or work gone bad. In the thick wall that separates thought and feeling from action, I sense cracks from the pressure of containment. I might impulsively hit on a student or blurt out "I want a divorce" when my wife yet again corrects my placement of the glasses in the dishwasher. I'll end up in a one-bedroom apartment or in a dead-end job uttering Dante's haunting lament:

In the middle of the journey of our life
I found myself in a dark wood,
For I had lost the right path.

I would feel more sanguine about middle age if I were better suited for family life. I'm Thoreau trying to play Ward Cleaver, and I'm barely pulling it off. At the ball field in town, I watch a father of twelve as if he were some freak. How unbothered he seems by the interruptions and squabbles and clamorous demands; how quick he is to feed into the chaos with zingers and laughter and mock indignation. If I were him, I'd starve the mayhem with aloofness. I have a hard enough time fitting a wife and daughter into my personal space.

So it is with a tinge of envy that I read the accounts of people who jumped off Beachy Head after losing a companion. A fifty-five-year-old man was found at the base of the cliffs, clutching a letter written by his just-buried mate. Her son told the inquest, "I wasn't shocked that he died on the day of her funeral. After my mother died, John felt like he had nothing to live for." An eighty-four-year-old widow had trouble eating and sleeping even seven months after her husband's death. She told her daughter after visiting his grave that she wished she could go to bed and not wake up. Three days later, she drove her Peugeot to Beachy Head and parked near the public bathroom. She put her car keys in the pocket of her cardigan, wrote a note thanking her daughter and asking for her forgiveness, and left it by her handbag in the car's footwell.

These two were prime candidates for suicide. Widows and widowers are two and a half times more likely to kill themselves during the first year of bereavement than married people in their age group. And the older they are, the greater the risk. In every country, the suicide rate for the elderly is higher than that of the general population; in the United States, it is 50 percent higher, a figure that doesn't include deaths from medical noncompliance, self-starvation or dehydration, "accidents," and other "silent suicides."

The golden years must seem like a cruel hoax to an elderly person in chronic physical pain. Medical illness plays an important role in 25 percent of suicides, and the percentage increases with age to over 70 percent in suicides older than sixty years of age.

While reading one sudden-death report, I am able to put a face to these statistics. In a photograph taken by her husband, Don, sixty-six-year-old Doris Haffenden stands serenely next to a pond, sportily dressed in a polo shirt and drawstring slacks and a white sun hat.

A former competitive tennis player, Doris Haffenden once told her husband that she was going to play tennis until she was ninety. That was before she began developing heart problems in her late fifties and was told by doctors that she'd have to stop playing sports. A few years later, she developed severe arthritis that didn't respond to treatment. She lived in constant pain and grew increasingly depressed. She felt she was the reason she and her husband could no longer go on holidays or take long walks.

The morning after attending her grammar school reunion and her grandson's christening, she woke up at six-thirty, a little later than usual. It was a hot July morning. Don noticed that she seemed very happy. Later in the morning, one of her best friends stopped by to visit. When the friend left twenty-five minutes later, Doris told her to "keep strong," a comment Don thought unusual but not worrisome.

Shortly after eleven, Doris prepared for her morning walk. She locked the side door and placed the key in the usual safe place. She walked to the backyard, where Don was working in the garden. She was wearing a broad-brimmed sun hat and a blue anorak. She said, "I'm going now, goodbye," something she'd said a thousand times before. Don had no cause for alarm: he hadn't noticed that she'd taken off her engagement and wedding rings.

She walked to the train station and took a cab to Beachy Head. On the way to the cliffs, she complimented the driver on the smoothness of the ride.

Shortly after Doris had left, Don finished working in the garden. He went into the house and found a note indicating that the baked potatoes were in the oven. When Doris didn't return home for lunch at one, he knew that something very bad had happened, because she was a person of great constancy. He phoned her best friend, thinking Doris might be there. He called the police. He retraced her walking route. He canvassed the town center. Two hours later, he returned home to find Doris's friend and two police officers talking in his driveway. The constables questioned Don about Doris's clothing and left with a photo of her. In an hour, they returned and told him that a body had been found at Beachy Head fitting the description of his wife.

IN THE RECORDS OFFICE IN LEWES, I crack open a leatherbound notebook with the ponderous title *List of Bills Submitted by the Coroner to the Eastbourne Sussex Quarter Sessions, 1753–1830.* Inside is a list of scrawled places, dates, and verdicts—the bills that coroners submitted to local justices for reimbursement of travel expenses. As one might expect, the verdicts offer a glimpse into a bygone era. People were killed by falling hay bales and by tumbles from horses and wheat stacks. One man was trampled by a team of oxen hitched to a plow; another was kicked in the head by a horse.

The suicide verdicts were rendered in language that, by today's standards, seems clumsy and tactless: "Henry, being a lunatic, hanged himself"; "Harriet, being a lunatic and distracted, cut her throat with a pair of scissors"; "Emmeline, having lost her reason through grief, hanged herself."

The ruling scrawled on a musty blue cardboard folder dated August 6, 1919, reads: "Found dead on the face of the cliff at Beachy Head, Eastbourne—suicide by throwing himself over the cliffs during temporary insanity." Inside lie the yellowed, handwritten witness statements and suicide notes gathered during the inquest into the death of Harry Poincilit, who, like Doris Haffenden, was in bad health, but unlike Haffenden, was only twenty-eight years old.

Born into a cosmopolitan upper-crust European family, Harry Poincilit had come to England eight years earlier, according to Kathleen O'Flynn, a female acquaintance, "for social purposes. He lived the life of a gentleman of leisure and was addicted to sport of all kinds." In language reminiscent of a Victorian novel, O'Flynn writes, "I met him at various places—in the way one ordinarily does—in society; that is, we went to the same houses and met occasionally."

But the good life was coming to an end for Poincilit. The war had rendered worthless a trust fund invested in Austrian and Turkish securities, and a chronic stomach ailment left him wasting away at a spa on the Thames. "I last saw him at Caterham Hydro about two months ago," O'Flynn writes. "The doctor gave hopes of a cure, but not a quick cure. He was then very ill which was the cause of the visit. He had written to me several times since then, rather despondent at times and at others cheerful, altogether as the mood was on him. He wanted to go to California or Spain, as he thought the climate would suit him. I last heard from him about a fortnight ago."

After seven months at the spa, Poincilit left on a Saturday morning in early August. That evening an Eastbourne resident was walking along the top of Beachy Head when he noticed, a few feet from the cliff edge, a walking stick, a novel, two sealed envelopes, and a letter in an unsealed envelope addressed to Miss K. O'Flynn and containing a check for sixty pounds. Some fifty minutes later, the two coast guards dispatched to the scene discovered Poincilit's "warm but quite dead" body on a grassy ledge three hundred feet above the beach. At some point, the police opened Poincilit's letters, which made his intentions clear. To Ms. O'Flynn: "Goodbye dear Kate. I am leaving this world. Please see that my sister gets the news. The enclosed cheque will cover all expenses and what is left over is a present to you. Yours, Harry."

He wrote to one brother that he "was looking forward to a

new home in a better world"; to his other brother, he revealed the depths of his despair. "When you receive this line everything will be over. I have had another relapse and there is no hope for me. I have no courage to struggle longer. I have the satisfaction that in my death, I can be useful to you, dear child."

The coroner concluded that Poincilit's "obscure stomach trouble" had developed into neurasthenia, or "insanity of the nerves."

MENTAL ILLNESS AND MISFORTUNE often feed on each other. The stress brought on by divorce, unemployment, or any other major setback can affect the sleep-wake cycle, which can trigger mania or depression in susceptible people. The reverse is also true: mentally ill people often create their own bad weather. Depressives, manic depressives, and schizophrenics are less likely to hold on to relationships and jobs, in part because they're more prone to abuse drugs or alcohol. Two thirds of people with manic depression and one quarter of people with depression are heavy drug or alcohol users—and suicide time bombs. Drugs and alcohol can trigger psychotic episodes, intensify depression, increase aggression, hinder treatment, and loosen inhibitions, costing jobs and relationships. One third of alcoholics who kill themselves have experienced the loss of a close personal relationship within six weeks of death.

Forty-two-year-old Besse Barnes was one of them. In the summer of 1915, Barnes worked as a cook in a hotel on the Eastbourne seafront. She was grieving the death of her boyfriend and drinking heavily. Her sister saw her ten days before her death and described the encounter to the coroner.

S: She was out shopping on Terminus Road and said she must get back again to her place of employment.

C: Did she tell you what she was going to do or whether anything was the matter with her?

S: No.

C: Didn't she tell you she was going to leave [her job]?

S: I knew she was going to leave but she said she promised to stay over Whitsun [the Pentecost].

C: Was she alright in health?

S: Yes, in health.

C: Was she sober?

S: Not quite, sir.

C: Had she had a drink that day?

S: She had been drinking before I saw her.

C: I'm afraid that was one of her failings?

S: It was.

C: And I suppose that was the reason of her leaving her situation?

S: I don't quite know. She came away before her time. She gave up on Whit Sunday, and I have not seen her since.

C: You know she had not been giving satisfaction owing to her drinking habit?

S: I understood so.

C: Had she ever told you she was inclined to take her own life?

S: She did about six weeks ago when she was in trouble. She said, "I will end my life. I will go and jump over Beachy Head." I did not take the threat seriously.

Two days after seeing her sister, Besse Barnes quit her job and found a room in an Eastbourne boardinghouse. Eight days later, she left, telling the landlady she would be staying with a friend and would not require a room anymore. The landlady assumed Barnes had found another job, until she read the note Barnes left behind.

Dear Mrs. Garnett,

I expect you will be surprised when you find I don't return, but I have made up my mind that after leaving the hotel I cannot face another place; so I am going to make away with myself and go where my poor Harry went six weeks ago today. I know there has not been a day pass but what I have prayed to die; but as I am not to have a natural death I must make an end of myself. I am truly sorry to give you all this trouble after your great kindness to me. Goodbye dear Mrs. Garnett. By the time you read this, I shall be gone to join Harry.

In summing up the case, the coroner said that "the deceased was addicted to drink and people in that state [are] very apt to commit suicide." The jury unanimously returned a verdict of "suicide whilst temporarily insane."

MOST BEACHY HEAD SUICIDE NOTES are brief and fall into one of four categories: apologetic, accusatory, explanatory, or practical (funeral instructions, life insurance arrangements, the settlement of property). They express feelings rather than ideas, in unembellished prose. Rare is the suicide note that is prolix, literary, philosophical, or funny; rarer still the note that is all of these. In Michael Davey's office, I happen upon one in the sudden-death report of fifty-year-old Kevin Hennessy, another alcoholic.

Hennessy was, according to his brother, the brightest member of their family. He obtained his A levels at university and went on to study law at the London School of Economics. But for some reason, he never became a lawyer; for most of his working life, he drove buses and trucks for nonprofit organizations. His brother remembers Kevin helping him get through a bad patch before withdrawing back into his own private miseries. "He always took other people's problems on board," his brother said, "but no one ever seemed to help *him*."

During the six months before his death, Hennessy was in desperate need of help. Deeply depressed, he seldom ventured outside the flat he shared with his girlfriend, and had started throwing away his belongings. When his girlfriend expressed her concern, Hennessy reassured her that he wasn't planning on doing anything silly.

On a Saturday morning in June, he left the apartment for the last time. He told his girlfriend he was going out for the day to attend a couple of Alcoholics Anonymous meetings. While he was out, she spent the morning shopping. When she returned home, she found a handwritten letter from Hennessy in the bread box, a location presumably chosen to prevent quick discovery. He wrote that he was going down south to sort himself out and to look for a place for them to live; he hated the northeast. Later in the afternoon, he actually phoned but then refused to tell her where he was. Right before he hung up, he said he'd be in touch.

Seventeen days later, a doctor was enjoying an evening stroll along the cliff top with his family when he saw a man run toward the cliff edge and leap off.

Kevin Hennessy's suicide note is a three-page, three-part, single-spaced meditation on life and death, filled with droll, telegram-like sentences ("Rotten job you've got. Letter to coroner in my sack with suggestions for identification"). In a section addressed to Emergency Services, Hennessy apologizes. He says he'd buy them a pint if he could, and hopes they never reach the point where they have to do the same thing. "It's not a bunch of laughs," he writes, "but there really was no other way."

In a section addressed to the undertaker, he again apologizes for the trouble he's caused. He's sorry as well for the pain he'll give his girlfriend, even though his death is "no great loss to the human race." He reveals that he paid for his funeral years in advance, knowing it might come to this, and gives a set of instructions: cancel the obituary notice, cancel the minister, use a cardboard coffin—anything to lower the cost. He expresses the hope that he'll be able to thank the undertaker personally in "a better world."

In the final section, addressed to the coroner, Hennessy mentions that he still has his own teeth—barely—for identification purposes. Though he recently celebrated seven years of sobriety, he says the coroner will undoubtedly discover alcohol in his system. He wants to make clear, though, that it wasn't the booze that drove him to suicide. "It was clinical depression, existential angst, cosmic alienation or whatever." A lottery win would have helped, but "better men and women than me" manage with little money. "So let's just blame my brain chemistry."

The note resonates. The self-abasement, the needless apologizing, the self-medicating—it struck me that Hennessy was much like me, and unlike all the other Beachy Head suicides I'd studied. He didn't seek to escape from a painful circumstance or a hopeless life. He hadn't been arrested, dumped, divorced, fired, laid off, bereaved, or incapacitated, and he wasn't institutionalized; he was a recovering alcoholic with a job, a girlfriend, and an apartment, who spent years "trying to make sense of the injustices on this demented planet" and believed that Britain was "sliding into anarchy." His suicide was more a response to meaninglessness than to loss or hopelessness; he wasn't disturbed or despondent so much as world-weary. If he was truly as much like me as I thought him to be, he instinctively recognized what Albert Camus described as "the ridiculous character of that habit" of "making the gestures commanded by existence," and he used alcohol to blunt that awareness. He was, in other words, susceptible.

READING THE SUDDEN-DEATH REPORTS, I'm well aware of their limitations. Mental illness, emotional upset, and alcoholism, alone or in combination, are not first causes of suicide. They trigger a predisposition that lies in the nether regions of biology and childhood, which lie well beyond the borders of the inquest.

To know why, of all the disenchanted alcoholics in the world, Kevin Hennessy was one of the few to take his own life, the pathologist would need to draw spinal fluid from his body to test for depressed levels of the neurotransmitter serotonin or the product of its metabolization, 5-hydroxyindoleacetic acid (5-HIAA), both of which have been linked to depression and violent, impulsive behavior, and the latter directly to suicide. The coroner's officer would need to inquire as to whether suicide ran in the family. If it did, perhaps Hennessy inherited a suicide gene (Canadian researchers have purportedly discovered a genetic marker for suicidal behavior) or a mental illness gene (children of parents who have suffered from depression are three times more likely to develop the condition) or an impulsive or violent temperament. The coroner's officer would also need to probe Hennessy's past for what suicidologist Edwin Shneidman calls, in one of the most moving passages in the suicide literature, "a vandalized childhood."

> I am totally willing to believe that suicide can occur in adults who could not stand the immediate pain of grief or loss that faced them, independent of a good or bad childhood or good or bad parental care and love. But I am somewhat more inclined to hold to the view that the subsoil, the root causes of being unable to withstand those adult assaults lie in the deepest recesses of personality that are laid down in rather early childhood. . . . Perhaps—I do not

know—every person who commits suicide, at *any* age, has been a victim of a vandalized childhood, in which that preadolescent child has been psychologically mugged or sacked, and has had psychological needs, important to *that* child, trampled on and frustrated by malicious, preoccupied, or obtuse adults. I tend to believe that, at rock bottom, the pains that drive suicide relate primarily not to the precipitous absence of equanimity or happiness in adulthood, but to the haunting losses of childhood's special joys.

Plenty of theories have been offered to explain the alarming increase—60 percent over the last fifty years—in the world suicide rate: the stresses of modern life; more accurate reporting of suicide (coroners are more willing to deliver suicide verdicts because suicide has lost some of its stigma); easier and earlier access to alcohol, drugs, and guns; an increase in the survival rate of premature babies, whose nervous systems may be especially fragile; and improvements in medicine that keep more people alive past the point of living, and allow more people who suffer from mental illness to marry and beget children who may inherit an increased risk for suicide. But it may be, too, that the world is producing more damaged children: more used, abused, bombed, neglected, malnourished, prenatally poisoned children who become suicidal adolescents and adults. More worrisome, in my mind, than the dire forecasts of climatologists and arms experts is the World Health Organization's prediction that by the year 2020, childhood neuropsychiatric disorders will increase by over 50 percent internationally, and that depression will become the second largest cause of death and disability.

According to his brother, Kevin Hennessy's childhood was not a happy one. If the coroner's officer had dug down to the "subsoil" of the deceased's suicide, he may have uncovered evidence of abuse (a number of studies have shown that physical and sexual abuse in childhood and adolescence are associated with later suicidality) or neglect (some psychiatrists believe the roots of suicide stretch back to mother-infant bonding: a well-cared-for baby develops what psychoanalyst Erik Erikson calls "basic trust," but one repeatedly left to cry alone, says psychologist Lee Salk, "ultimately learns to give up and tune out the world. This is learned helplessness and possibly the beginning of adult depression"). Maybe Hennessy was never allowed to be a kid: one group of researchers looked at adolescent boys who attempted suicide and discovered that, in many cases, the boys had assumed the responsibilities of their absent fathers, functioning, in effect, as their mothers' "husbands." Maybe it wasn't innocence or trust he lost but something even more devastating: the death of a close relation. Psychiatrist Gregory Zilboorg calls it "probably the most primordial cause of suicide in the human breast." In a study of fifty attempted suicides of all ages, researchers found that 95 percent of the subjects experienced "the death or loss under dramatic and often tragic circumstances of individuals closely related to the patient," generally parents and siblings; in 75 percent of the cases, the loss had occurred before the end of adolescence.

It's impossible to know. Out of shame or ignorance, families seldom reveal their past contributions to a loved one's suicide, and coroners rarely ask. Though the inquest is open to the public, the door to a victim's childhood is closed and the window into the biological mechanisms of his or her suicide shrouded in darkness.

THE IDEA THAT SUICIDE is a susceptibility rooted in nature or nurture explains some of the more puzzling acts of self-destruction—those, for example, that seem more like the consummation of a lifelong courtship than a combustion of cause and precipitant: "obsessive suicides," as French sociologist Emile Durkheim called them, because they're "caused by no motive, real or imaginary, but solely by the fixed idea of death which, without clear reason, has taken complete possession of the patient's mind. . . . It is an instinctive need beyond the control of reflection and reasoning, like the needs to steal, to kill, to commit arson. . . ." Coast guard Bob Jewson put it this way: "There are people who have a gene or something in their history, and it's like a little time bomb ticking away that they just can't turn down until they commit suicide." Italian writer Cesare Pavese echoes Jewson: "I know that I am forever condemned to think of suicide when faced with no matter what difficulty or grief," he wrote in his journal at age twenty-eight. Fourteen years later, Pavese won Italy's top literary prize, and a month later, he overdosed in a hotel room and died.

The idea that suicide is, like alcoholism and gambling, a predisposition also explains why some people, like a homeless schizophrenic, endure miserable circumstances, while others, like a baker who drove off Beachy Head after his uninsured car struck a car parked along the seafront drive, snap over trifles. "A suicide's excuses," writes the poet A. Alvarez, "are like a trivial border incident which triggers a major war. The real motives which impel a man to take his own life are elsewhere; they belong to the internal world, devious, contradictory, labyrinthine, and mostly out of sight."

I don't know where in this internal world the answer to Conrad's suicide is to be found. He wasn't, by nature, impetuous or violent. He was much loved. Suicide doesn't run in his family. Was he short a few nanograms of 5-HIAA? We'll never know. My guess is that his schizophrenia acted alone; he was an exception to the cause-precipitant, or "double-hit," theory of suicide.

Just as some people might kill themselves in the absence of a clear precipitant, so strong is their compulsion toward self-destruction, others might commit suicide who aren't inclined to, so excruciating is the pain of their mental illness.

But the precise nature of this pain is still a mystery to me when I've finished reading the sudden-death reports. I feel the same frustration voiced by the coast guard Chris Turner. *I can't understand what goes through their mind.* And yet I desperately want to. What does unbearable psychological pain feel like? How does it affect thinking and perception? To perform an inquest of this depth, I need more than suicide notes and witness statements. I need a living body. A week later, I find one.

8

The Suicidal Mind

Cabdriver Manny de Silva is about to tell me his Beachy Head story. We're passing through the Langney section of Eastbourne, widely considered its most undesirable address, an abscess of strip malls, industrial parks, and construction sites on the city's eastern flank. I was in this very area a week before, knocking on house doors in a potholed cul-de-sac, hoping that Bill Hull would open one of them. He never did. He had moved out of the neighborhood, a woman told me. But her husband had his address if I wanted to leave my phone number.

Several days later, in a driving rainstorm, I slipped a letter of introduction through a mail slot in what I believed was Hull's apartment door. He called after four days, apologizing for the delay. He explained that the letter had been delivered to the wrong apartment—and that he'd had trouble deciding whether to meet with me.

With a thumb and finger on the wheel and an arm slung outside the window, de Silva jockeys for position with another one-armed driver before entering a rotary that spits out cars like wood chips. My body leaning against the door, I feel a strange mix of exhilarating anticipation and doubt that I imagine sailors feel when they finally see land and wonder if it's too good to be true. The cab might break down (it looks like it could). Hull might not answer the door. I might have the wrong address—again. De Silva glances into the rearview mirror. His eyes look strained under his bushy eyebrows; the whites are yellow.

"It was in the evening. I was driving the girl to the pub, and she was very quiet," he's saying in a strongly accented voice. "I asked her if she was okay, and she started crying. She said she and her boyfriend had come to Eastbourne for a little away time, to try to patch up their relationship, and then he left her. I listened, of course, tried to help her sort things out. She was obviously upset, but I thought she'd be okay, you know? So I left her at the pub, she went inside, and two months later, my boss says he got this letter for me. It was from the girl, thanking me for saving her life. Couldn't believe it." He shakes his head, and as we emerge from the rotary, I sit up straight and see de Silva looking at me in the mirror. "I have it here, if you'd like to see it." He reaches for the glove compartment and takes out an envelope.

Outside the business district of Langney, the road begins to climb. Drab concrete bungalows ribbon a treeless hillside where stately Victorian houses once stood, before German bombers flattened them. From above, the bungalows appear connected by the clotheslines running between them, like rectangular beads on a choker. I take the envelope and pull out a thank-you card embossed with stenciled fruit and flower designs.

The girl wrote how frightening it was to look over a cliff in the darkness, wishing you were at the bottom of it. Walking along the seafront at two in the morning, she thought about everything de Silva had told her. Maybe the man in the clouds sent him. Anyway, she was going back to Derbyshire. She thanked de Silva "for proving that there are a few people who care about others." She signed the letter "Toni."

I slip the card in the envelope and hand it back to de Silva, who says nothing. I gaze out the window at a line of low-income brick apartments, imagining Toni peering over the cliff edge in the darkness. I've heard stories of cabbies physically restraining suicidal passengers on the cliff top, but there must be at least as many aborted suicide attempts, passengers who, unbeknownst to the driver, travel to Beachy Head fully intent on jumping but are pulled back by the memory of something the driver said or did—a compliment, an expression of interest, a willingness to listen—some small act of humanity that cabdrivers and bartenders seem to specialize in. "She's lucky you picked her up," I say.

"I was only doing my job," he says without a trace of false modesty. He glances into the side mirror and pulls the cab over to the sidewalk. He turns around to collect the fare. His caramel-colored cheeks are pockmarked, his short black hair flecked with silver. He looks subdued. I hand him the money. He smiles weakly and says, "Cheers."

I stroll down Malvern Close and turn off the sidewalk onto a narrow walkway clefting two apartment buildings. It's damp and dark between the brick walls, which rise two stories to a strip of cloudless blue. There is life and light at the end of the tunnel-like walkway: a man and a woman tend a raised flower bed in a bright yard. The man is in a wheelchair, picking at flowers level with his lap, and the woman stands close to him, doing the same. Behind the garden sits a small greenhouse, and behind the greenhouse, another apartment building rises up.

From afar, there's something dreamy about the two gardeners. Their movements are languid, their figures fuzzy, as if they're suspended and partially dissolved in a clear liquid. When I draw close enough for them to hear, see, or sense me, their movements quicken. The woman's head snaps up. Her face is round and pale, and her cheeks turn to balls when she smiles. She says hello. The wheelchair pivots sharply. A fiftyish man wearing a black T-shirt and black sweatpants smiles shyly and lopsidedly. His gray-streaked hair is pulled back in a ponytail, exposing a pierced ear. His head is large; his freshly shaven face seems pasted onto his hunched torso. He extends his hand and, holding rather than shaking mine, softly concludes that I must be Tom.

He introduces me to Steffanie, his upstairs neighbor, and asks her to stop by in the evening. Then he wheels toward the ramped entrance of his apartment a few yards away. Inside, we pass through a galley kitchen. An old radio sits on the countertop next to a jar of instant coffee. The living room is dimly lit. On one wall, spooky tribal masks encircle an abstract drawing with mazelike patterns and explosive yellow hues.

"I did that when I was on an acid trip," Hull says matter-of-factly.

On another wall hangs a black-and-white photograph of a hippieish Hull peering into a cup. "That," he says, "was taken at the National Botanical Gardens in the blistering summer of seventy-six. We were all very high on hashish, sun, scenery, and good fellowship. The photographer caught me contemplating my reflection in my drink. Halcyon days!"

He pivots his wheelchair and directs me to a corner table near the kitchen doorway. I sit by the room's lone window, which is covered by a closed blind.

Hull asks if I'd like some tea and wheels back into the kitchen. I take a moment to survey the tabletop's terrain: a telephone, a ghastly silver lamp in the shape of a female head, a large earthenware fruit bowl, videotapes, remote controls, a transparent container of felt-tip markers, a jar of cheese sticks, a tin box, a copy of Tom Wolfe's *A Man in Full*, a pack of Gitane cigarettes, and a brass Zippo lighter. Hull inquires about my stay—who and what I've seen—and I give him the short version. I don't mention that I heard him discuss his suicide attempt on a German documentary about Beachy Head or that I'd spoken to his rescuer, Bob Jewson.

I'm nervous. I'm about to have a conversation with a stranger who made a sincere attempt to kill himself six years before. How do those confessional talk-show hosts do it—delve so comfortably into the private lives of their troubled guests, as if there's no line they could possibly cross? If knowledge of a man is Y and time spent with him X, I've plotted an unnaturally steep climb along the edge of Hull's private self. Watching him fill two cups with steaming water, I consider the hazards of such a venture: reopening wounds long closed, opening ones long hidden. Perhaps Hull was reluctant to meet for these very reasons.

Dictionaries, multivolume histories of the British Empire and twentieth-century art, LPs and CDs of Aaron Copland, Laurie Anderson, Joni Mitchell, John Lee Hooker, and others pack the glass-fronted cupboard next to the doorway. I glance at the copy of *A Man in Full*. Could a shared sensibility possibly compensate for the lack of a shared history?

He returns with the tea and asks if I mind him smoking.

"Not at all," I lie.

He lets out a small gasp as he reaches for his lighter; tremulously, he lights up. He props his elbow on the arm of his wheelchair and watches me intently through tendrils of smoke. His eyes are hazel, flecked with green. "So."

I repeat the contents of my letter: the circumstances surrounding my brother-in-law's death, the questions I've had since, and the hope that he might be able to answer some of them. I don't tell him that I resolved to track him down because I want to explore the unconscious motives that impelled him to make an attempt on his life, and, even more, to know what it *feels* like to be suicidal. How does acute psychological pain coerce the mind into destroying itself? Better to start with an easier question.

"Why did you do it?" I ask.

Hull regards his cigarette gravely as he taps it over the ashtray. There is no sign that he relishes the attention his story brings him. In the brief interval between fixing his gaze on my face and speaking, he looks like a man who wants to be rescued. His voice is husky, and I find myself leaning to hear.

Hull was a production-line worker for Birds Eye Foods, and a senior shop steward for the Transport and General Workers' Union when the factory shut down. He couldn't find another factory job—couldn't even get an interview—because no one wanted to hire someone with a reputation as an agitator. So he worked as a landscaper and mover, jobs that barely paid the bills. He didn't think his problems could get any worse.

Then, three years later, he developed myalgic encephelomyelitis (ME), a viral illness of unknown origin, with symptoms— muscle aches and mental confusion—that become full-blown very quickly. "I couldn't really work at all then." He turns away to exhale a plume of smoke. "My wife would always be saying, 'Don't overdo it, don't overdo it.' I'm a very enthusiastic sort of person, you know. I'm doing something in the garden, going from one thing to the other, and the next day I'd just be flat. It's like suddenly your account is empty. Still, I managed to get by and stay happy."

For four years, Hull was annually evaluated and pronounced unfit for work. Then a doctor for the Department of Social Security cleared him to do light, unstressful work, over Hull's and his personal physician's objections. "He said I could be a receptionist, or a museum or car park attendant." Hull laughs and shakes his head. "Well, they don't have male receptionists, there's only one museum in Eastbourne, and the car parks are run by machines."

Jobless and benefitless, he appealed the assessment. Though he won the appeal, and back pay, the damage was done. Three months into the six-month appeal, he'd slipped into a deep depression. His physician prescribed Prozac, which, Hull says, made him crazy. He couldn't sleep for more than half an hour at a time; he'd read the same line in a book over and over again; he experienced strobelike, psychedelic hallucinations; and he entered states that he now knows as "depersonalization" and "derealization." "Everything seemed like a dream around me," he says as if he still can't quite believe it. "That was the derealization. And the depersonalization means you become alien to yourself. I'd be making a sandwich and look down at my hands buttering a slice of bread, and they'd be like somebody else's hands. There was no connection between the two. It was like being in a bad dream."*

* *The Diagnostic and Statistical Manual of Mental Disorders,* the bible of the mental health profession, describes "depersonalization" as a disassociative disorder characterized by persistent feelings of "detachment or estrangement from one's self, a sensation of being an outside observer of one's mental process, one's body, or parts of one's body." It's frequently a stressed response to life-threatening dangers such as accidents, assaults, and serious illnesses and injuries, but it also occurs as a symptom in many psychiatric disorders. Approximately one in a thousand people who take Prozac experience extreme side effects like psychosis and depersonalization.

Desperate for a change in medication, Hull again saw his physician, who insisted that Prozac couldn't possibly cause such symptoms. He adopted a wait-and-see approach, leaving Hull to fend for himself over the holidays, which were a disaster. Hull cried before he and his wife left for a friend's house in Hastings, because the thought of spending Christmas Day in someone else's home while in the throes of madness was terrifying. Once there, he was withdrawn and agitated. So he stopped taking Prozac, and the next day he and his wife decided to cut short their visit and return to Eastbourne. Because his doctor was on holiday, he saw an on-call physician who prescribed the tricyclic antidepressant Prothiaden over Hull's objections. Hull felt a quarantine period was necessary, as Prozac was still in his system; the doctor insisted that Prozac leaves the body quickly.*

The piggybacking of antidepressants perturbed Hull even further. His hallucinations continued. He was terrified of being alone or away from home, he couldn't tolerate silence, and he was emotionally raw. "My emotions were just completely overwhelmed by everything," he recalls. As he talks, his arms rest comfortably along the arms of his wheelchair; his right hand dangles over the side, a cigarette smoldering between two long fingers. "I mean, I like music. I had a Neil Young concert on the television. I couldn't watch it. I went down to the basement, and I could hear it, the sound of his voice coming through the floor, and I just sat there and cried and cried. He always touches me a bit emotionally anyway, but this was completely over the top. It was like the feeling after there's been a very bad storm. You feel like you're underwater. You're all stirred up inside."

Longing for relief, Hull stopped taking Prothiaden shortly

---

* According to the makers of Prozac, it may take as long as one to two months for the drug to disappear from the body.

after he started and saw an Eastbourne District General Hospital psychiatrist his physician had referred him to. "He was a pill-prescribing machine. Didn't investigate me at all. He said there's no such thing as ME. He said I had mild depression and asked me no further questions." He smiles scornfully. "He asked me three questions, actually: 'Do you have any children? Do you own your own home? And do you still smoke marijuana?' And that was it. End of story. 'And here's some drugs.' "

The psychiatrist prescribed the antidepressant Seroxat. Hull knew that Prothiaden was still in his system (his daughter, who worked for a major pharmaceutical chain, had supplied him with technical information on a number of antidepressants), and he feared that taking Seroxat would guarantee another chemical crisis. "When you're in the sort of state I was in, all your intellectual weapons for arguing with somebody go out the window just when you need them. You can't defend yourself verbally, you can't sort your psychiatrist out, and your insight goes. It's just not clear anymore. So you really end up being bullied into doing what they want you to do. And that's why I took these drugs as they advised, one after the other, with no sort of quarancy period in between."

When he tried to switch psychiatrists, his shrink said that he needed his physician's permission and that the process would take time. It was then that Hull wrote his first suicide notes. "I just felt stuck in the middle of the system, and I couldn't get out," he says in a voice barely above a whisper. "I didn't feel like a worthwhile person anymore and thought my family would be better off without me." He shared these thoughts with his wife, thinking that if he externalized them, they would go away. They didn't. "I thought another way to externalize it would be to write letters—you know, suicide letters to bring this outside myself. And for a couple of months, it worked."

On a cool, clear April afternoon, Hull dated the letters and placed them in a desk drawer. He then told his wife, who'd been going everywhere with him the last few months, that she needn't accompany him to his doctor's appointment. She didn't argue; she'd noticed he seemed in better spirits lately.

Leaving home, he spotted some weeds in his garden. "Let's get those when I come back," he thought. He took a bus from Seaside to Eastbourne center. Crossing the street to board the connecting bus to Meads, he felt as if the bus were sitting there waiting for him. Everything was happening perfectly. All the lights were green, all the way down the line. If he still had any doubt about his decision, it was pushed aside by the fact that everything was laid out for him to carry through.

From Meads, he walked up the steep hillside in a Zenlike state. He felt divorced from himself, the way he imagines a samurai feels when calmly plunging a disemboweling knife into his own stomach and twisting it. When Hull arrived at Beachy Head, he noticed the Samaritans' number posted on a sign in front of the coast road phone booth. He called and asked them to tell his wife where she could find his letters.

He walked across the cliff top toward the edge. He wasn't afraid. Though he doesn't believe in an afterlife, he saw his deceased aunts and mother waiting for him on the other side of the cliff edge, beckoning him to join them.

Ten feet from the edge, he stepped over sagging strands of barbed wire bounding fissured earth. Then, without breaking stride, he walked off the cliffs. His mind was blank during the three-second fall. Then he saw a flash.

When he opened his eyes, he saw two men in harnesses and helmets crouching above him, and over them, a helicopter dangling a long rope. One of the men had a black beard; the other had a red cross on the chest of his jumpsuit. The man with the beard explained that Hull was on a ledge a hundred feet below the cliff top at Beachy Head. It was then that Hull was aware of the pain in his right wrist and ribs, and the ominous absence of feeling below his chest. Still, he was happy to be alive. He felt as if he'd just awakened from a very bad dream. During the three hours it took for the two rescuers to stabilize him, he couldn't stop talking.

Following the attempt, Hull lay heavily sedated in Eastbourne District General Hospital for two weeks. It was a nightmare inside his head, these terrible scenes, unimaginable. But when he finally came to, the hallucinations were gone, the depression was gone, everything was right in his head. Was it the long period of sedation? Or did a massive blood transfusion flush the offending chemicals out of his system? He's not sure.

After five weeks in intensive care, he was taken to the National Spinal Injury Centre, where, in addition to undergoing ten months of grueling physical therapy, he began the long, painful process of coming to terms with what he had done. Still, he felt at peace. Returning home was, in some ways, harder than the rehabilitation. He called two of his best friends, whom he hadn't heard from during his time at the center. They promised to visit him but never did. He phoned a former co-worker whom he'd once befriended while the man was recovering from an amphetamine psychosis in a mental hospital. Just the sort of person he thought would understand. Never heard a word from him. Then Hull's wife asked for a divorce, and he lost his house. While adjusting to life as a disabled bachelor, Hull filed a malpractice suit against his doctors that was eventually dismissed by the high court. Though the court found fault with the doctors' medication practices, it couldn't prove that the pharmaceutical follies had caused Hull to attempt suicide.

———

THE CRACKS IN THE BLINDS are strips of black, and the room has grown cooler.

"We need heat. A cold front's moving in." Hull wheels across the living room and turns on a small electric heater. The coils glow orange in the darkening room. When he returns, he reaches for his cigarettes and, with a jerk of the wrist, ejects one from the pack. He squints as he lights up, the flame briefly illuminating his face. "I didn't attempt suicide because I couldn't work, because of my chronic fatigue. It's the illness itself that makes you do it. It's not the circumstances that bring the illness about."

Like most people, I tend to think of depression as a fairly ordinary occurrence, a temporary black cloud brought on by seasonal changes, hormonal surges, and standard setbacks—the mental equivalent of a common cold. But severe depression's "veritable howling tempest in the brain," as author William Styron calls it, is an altogether different weather system. Garden-variety depression provides intimations of madness—disturbed sleep and concentration, distorted thinking—while, as Styron writes about his own brush with suicide, "depression, in its extreme form, is madness." In a Swedish study, severely depressed subjects displayed "impaired reality testing, often of psychotic proportions," and were seventeen times more likely to kill themselves than moderately depressed subjects.

The storm of severe depression is so enveloping that the afflicted often feel as if they're suffocating. A twenty-three-year-old silversmith from Massachusetts wrote before killing herself, "I feel as if I am encased in foam rubber packing." Sylvia Plath felt as if she were being "stuffed further and further into a black, airless sack with no way out." Andrew Solomon, author of *The Noonday Demon,* part of which chronicles his descent into suicidal depression, felt as if he were "constantly vomiting but had no mouth. . . . The air seemed thick and resistant, as though it were full of mushed-up bread."

Having never experienced such a state, I had difficulty imagining it. Even after reading personal accounts of severe depression, I had trouble really believing that one could be depressed to the point of madness. I suspected suicidal people embellished their inner turmoil to gain sympathy or to justify their suicide attempt, in the same way that type A personalities might exaggerate how little sleep they get to impress people. Insanity was the province of more "serious" mental illnesses, such as manic depression and schizophrenia.

But as I sit listening to Hull for close to three hours, I've become a believer, even though his psychosis may have been partly the result of mismedication. I've entered into Hull's experience without having to pay the normal price of admission, escaping the heavy cost of a comparable experience of my own. What I find most frightening from my front-row seat is the cruel irony of severe depression: the very despair that compels suicide erodes the faculties needed to defend against it.

"When I came out of the hospital, I had my share of disillusionments," Hull goes on. "If anything was going to push me over the edge to try to kill myself again, it would have been my friends avoiding me and my wife leaving. But I was in my right frame of mind. I had the tools to deal with it. I had all this positive experience from my past that I could draw on. But when you're depressed, your personal experience doesn't matter anymore."

That's because you can't remember much of it. Research shows that highly specific memories of positive events—the kinds of memories that suggest solutions and offer strength—are largely inaccessible to severely depressed people.

"What about your family?" I ask. "Did you think of them?"

"No. No, I didn't." Hull stares into the air as if transported to some painful, private place. For the first time I notice that the downward slant of his eyes is a permanent feature of his face, like a scar. "My wife talked to God knows how many people when I was in hospital, and she said some totally ridiculous things. Said that I went up to Beachy Head before to jump, but then I thought about her and the kids and couldn't do it. I tried to explain to her it's totally ridiculous, it doesn't work that way. There's nothing else in your life. It's a very cold solution in that way. You're just so focused on what you're doing, there's nothing else there." He pauses. "A friend of mine expressed it quite well. She attempted suicide a couple times herself in the past, and she said it's the feeling like your head's in a globe. It's in a goldfish bowl. It's just you in there."

"Are you aware that it's you in that goldfish bowl?" I ask. Was Hull's calmness the result of depersonalization? Was he so detached that he didn't recognize himself in this drama?

He shakes his head. "No. Somehow the fact of you gets lost. It's an egoless state. Your id has taken over, if you like. It's a response to something deeper inside you that you can't even recognize."

The suicide literature is filled with references to constriction, a perceptual narrowing that is as much a hallmark of the suicidal mind as auditory hallucinations are of the schizophrenic mind. Psychologists liken it to the closing diaphragm of a camera, and understand it as a sort of functional madness that allows people to kill themselves.

"Is it a rational state?" I ask.

Hull pushes off the arms of his wheelchair to shift himself, but the effect is negligible; his limp legs barely move. "It was rational in the state of mind that I was in at the time. Totally irrational, from a normal state of mind. If that's plain; I don't know if it is." He laughs, then turns thoughtful. "It's rational, but it's rational prior—before the actual act. The consideration of all the possibilities of getting out of the situation without killing yourself has happened before. You try a pyschiatrist, you try antidepressants, you try talking to people, you try reasoning with yourself, you try writing it down. You go every way that you can, but every door is closed to you, and there's only one that's open." He pauses. "But to actually take that door is a totally mad thing to do."

He takes a deep drag on the pencil stub of his cigarette. The cool squint of his eyes, the orange glow of his cigarette, the blue smoke rising in the darkness, and now, the edgy tone of his voice, create a film-noir effect. Suddenly, Hull feels far away. "My wife," he goes on, "one of the things she held against me more than anything, she said, 'You seemed happier. You seemed so icy calm when you went out. I had no inkling of what was going to happen.'" He lets out a small, sardonic laugh. "Her idea of madness is being like a maniac, which is an outdated concept. You're going to be rolling and tearing your hair out and banging your head against the wall. But what is more mad than to be so totally calm and lucid inside yourself, knowing you're gonna do yourself in?"

"But if you know your pain is about to end, wouldn't it be normal to be calm?"

He smiles as if he's about to let me in on an inside joke. "But that is the madness of it. You see the relief of the pain, but you don't see the fact that you'll cease to exist." He pauses. "I thought I was going to get my bucket of peace and then return home and weed the garden."

I find myself stuck on the same question that I posed to coast guards Bob Jewson and Chris Turner. "I guess I'm challenging the idea that you have to be mad to kill yourself."

Hull watches me intently, his mouth set in a compassionate half smile.

I go on. "I think about people who've been institutionalized off and on, their whole lives, and reach the point where they've had enough. Isn't it possible that they know exactly what they're doing when they jump?"

Hull ponders the question. "You can say to yourself, 'What sane person would want to go on living in institutions and being treated badly and never feeling happy all their lives?' If you haven't got a positive experience, you can't think to yourself, 'Well, things are going to get better somehow. I'm going to get over this.' You haven't got that to rely on, yeah?" He pauses and looks as if he's trying to find the road he meant to go down. "I still think it's a mad thing to do. You've got to be in that state of mind where it's egoless, because the thing that thinks inside you, you're destroying that. Our prime directive for ourselves is self-preservation, isn't it? We're a gene-scattering machine, aren't we? Nature wouldn't put in a self-destruct facility for a machine which is there to spread genes."

HULL IS IN GOOD COMPANY in thinking that suicide is unnatural. Saint Thomas Aquinas claimed that suicide was "contrary to the inclination of nature" because "everything naturally loves itself, the result being that everything naturally keeps itself in being." Some five hundred years later, Immanuel Kant wrote, "We shrink in horror from suicide because all nature seeks its own preservation; an injured tree, a living body, an animal does so. . . ." Suicide, Primo Levi believed, "is an act of man and not of the animal. It is a meditative, noninstinctive, unnatural choice."

And yet each year approximately one million people worldwide kill themselves, thirty thousand of them Americans. Why *would* nature give us this capability? Perhaps minds that were adaptive in their original environment have become increasingly maladaptive in our modern one; the relatively late addition of frontal lobes to human headgear may have had unintended consequences. Designed to allow our hirsute, highly communal ancestors to suspend visions of tools and weapons in memory while pondering their construction, our forebrains enable today's visionaries to fashion tools of survival—water purification systems, MRI machines—that, in their mind-boggling complexity, would have bewildered our scantily clad forebears. But they also enable divorcées, unemployed workers, nursing home residents, and adolescents to ruminate upon their disappointments and disconnectedness. We've remade our social environment in such a way that the faculty of working memory has become an increasingly mixed blessing, which is, I suppose, another way of saying that consciousness has become increasingly painful. Human beings are uniquely equipped for self-destruction; we're the only animals that can hate, blame, and shame ourselves, envision a bleak future, question the meaning of life, and imagine our own death.

Is it fair, then, to expect such a highly conscious, psychologically burdened animal to abide by the law of self-preservation as faithfully as an injured tree or frog? I don't think so. "Unlike other animals," writes Daniel Callahan in his book *The Tyranny of Survival*, "human beings are consciously able to kill themselves by suicide; some people choose to die. They want more than mere survival. Models which work with ants do not work well when extrapolated to human beings."

It seems to me as unnatural to endure intolerable, irremediable pain when you have the means to end it as it is to kill yourself.

We're as averse to suffering as we are to death. We destroy shattered horses and put sick dogs to sleep because we feel it is the humane thing to do; we feel, in a sense, that we are doing what they cannot do for themselves and what we would want done if we were in their place. But when humans who suffer from chronic psychological pain are their own executioners, they run the risk of being called crazy. Why is that?

I can think of a few reasons. Physical agony is usually visible, and mental anguish usually isn't. People have trouble believing in the existence of things they can't see, which explains why employers offer sick days but frown on "mental health" days; why most health insurers don't treat mental and physical illnesses with full parity; and why suicide is more easily accepted in cases of physical suffering. A hostage who chooses to commit suicide rather than subject himself to another round of torture would earn mostly sympathy. Some people might even think him brave for hanging on as long as he did. Sufferers of severe and recurring depression await its return with the same dread and feeling of powerlessness that the hostage awaits his next bout of torture. Describing her own struggle with depression, poet Jane Kenyon wrote, "I believe only in this moment of well-being. Unholy ghost, / You are certain to come again / . . . and turn me into someone who can't / Take the trouble to speak; someone / Who can't sleep, or does nothing / But sleep; can't read, or call / For an appointment for help. There is nothing I can do / Against your coming." Unlike the hostage, the chronic depressive will almost certainly be judged mad or irrational should she decide to kill herself to avoid further torture.

In the same way, most people would consider the suicide of an eighty-year-old terminally ill man to be more rational than the suicide of a twenty-five-year-old chronic schizophrenic because the fact of the old man's dying—the gaunt, bedridden, intravenously fed body—is apparent, and the chronic schizophrenic is presumed incapable of clear thought. It's hard for healthy minds to imagine that for the young paranoid schizophrenic who doesn't respond to treatment (or is never treated), who can't work or keep relationships, whose "consciousness" is a toxic stream of self-hatred, delusions, depressions, and hopelessness, the experience of living might feel like dying. There's a reason why mental illness raises the suicide risk significantly more than physical illness does.

The belief that suicide is an act of madness is held not only by people who can't imagine the crushing weight of despair, or who instinctively feel that suicide is unnatural, but by people who value life above all else, which probably describes most Americans. Though we care about quality of life, many of us tend to think of life as an absolute value. Our hospitals take extraordinary measures to prolong lives that are hopeless, and only 12 percent of us, according to a recent Gallup Poll, believe that suicide is morally acceptable. This shouldn't be surprising. Life has been good to most Americans, and most Americans are Christians. They believe that life is a gift from God and suffering is redemptive.

It is quite a different view from that of a Buddhist, who believes that biological life is not only meaningless but filled with suffering; or that of an eighteenth-century rationalist like David Hume, who, in defending suicide, famously declared, "The life of a man is of no greater importance to the universe than that of an oyster"; or that of Immanuel Kant, who, though believing most suicides to be "abominable," admired the Roman warrior Cato's suicide because "there is much in the world far more important than life. . . . To live is not a necessity; but to live honourably while life lasts is a necessity. . . . It is cowardly to place a high value upon physical life."

Thus Cato stabbed himself in the breast and plucked out his bowels, preferring death to life under Caesar, and the early Christian martyrs begged to be executed, one woman reportedly celebrating her death sentence by "rejoicing and exulting at her departure as if invited to a wedding supper, not thrown to the beasts."

In precolonial India, a Hindu wife was expected to show her devotion to her husband by throwing herself on his funeral pyre, a practice known as *suttee*. Though the British outlawed the practice in 1829, it has still not been entirely eliminated, so embedded is it in traditional Hindu culture. In Japan, where being an orphan is considered a fate worse than death, *oyako shinju* (parent-child suicide) has been traditionally viewed as an act of devotion and caring. Several hundred cases occur each year, most involving mothers plagued by poverty or shamed by divorce. In a recent survey of married female Japanese college students, over two thirds said they would kill themselves and their children if their husbands deserted them, a statistic that beggars belief.

Buddhist monks immolated themselves to protest Nguyen Van Thieu's dictatorship in South Vietnam. More recently, the friend of an eighteen-year-old Arab suicide bomber told reporters, "It was a courageous act and all of us wish to be in her shoes."

Each of these suicides was considered natural and rational by people in cultures that valued devotion, honor, heroism, or paradise more than life itself. But to Americans, such suicides seem fanatical and dangerously subversive. "The suicide does not play the game, does not observe the rules," writes Joyce Carol Oates, "he leaves the party too soon, and leaves the other guests painfully uncomfortable. The world which has struck them as tolerable, or even enjoyable, is, perhaps to a more discerning temperament, simply impossible. . . ."

HULL IS IN THE KITCHEN, on the phone with Steffanie, laughing. Maybe that's why he believes so adamantly that "the prime directive for ourselves is self-preservation." He's happy. Life is good. Since his suicide attempt, he's realized what a friend his daughter has been to him. He no longer argues with his brother, a businessman and Hull's ideological opposite, who was the first person to see him in the hospital and continues to stay in touch. And Hull hasn't had a suicidal thought since his attempt. His life is filled with loyal companionships and solitary pleasures: reading, drawing, listening to plays on the radio, "putting the world to rights" with friends, and gardening and smoking marijuana, both of which "allow you to notice things you didn't before. It's a feeling of a life force that ties everything together."

Dinnertime is fast approaching, but the question I've been avoiding lingers. I feel the same way I did when I was about to broach the subject of the suicides with Mark Roberts: gearing up to strike a nerve. Hull said to me, "Suicide is a response to something which is deeper inside you that you can't even recognize." So what was he responding to? The depression that preceded his suicide attempt was not his first. He said he'd been depressed sixteen years earlier, for a period of two years. He was jobless then, too, after five years of working night shifts and overtime. What hidden wound made Hull so vulnerable?

Hull hangs up the phone and wheels back to the table. "Sorry about that." He glances at his rumpled cigarette pack and empty teacup, the discarded provisions of a psychological dig, then looks at me.

"Bill," I ask, "did anyone close to you die when you were younger?"

He blinks, and his mouth opens seconds before the words come. "My mother died when I was thirteen. Why?"

I tell him about a highly regarded Freudian case study of Abraham Lincoln in Harold Kushner's book *Self-Destruction in the Promised Land*. Lincoln reneged on a promise to marry Mary Owens and later broke off his engagement with Mary Todd, triggering a six-month-long episode of severe depression during which he threatened suicide; he told a friend he'd done nothing to make people remember him. Kushner hypothesizes that Lincoln's unresolved grief, or "incomplete mourning," over the death of his mother when he was nine, and over his sister's death ten years later, caused him to abandon lovers before they could abandon him. Lincoln may have seen suicide as a hedge against desertion, Kushner surmises, a way for him to live on in people's memories. Or perhaps he was angry at his mother and sister for dying; guilty about feeling that way, he may have turned his anger against himself by inviting thoughts of suicide.

Hull listens intently. When I finish, he folds his hands in his lap. He says that when his mother died, his brother, who was four years old, couldn't sleep. Hull, on the other hand, acted as if nothing had happened. The only time he cried was when he saw his grandmother upset at the funeral. When he later read *Darkness Visible* and discovered that William Styron's mother had died when he was thirteen, it clicked. "So I think it's quite possible that there are elements of incomplete mourning. I think I lost my emotions for a lot of years. When I was a teenager, I had a very hard exterior. That's why I was a bit of a juvenile delinquent. When I look back now at some of the girls I went out with, I would never get involved with anybody. I'd dump them just like that. No thought about feelings."

"What about your father?"

Hull looks stricken. His eyes soften. "After I was married, I had a falling-out with my stepmother, and for a number of years, I hardly ever saw my father. My stepmother had quite a dominant personality and a temper to her; you could never fall out with my father. He's the most balanced of men." He pauses as if to reconsider his words, says that as an eighteen-year-old soldier, his father witnessed the liberation of the Nazi concentration camp at Bergen-Belsen. According to Hull's aunt, he was a changed man when he came home. "She said before he left for the army, he was up at six in the morning whistling and singing, and he just never shut up. When he returned home, he would just sit and stare at the walls all the time. So maybe there was some emotional damage to him. He's talked a little about it, but I don't think it's something he's ever met head-on."

Rain beats lightly against the window. It is almost time to go. "You said that suicide was a cold solution. What are some of the emotions you lost touch with that, if you could have felt them, might have prevented you from attempting to take your life?"

"The love of the world all around you and your love for your family. Well, love generally, I suppose. And the feeling for every good thing you've ever felt. Yeah." He nods. "I felt there was nobody else I could rely on. I was the only person I could rely on. Nobody else could affect what was happening inside me. But you really feel, 'I wish I had somebody to lean on.' " He pauses. "Maybe this is where people who do believe about the old-man-in-the-sky stuff have an advantage."

I'M STANDING IN THE RAIN, second-guessing my decision to leave. Hull's wheelchair fills the front door's frame. He sits slumped, and he looks at me intently, almost wistfully. Does he want me to stay? Should I stay? I catch the tail end of Hull saying something about his garden, and I remember that Steffanie is coming over tonight.

"Keep in touch," he says.

How could I not? Hull told me more about himself in four

hours than some people reveal in a lifetime. But I know that I probably won't. I rarely do.

As I walk down the dank alleyway, I imagine Hull closing his front door and wheeling back into his living room, now filled with my absence. I hesitate. Then I continue on, through a shaft of light, over tobacco-colored puddles, and finally into open air.

9

The Long Goodbye

During my first visit to Beachy Head, I left Black Robin Farm each night at ten and walked to the pub, where I nursed a pint at one of the many empty tables while taking in the sights and sounds of closing: the call for last orders, the counting of money, the plunk of overturned chairs on tabletops. When the doors closed at eleven, I strolled along the cliff top, where, enveloped in darkness and wind, I felt I'd temporarily given the world the slip. Sometimes I walked all the way to the foot of Belle Tout lighthouse. One Saturday night, I regret that I didn't.

IT'S THE DAY BEFORE England's Mother's Day. Twenty-four-year-old Duncan Copper sits in his car outside his girlfriend's home in Westerham, a small town twenty miles south of London. He tips back a bottle of Budweiser while listening to a Nine Inch Nails CD. He and Kath have a date, but it's beginning to look as if it isn't going to happen. When he arrived forty minutes earlier, Kath turned him away at the door. She said she had to help a friend sort out some personal problems, which is a convenient excuse for what Duncan refuses to acknowledge: she's trying to ease him out of her life. So he returned to his car and waited. In the space of twenty minutes, he knocked several times more, but each time she sent him away. Eventually, she came out, and together they drove to a supermarket to buy some wine—which was what made it so hard. Rather than make a clean break of it, she gave him a rickety reason for hope. But when they returned to her house, she still refused to invite him in. She did bring him a small consolation prize: a bottle of Bud.

After stewing for another twenty minutes, he gives it one more try. He walks up the steps and knocks on the door. The door swings open, and there's Kath, cutting a boyish figure in the bright doorway. She looks at Duncan coldly. He takes off his jacket and shows her a burn mark on his shoulder. He claims it's work-related, but she's skeptical; it looks like a freshly self-inflicted cigarette burn, a final bid for attention. She isn't impressed. He says he's having problems at work. Her mouth tightens. "What's the *problem?*"

"Oh, I'll tell you sometime." He gives her a long, hard stare. Then he leaves. Twenty minutes later, he arrives at his home in Tunbridge Wells, a mid-sized city equidistant between London and Eastbourne. It's ten-forty-five. The house is quiet. His mother is in bed reading. His father is in the backyard with the dog. He walks up the stairs.

"You're home early, son," says his mother, Lesley.

"Yes, I am, aren't I?" he says from the hallway. He closes the door of his bedroom and takes two sheets of computer paper off his desk. He sits down on his bed and begins to write.

Dear Kathy,

Please don't blame yourself. I really couldn't have gone through life the way I was. . . . Four months, that's all I knew you for, but in that short time you made me happier than anyone else. Thank you. I just wish that I had met you when I wasn't crazy. Do me a favor, come up here, watch the sun rise and think of me, will you?

Love,
Duncan

He folds the note and slips it into his pocket. Then he writes a shorter, second note:

To My Family,

I'm so sorry. I just can't take life anymore. I love you all and in everything I did, I thought of you. Tell Kath I love her and I hope she finds happiness one day.

Sorry,
Duncan XXX

Quietly, he leaves his bedroom and heads for the stairs. It's eleven-fifteen.

"Where are you off to, then?" his mother calls out.

"Puttin' my car in the garage."

"All right, don't be long."

"No, all right." Halfway down the stairs, he wishes her a happy Mother's Day.

She thinks, "You're not getting up very early in the morning, then, sunshine."

At the bottom of the stairs, he yells up, "I love you."

"How odd," she thinks. She's no longer reading, just listening. She believes she hears Duncan open the back door, perhaps to say good night to his father, but she can't quite tell. Then she hears the front door close and, moments later, the slam of the car door and the start of the engine. In seconds, she expects to hear the engine fade toward the neighborhood garage, a reassuring sound she's heard hundreds of times before, but instead the engine fades away from the garage.

She puts down her book and picks it back up. After fifteen minutes of trying to read, she gives up. She walks to his room. She heard the scrabbling and paper rustlings when he was in there and wondered what that was all about. She opens the door, turns on the light, and scans the room. Her eyes come to rest on a folded piece of paper on the night table. She picks it up, unfolds it, and reads. Her heart begins to race, her knees weaken. "Peter!"

Her husband drops the dog's leash and dashes inside, up the stairs, and into Duncan's room. Lesley sits on Duncan's bed, slumped and crying. She hands him the paper, and seconds later, he's racing down the stairs, out of the house, and down the road to Duncan's garage. Time is critical. He knows that Duncan means business; he never does anything by half.

The garage is locked. Peter puts his ear against the door. He hears nothing. Still, he has to be sure, to rule out all the possibilities. He runs back to the house for the spare keys. When he returns to the garage, he frantically opens the door. No car, no Duncan. Beachy Head. He's going to Beachy Head. When he was a child, Duncan, Peter, and their dog would tramp all over Beachy Head during their annual vacation to nearby Pevensey. As an adult, Duncan would go there alone and walk along the Downs or sit on the cliff edge and think. He'd said that when his decrepit cat, Domino, died, he'd bury her at Beachy Head. It was one of Duncan's favorite places in the world. By Peter's estimation, his son would be there in half an hour.

Back at the house, Lesley rings her daughter, Nikki, who volunteers to call Duncan's friends and the Eastbourne police. Lesley then phones the local police, who say they'll send someone out to collect the suicide note and to take statements.

The waiting is excruciating. Neither Nikki nor her husband, Simon, can drive to Beachy Head because they've had a bottle of wine between them. Peter's been drinking, too. The only one who hasn't been drinking is Lesley, who can't drive. They contemplate getting a taxi, but there's no guarantee that Duncan is at Beachy Head. So they wait by the phone. It seems the quickest way to make anything happen. Nikki calls back to say that none of Duncan's friends, including Kath, know his whereabouts, and that the Eastbourne police are dispatching a helicopter. Throughout the waiting and calling, they hold out hope that Duncan will return. His sister thinks, "Oh God, Duncan, you're going to get in so much trouble when you get home."

DUNCAN ARRIVES AT BEACHY HEAD shortly after midnight, unaware that an Eastbourne police cruiser is rushing toward the same spot. He pulls into a parking area near Belle Tout lighthouse, turns off his headlights, and uncaps a half-pint of rum. He takes several swigs and throws the bottle in the backseat, where it joins the empty Budweiser bottle. He takes his note to Kath out of his pocket and holds the corner to his lighter flame. When the paper begins to burn, he blows out the fire. He stares at the oversize furry dice dangling from his rearview mirror. He gently removes the dice, which his mother and father gave him as a joke for his eighteenth birthday, and clutches them in his hand. He opens the car door, locks it, puts the keys in his pocket, and climbs over a four-foot-tall berm. The sky is moonless and the clouds invisible in the misty darkness.

What happens in the seventy-five feet between the embankment and the cliff edge, nobody knows. Maybe he runs and dives off. Maybe he slips on the grass or a piece of cliff edge breaks away and he dies before he wants to. Maybe he sits down, shuts his eyes, and leans over, or maybe he stands on the edge and puts one foot forward. Maybe he cries.

THE EASTBOURNE POLICE arrive ten minutes later. Duncan's car is easy to find; it's the only one in the parking area. One constable checks the license plate and shines a flashlight inside. The other climbs the berm and runs the beam of his flashlight along the cliff edge. Nothing. He yells, "Hello!" into the wind. Nothing. He rejoins his partner, who's broken into the car and extracted some of its contents: a partially charred suicide note and a gym pass showing a young man with a strong chin, deep-set eyes, and closely cropped blond hair.

The helicopter arrives minutes later, concentrating its search on an area of the cliffs in line with Duncan's car. Peering through a thermal imaging device, the air observer spots a warm body on a ledge some two hundred feet below the cliff top and directly in line with the abandoned car. The pilot radios the constables on the cliff top, who radio the Tunbridge Wells police that a body of unknown identity has been discovered at Beachy Head.

IT'S SHORTLY AFTER TWO in the morning, and Lesley and Peter are standing in the middle of the living room with two Tunbridge Wells police officers, finishing up an interview for the missing-persons report, when they're interrupted by a staticky voice. They glance at the radios in the constables' holsters as if startled by a loud crash. The female constable, a chunky, purse-lipped woman with the posture of a drill sergeant, quickly lowers the volume and turns her back on Peter and Lesley to take the call.

"It's about Duncan, isn't it?" Lesley asks when the constable turns back around.

"No, no, no," she says. "We wouldn't be sittin' here takin' statements from you if it was." Her partner, a slim-hipped, full-bellied man with an air of relaxed authority, nods unconvincingly.

"Yes, it is. It's about Duncan," Lesley repeats.

The constables abruptly wrap up and say they'll keep in touch. Through the window, Peter watches them walk across the front lawn toward the patrol car. Then he sits with Lesley in the living room.

"They *must* have been able to get up there, they *must* have been able to find him," Lesley says, dabbing her eyes with a tissue.

Peter shakes his head. "People aren't acting fast enough."

Under a minute later, they hear a gentle knock. Peter shoots up out of his chair and opens the door. The constables stand on the stoop, their air of efficiency gone. The male officer solemnly asks if they can come in, but Peter is already opening the screen door as if he has prepared for this very moment. The officer, his partner standing stiffly by his side, informs Peter and Lesley that a helicopter located a man's body, thought not to be alive, lying on a ledge at Beachy Head. A car with matching plates was found in a car park near Belle Tout with Duncan's gym card inside. He adds that because of the weather, the police won't be able to recover the body until morning. He regrets that they couldn't offer better news.

After they leave, Peter holds Lesley, and they cry in the quiet, empty house. Having just received the most devastating news imaginable, they must now call Nikki, the big sister who once overheard her brother tell friends how much he loved her, how their personalities were so similar it was as if they were twins.

Nikki and Simon grab their jackets and head out the door. The streets are quiet except for the buzzing streetlights, the houses dark save for the occasional flickering glow of a television set. They walk almost two miles before Nikki stops at a lamppost. She kicks it repeatedly, then falls into her husband's arms.

"Be strong for Mum and Dad," she says to herself as they approach the front steps of her parents' home.

The family spends the rest of the long night trying to make sense of Duncan's death. They try to imagine what was going through his mind and where his body is now. The thought of Duncan spending all night on a dark, cold, wet, windswept ledge far from home, visited by one of his worst fears—slugs—is almost too much for Peter to bear. "It doesn't make any difference to him, does it?" he says. "The lad is dead. But it does to me."

At eight the next morning, the coast guard's cliff team recovers Duncan's body.

The following morning, Simon drives Peter, Lesley, and Nikki to Eastbourne District General Hospital, where Peter, later joined by Nikki, identifies the body. Duncan lies in a bier in the mortuary's viewing room. His head is heavily bandaged, and he strikes a characteristically proud pose, his prominent chin tilted upward, as if to say, "I've done what I wanted to do, and I'm proud of it."

Sharon Debenham, the attending mortician, tells Peter and Lesley that Duncan died instantly, the result of a process known as deceleration: the "shell" of the body stops on impact, but the insides try to keep going. Later, they'll learn that Duncan broke virtually every bone in his body: skull, nose, jaw, shoulders, arms, spine, and legs.*

From the hospital, the family drives to the Eastbourne police station, where they're given a bag containing Duncan's possessions: wallet, cigarette lighter, gym card, change, and his suicide note to Kath.

SEVENTEEN MONTHS EARLIER, on the other side of the ocean, my twenty-five-year-old brother-in-law had been watching TV at the foot of his parents' bed as they played cards at the head of it, when he abruptly left to go to his room because of some perceived insult. Seconds later, they heard through the wall a click, then a pop. My mother-in-law rushed to his bedroom door. She called his name. Nothing. She opened the door. He lay on the bed, his eyes staring lifelessly up at the ceiling. She walked toward the bed, calling his name again, this time more urgently, as if trying to shake him awake with her voice. She bent over the body and called again, softly, in tears. She sat on the edge of the bed and cradled the bloodied head of her youngest child as her stunned husband watched from the doorway.

They are still mourning his death, consumed by "why" and "what ifs," depleted by sleepless nights and endless replays. Ordinary movements—reaching for the phone, closing the oven door—are an effort. Occasionally, they discuss Conrad's death with their children, but for the most part, they bear the heavy burden alone. At times it seems to me that they are counting the days until their own deaths. Will they ever feel the same attach-

---

* Duncan died not only instantly but painlessly. A falling human quickly reaches a terminal velocity of 150 to 180 mph, while the sensory nerves conduct pain impulses at a maximum speed of 100 to 120 mph, which means any impact occurring faster than 120 mph will result in death before those pain signals ever reach the brain.

ment to life that they did before Conrad's death? And if so, how can they get to that point? They won't attend suicide survivor support groups, but maybe I can bring the experiences of fellow survivors to them. With that thought in mind, I take down the addresses of eight mothers and fathers whose depositions I've read in the sudden-death reports. I write each a letter. Peter Copper is the only one who answers.

ON A PLEASANT SATURDAY MORNING, a short, wiry man with a closely cropped silver beard rounds the corner of the Eastbourne train station. We catch eyes. Striding forward with an outstretched hand, he introduces himself to me. During the fifty-minute drive to his home in Tunbridge Wells, he tells me about Duncan, who died almost a year ago to the day. In a voice that fades in and out like a weak radio signal, he says that Duncan left school at sixteen and worked for three years in the silk-screen printing industry before being made redundant; that he'd laid lines for an electric company since he was nineteen, turning down several opportunities for promotion because he didn't want to abandon his supervisor and loyal friend, Rex; and that he'd finally accepted a promotion two days before his death. Peter proudly recites Duncan's many talents. He was a gifted cartoonist. He could speed-read—books about military history were his favorite—and he was a great multitasker, someone who could read, watch TV, and hold a conversation all at the same time. If you quizzed him on what he'd read, he'd remember it all.

"He never gave us any problems," Peter says, shifting his rugged hands on the steering wheel. "He was just too good." He pauses. "There's an unwritten rule that parents don't outlive their children. It should have been me."

An awkward silence fills the car.

He asks about Conrad—the circumstances of his death, what he was like. Somewhere in the conversation, he stops at a traffic light and glances in the rearview mirror. His gaze freezes and doesn't fully return to the road until we're well past the intersection.

"He looked just like Duncan," he says more to himself than to me. "The guy in the car behind me. He was probably totally different from him, but in the mirror, through my back window to his windscreen, he looked like Duncan. He was just watching me."

I turn around and see only an indistinct head in the car behind us. Ten minutes later, we pull up in front of a two-story brick duplex in a quiet neighborhood. A budding sumac tree overarches a postage-stamp yard enclosed by a wrought-iron rococo fence. I comment on the fence, and Peter says he designed and welded it. He repairs industrial heaters and air conditioners, he adds, so he knows a little bit about welding.

A large woman in a floral-patterned summer dress greets us at the front door. Her thin lips break into a weary smile. At her feet yips Jaffa, an adopted spaniel whom Peter showers with endearments and playfully swipes across the head.

The living room is a cozy, unpretentious space. Ceramic vases and mugs and a fruit bowl full of painted wooden eggs line the shelves of a glass-enclosed cupboard; shot glasses and bottles of whiskey and ouzo stand behind its cabinet doors. A peaceful needlepoint sea scene of a mother and her children hangs above a small kerosene heater; another picture spans a stretching frame next to the couch—a project, perhaps, that helps Lesley to forget during her lonely days at home. On the other side of the sofa, a framed photograph of Duncan sits atop a giant stereo speaker.

Jaffa barks at the front door as I settle onto the couch. A compact young woman in tight jeans and a turtleneck shirt appears inside the doorway. She has short frosted hair and a toothy smile that makes her eyes crinkle at the corners. She kisses Peter, then Lesley, on the cheek. When she turns to me, I see her brother's high cheekbones and father's aquiline nose on a longer face. Her attractiveness, I discover, is the type that sneaks up on you. She smiles easily and extends her hand, as if I am the last of a brood to be gathered under her wing.

She steps aside and introduces her husband, Simon, a slender man with a crooked smile, protruding ears, and a gentle, watchful demeanor. After offers of water and tea, Lesley heads to the kitchen. I return to the couch. Nikki pulls up an ottoman in front of a large-screen TV and stretches out her legs; Peter and Simon sit Indian-style on the floor. Simon unzips his fleece jacket and drapes it across his lap. With his boyish looks, Harley-Davidson T-shirt, and faded jeans, he could pass as a college student.

"Dad told us about your brother-in-law," Nikki says. "I'm sorry."

Her tenderness makes me uncomfortable. Since meeting Peter at the train station, I've felt fraudulent, as if I'm trading on Conrad's suicide to gain access to the Coppers' grief. Though Conrad's death affected me deeply for reasons I'm just beginning to understand, it wasn't devastating. He didn't leave a huge hole in my life. I didn't become depressed or guilt-ridden or have nightmares. He was the brother-in-law I didn't really know, not a son or brother. My loss can't compete with the Coppers', and I want them to know that, no matter how much their misery may long for company. So I downplay Conrad's death. I explain, tersely and dispassionately, that he was mentally ill and that his death was not wholly unexpected—at least not by me.

Nikki's eyes soften. "It must have been hard. I mean, knowing that it could happen. We had no idea, which in a way makes it easier."

"It was hard for my wife and her brothers," I say, "and hardest of all for my mother- and father-in-law."

"Of course," she says, nodding. Lesley returns with a tray of hot tea and ice water and makes the rounds.

"What was Duncan like?" I ask.

The question elicits instantaneous and glowing smiles. During the next twenty minutes, the conversation flows without pause as the Coppers bounce around the subject of Duncan.

"If he got into something, like . . . spaghetti Westerns, he had to have every one. He was fanatical about that, wasn't he? And clean hands, too. He had to have clean hands, he was terribly untidy in his bedroom, oh dear, but in himself, that was another matter. . . . He was always playing practical jokes on people. He kidnapped a garden gnome. He took pictures of it and sent a ransom note like, 'Give me the money or the gnome gets it.' That was life, wasn't it, with Duncan? It was just a great laugh. He used to laugh until he coughed, didn't he? . . . We'd have to go get water. . . . He was strong as an ox, but he was so sensitive, wasn't he? He was a tender, sensitive person. . . . He was shy with a crowd of people. At the same time, he was very confident, I mean, the two things belie each other. . . . And animals, he went mad when he saw people baiting badgers on an animal show. . . . He'd do absolutely everything for you. If anybody had said anything about Mom or Dad or me or Simon, he'd risk going to prison doing anything. He was very, very protective . . . 'cause he was big enough to carry it off! . . . He was very, very, very generous. When I was a little tight, he'd give me more money than I needed, or when I tried to return borrowed CDs I hadn't had a chance to listen to, he'd tell me to keep them—'And here's some more,' even though I didn't want any more. His generosity was overpowering at times."

"He was too nice," Peter mutters.

"He was too nice," says Nikki.

If the day Duncan Copper leaped off Beachy Head was a typical day for suicide in England, he would have been one of two people between the ages of fifteen and thirty-four to take his life. According to the Samaritans, suicide accounts for 20 percent of deaths among people aged fifteen to thirty-four and is second only to car accidents as a cause of death of young men. But Duncan better fits the profile of an *attempted* suicide, someone who is likely impelled more by emotional upset than by mental illness— upsets of the sort that drove Goethe's Werther to shoot himself after he was spurned by a married woman, inspiring legions of frustrated romantics in eighteen-century Europe to dress in blue tailcoats and yellow waistcoats and dust off their attic pistols. The Samaritans claim that unrequited love is responsible for 74 percent of adult and adolescent suicide attempts, and an increasing number of them are made by men, many of whom are probably like Duncan: "tender," "sensitive," "too nice": men for whom loving hard carries the risk of falling hard.

Duncan met Kath through a friend who worked with her, and they started dating four months before his death. It wasn't long before his family noticed changes in his spending habits. He showered Kath with expensive gifts, flowers, and dinners out. Two months after meeting her, he'd drained most of his savings. To raise cash, he sold one of his favorite possessions, a large Russian telescope. On the first business day of the New Year, he took two large Nescafé tins full of coins from his dresser and deposited the change into his bank account.

"It's almost like he was buying love," Nikki says, wiping away a tear, "because he didn't think he was good enough to be loved for himself."

But Kath's love couldn't be bought. She didn't give Duncan a Christmas present. She canceled dates at the last minute. It always seemed to be Duncan who was making the effort.

"We didn't interfere with the relationship," Peter says. "You can't protect him and decide what girlfriend your son should have when he's comin' up twenty-five years old. You can only say, 'Well, you sure she's the one for you?' And he'd say, 'Yeah.' But we said many, many times, 'I hope she doesn't hurt him.' "

Duncan nursed his hurt in private. Only later, after talking to Duncan's friends, would the Coppers learn that he once arranged a phony double date at a restaurant in a desperate bid for alone time with Kath. As Nikki tells it, while Kath and her friend Nicole waited in the pub for Duncan's "friend" to arrive, Duncan borrowed Kath's phone, went outside to call his "friend," and then returned to tell Kath and Nicole that his "friend" couldn't make it. Kath later tried the number and discovered it was bogus. "That to me says, 'Two's company, three's a crowd, can't you get the hint' type of thing," Nikki says. "But she didn't."

Only when sorting through Duncan's receipts and credit-card statements after the funeral would they discover that the car stereo Duncan said Kath gave him for Christmas, occasioning a cheerful "I'm a lucky fellow!" was bought by Duncan himself. Only later, while cleaning out Duncan's eerily vacant garage, would Peter find the two empty whiskey bottles and dead flowers scattered across the floor, probable evidence of a canceled date.

But some things Duncan didn't or couldn't hide. There was the depressing, nihilistic music—so unlike the "normal music" Nikki and Duncan were used to sharing with each other. Nikki imagines Duncan lying in bed with his headphones on, listening to lines like "I shot myself and it doesn't hurt," and getting ideas. She said he stopped caring for his car, which he'd always been very particular about. The gearbox was going, the brakes. At the time they thought maybe he couldn't afford the repairs, but now Nikki wonders if he simply lost interest. He was losing weight as well—to please Kath, they assumed, who was very slim.

"I said to him, 'Boy, you're losing weight,' " Nikki recalls. "And he said, 'Shh, I'm going to get into trouble with Mum.' "

Lesley nods. "I had already had a go with him about it. I didn't notice until I saw his legs. He must have lost about two stone."*

Nikki turns to me. "It almost seemed like he was winding down."

I describe Conrad's secret winding down: the neatly packed boxes in the furnace room of the basement; the junking of nearly all photographs of himself, as if he'd tried to erase all signs that he ever existed; the endless scroll of "file deleted 12:10 p.m., Wednesday, October 2, 1996" on the hard drive of his computer; and the one bit of housekeeping we were aware of at the time that should have given us pause: the unloading of his possessions. I let him give me his tennis racquet, hiking boots, and some CDs. How could I have been so aware of the possibility of suicide and so unaware of its imminence?

"You could *kick* yourself now, couldn't you?" Lesley says.

"Yes—"

"It's like I told you on the way here, Tom," Peter says. "Each human has many facets, and Duncan showed each of us a different one, so there was nobody who could sort of lot the whole lump together and say, 'Oh, it sounds like he's got a problem.' "

And so, when Duncan didn't touch the curried vegetable dish

---

* Twenty-eight pounds.

Nikki cooked for him four nights before his death—the last time she saw him—she assumed he didn't like it. She did notice, though, that he seemed contemplative and irritable. "God, you're a grumpy old kid," she joked.

On Saturday, the day of his death, Duncan seemed fine. In two days, he'd report to work in a suit and tie for the first time, and check up on the job sites he'd mucked around in only days before. He was up for it, Lesley says. In the morning, he'd had his picture taken for the company ID card. The photo showed a gaunt, hollow-eyed young man.

In the afternoon, he bought a new tire for his car. Then he returned home, put the tire on, and retired to his room to play computer games and watch one of his favorite movies, *The Great Escape*. After dinner, he spoke to his sister for the last time, but only secondhand, relaying to Lesley—who was on the phone with Nikki—that he'd see her when she and Simon came over for Mother's Day supper. When he left for his date shortly after nine, he seemed in good spirits.

"And then," Lesley says, staring out the window, "something went in him on his way home from seeing Kath."

A WEEK AFTER HIS CREMATION, Nikki and Simon visited the spot where Duncan jumped—the same spot, friends said, where he used to sit and think. They attempted to throw white roses with attached letters over the cliff edge, but the wind kept blowing them back onto the cliff top and, in one instance, against the cliff face, requiring Simon to retrieve it with an ungainly belly crawl. After he finally managed to throw the flowers over the edge by wedging a chunk of chalk among the stems, they stood together in silence. But the moment was quickly spoiled when a group of college-aged kids walked by, laughing and joking about what a good place it would be to kill yourself.

"It was really insensitive," Nikki recalls. "But then, on the way back to the car, this little ice-cream man said, 'Excuse me, you just laid flowers.' And we said, 'Yes, we have,' thinking we're going to get in trouble for littering or something. Then he said, 'Would you like an ice cream? It's on the house.' " She smiles and turns to Simon. "That sort of restored our faith in human nature, didn't it?"

In the months that followed Duncan's death, that faith would be challenged repeatedly. The crematorium people took several months instead of the expected six weeks to install the memorial plaque at Duncan's burial site. The Coppers missed the deadline for putting Duncan's name in the Book of Remembrance, a place for epitaphs from family and friends; no one at the crematorium had explained the procedure. They had to wait fourteen weeks for the inquest, while a "bitty" actress who jumped shortly after Duncan had hers within two weeks. When they finally received the certificate of death that would allow them to settle Duncan's accounts, they discovered that the bank had "foolishly" cleared his account of all but two pounds, repossessing a loan that was actually covered under Duncan's life insurance policy. The mess took two months to clear up.

Lesley shakes her head and mutters, "Every single path we went down—"

"Mum and I are going through a bit of an angry stage now, aren't we?" Nikki says.

"Oh, yes."

"Duncan was very much into the unknown—ghosties and ghoulies and that sort of thing. He said to his friends, 'When I die, I'm going to come back in twenty-four hours and visit.' So now they're obviously terrified." One friend believes that the image of a dog on her steamed-up bathroom mirror was drawn by Duncan. A girl who never met Duncan claims he visited her in her bedroom on Halloween. "It's getting silly now." Nikki's voice rises with emotion. "It's like he's a freak, and he wasn't a freak. He was just a very upset person. I find that quite distressing at the moment. Just lay him to rest, okay?"

"Actually, we're sort of guilty of the same thing, aren't we?" Peter says. He remembers the vacuum cleaner fuse blowing while he was cleaning Duncan's car, and thinking Duncan caused it. Lesley recalls Duncan's hair clippers shutting off while she was cutting Peter's hair, as if he didn't want them using his stuff. Simon remembers a wedding video, showing Duncan fainting, jamming in the VCR.

There's an awkward pause. Nikki turns to Simon. "You can smell him, can't you?"

He nods and begins to speak but isn't quick enough.

"*I* smell him," Lesley says.

"I smelled him a minute ago," Nikki says. "You can smell his aftershave. You can smell him on the cover of his CDs. You can smell him at my house."

"Duncan's a common person in this area," Lesley says.

It all sounds very familiar. My mother-in-law said that shortly after Conrad's death, she went into his room to meditate and saw his disembodied face floating in the air. Another time, while sitting alone in the living room, she heard a strange voice. Her granddaughter later heard the same voice in the same place and was terrified. My mother-in-law reports household quirks—the erratic cutting on and off of the dishwasher, a late-night tapping on the bathroom mirror—that started occurring only after Conrad's death.

Are ghosts independent spirits? Or are they, like the ghost of Banquo, projections of guilt? Or, like Constance's captured son Arthur in Shakespeare's *King John,* a wish fulfillment, a presence invoked to fill an absence?

Grief fills the room up of my absent child,
Puts on his pretty looks, repeats his words,
Remembers me of all his gracious parts,
Stuffs out his vacant garments with his form . . .

"He's still got a terrible influence on us, on all our thoughts, on everything," Peter says softly.

Duncan is the subject of Simon's dreams: he holds Duncan on the cliff edge. The editor of Nikki's ruminations: she thinks "nasty thoughts" about Kath, then catches herself because she knows Duncan loved her. The author of their guilt: Peter feels guilty for outliving Duncan, and Nikki for enjoying a sunny day; they all feel guilty for putting Duncan's hepatitis-ravaged cat, Domino, to sleep rather than pay another expensive vet bill. He is the topic of every conversation—"Whoever came, it was 'Duncan, Duncan, Duncan, Duncan, Duncan,' wasn't it?"—and the object of Peter's disappointment.

"Duncan and I had a pact that if either of us had an accident, where we were sort of left wanting for life, so to speak, a little bit of a vegetable, we'd be there for each other," Peter says, picking at the carpet. "He said, 'When you're old, Pops, if you put your slippers on the wrong feet, I'll change them for you and put them on the right feet. If you dribble, I'll wipe your mouth.' And he's let me down."

"You should hate him for what he did," Lesley says, leaning forward and glancing at each of the assembled as though trying to solicit their support on this one point. "Not hate himself, but hate him for what he did to me and to you."

A rare hush falls on the room. Peter strokes Jaffa's head; Nikki and Simon stare at the carpet. Finally, Nikki looks up. "Mum's been really upset sometimes because she didn't think he cared about her when he said, 'Have a happy Mother's Day' before he left." She turns to Lesley. Her voice softens. "I don't think that's the case at all. I think he was trying to cover up."

Lesley nods, dabbing at her eyes, as Nikki deftly steers the conversation to an easier target of resentment: Kath. How could she date a chap so soon after Duncan's death? How could she not cry during the memorial service? And now she isn't talking. They know she turned Duncan away at the door, but did something else happen? Did she break off the relationship? Did they have an argument? If only she would come forward, it might help them with their grieving, because then there would be a reason. On some level, Peter believes *she* was the reason. "Duncan had stronger feelings for her than she had for him. In a way, she was the cause of his death."

Nikki flushes slightly. She is the keeper of the conversation: monitor of tones, plugger of awkward silences, restorer of balance. "We don't want to sound like we're bitching about her. We can't blame her. We know that Duncan made this decision."

"We just want to know why," Lesley says, grimacing, as if the very word makes her head hurt.

Of course. If you strip a suicide survivor's bereavement of all emotion, peel off the layers of anger, grief, and guilt, you inevitably find the bare bone of "Why?" The question imbues the grief of suicide survivors with a metaphysical anguish as oppressive as their emotional distress—especially when the deceased was a highly functioning young person with prospects.

"I'm sure I heard two doors shut on that car," Lesley says, glancing at Peter. "I thought somebody forced him down there and pushed him off." She laughs and shakes her head. "You think all these stupid things. He was big enough to flatten anybody."

"God, your mind," Nikki says. "All the things that you go

over." She turns to Lesley. "You just go over everything, don't you? You read all sorts of things into silly little things and imagine things that might have happened."

"He desperately didn't want to let us down," Peter adds. "Did we pressure him? Were our expectations too high?" He's the only one in the room who hasn't laughed, whose voice never rises above a soft, husky monotone, and who seems to find only small consolation in the memory of Duncan, who wasn't just his son but his closest male friend. They played video games and toy trains together ("How about a steam-up, Pops?") and watched *The Simpsons*. They took long walks along Beachy Head, just the two of them. They fought over portions of ice cream ("You've got more than me, you bastard!") and measured their cheesecake. "Loads and loads of times," Peter goes on, "when you're saying to yourself, 'Why did you have to do it, Duncan?' you lay the guilt on yourself. You shouldn't be blaming him."

"It's the way your head goes round and round," Lesley says. "You know, on some level, there's nothing you did that caused him—even though you feel guilty and wonder two, three years ago, if you didn't do what you should have done or whatever. It comes back to 'Why?' Why, why, why, why?"

Nikki says that Duncan was fascinated by death because of Mark, Lesley and Peter's first son, who died of spina bifida when he was nine months old. He spoke a lot about his brother to friends, as if he had some sort of bond with Mark. Shortly after Duncan's death, Nikki saw a medium who said that Duncan didn't want to grow old. The medium also mentioned the name Mark.

"Obviously, deep down, Duncan kept things in," Nikki says, still trolling for explanations. "In his letter to Kath, he said, 'I wish I had met you before I was—' You know, something to do with sane. I think he thought he was insane. Nobody else thought that, but he did."

It's the first time anyone has brought up the question of Duncan's sanity. They'd imagined his death, replaying it ad nauseam. Lesley pictured him holding his furry dice and running over the cliff; Nikki envisioned him sitting, closing his eyes, and leaning over; Simon saw him standing and putting one step forward; Peter imagined him crying as he went over the edge. But what about his mind? What was going on in there?

"You didn't think he was insane before he jumped," I say.

"That's right," Nikki says.

"What about *when* he jumped?"

Peter stops stroking Jaffa's head. "Something I am very, very pleased about. I know it might sound strange, it might sound peculiar, even. At the end of the inquest, the coroner didn't say 'while the balance of mind was disturbed.' I was dreadin' him saying that. Duncan's mind *wasn't* disturbed, the balance *wasn't* disturbed."

Lesley shakes her head. "Duncan went over the edge and over the edge—over the edge mentally, to be able to do that, to have the courage to do that." Her eyes sweep the room. "Don't you think the majority of us haven't got the courage to do that? If more of us had the courage to commit suicide, if we had a terminal illness or anything like that, then there would be no need to talk about euthanasia, because we'd all be doing it for ourselves, wouldn't we? Not necessarily jumping or shooting, but we would sort ourselves out in the end, wouldn't we?"

It's an intriguing question. If suicide were guaranteed painless at the push of a button, would more people kill themselves? Or is the fear more psychological than physical, a fear of death rather than of skull-breaking bullets and neck-snapping nooses?

Or is the greatest inhibitor of suicide not fear at all but family? It's hard to imagine a lucid Lesley killing herself as long as Peter and Nikki were around, even if fear weren't a factor. But then Duncan's love for his family didn't stop him. Maybe he *was* crazy.

Nikki looks tenderly at her father. "I think he was disturbed, compared to you and I in our normal everyday," she says. "I don't mean that he'd gone mad or anything, but for him to do that, there's got to be something wrong. That isn't human nature to do that."

"No, no. Duncan had made up his mind he was going to do that. Duncan knew what he was doing. Duncan did what he wanted. That was his solution."

"Because he couldn't see a way out of it," Nikki says. "Most people can see a way out. They will go and get help. I'm not saying he was mad or insane or anything, but he must have been disturbed to do that, because most people would go and speak to someone. There was a solution, but Duncan couldn't see that far. So you've got to be a different person."

"But Duncan didn't want help—"

"Because he couldn't see a way out."

Peter clamps his mouth in frustration. He'd told me in the car that he always included the children in conversations when they were young, and he valued what they said, because he didn't believe that children should be seen and not heard. But at the moment, he doesn't appear to be enjoying the consequences of his child-rearing philosophy. He appears unable to see a way out of this circular argument.

"If you got him out of this problem," he says slowly, as if still formulating his thought, "he'd think, 'Well, I still got life,' and he wasn't particularly interested in life, not in its present form. That's why he wrote in his note, 'I can't take this life anymore.' "

Their disagreement mirrors a debate that has been going on

in my own mind for some time: can the tunnel vision that Nikki describes be anything other than the blindness of an unbalanced mind? Can it ever be the single-minded resolve of a balanced one? The mental constriction that characterizes the suicidal mind is similar in many ways to the "flow" state experienced by brain surgeons, chess players, writers, and anybody else who, according to psychologist Mihaly Csikszentmihalyi, "is so involved in an activity that nothing else seems to matter." He explains that in the flow state, "psychic disorder," which he describes as "information that conflicts with existing intentions," is blissfully absent. Is it possible that some jumpers who stand on the cliff edge focus on suicide in the same way that a free climber on a sheer rock face keys into a life-or-death handhold—intently, lucidly, vitally? It's easy to see how a state free of psychic disorder might appeal to someone who's chronically mentally ill, and it's tempting to speculate that some people might court suicide as a way of clearing the static from their minds. But it's harder to see the tunnel vision of a crazy-in-love, temporarily despondent young man with much to live for as anything but madness, and the outcome as anything but a terrible waste.

Peter takes a sip of water. Nikki and Simon talk to each other with their eyes.

Lesley, her forearms resting comfortably on the arms of her chair, searches the air for a thought. "That was a different person down there," she says. "That was not our Duncan."

Silence fills the room, and no one seems keen to break it. I take the opportunity to lob another bomb. "Do you think what Duncan did was selfish?"

Peter considers the question. The island of sunlight he and Jaffa shared is gone, and Jaffa, too. "We don't agree with what he did," he says. "The problem could have been solved. But we bear him no malice. People have said to me that he was selfish to do that. But I said, 'Aren't we selfish for wanting him to still be here in spite of his problems?' I mean, from a religious aspect, they'll say, 'How dare he take his life. It's not his to take.' But, you know, they're sort of taking it to the other extreme. It *is* a gift, but the gift is to use however you feel fit."

Nikki nods. "If you're in that state, you're thinking of yourself, aren't you? You're thinking, 'I can't get out of this, I want to do something for me.' If you were really to think and see the pain that you'd cause, you wouldn't do it. He was just thinking about what he needed to do, and his life, and 'I can't go on.' It was tunnel vision."

Can a suicide be considered selfish if the people left behind are beyond his field of awareness when he pulls the trigger or jumps off the cliff? We absolve insane murderers of guilt on the grounds of diminished responsibility; why not exonerate disturbed suicides of selfishness on the grounds of diminished perception?

"Duncan wasn't a selfish person," Lesley says wearily. "He did this one thing for himself."

There are nods all around and then a long silence, and again no one is in a rush to fill it.

AFTER MY TALK WITH THE FAMILY, Peter takes me to his garden in the backyard. There's a popular television show in England on which master gardeners perform spectacular backyard makeovers, transforming tiny, derelict plots into garden paradises for unsuspecting homeowners. Peter's garden isn't quite as ambitious as the ones on TV, but it does have the feel of something created from nothing. A brick walk leads to dormant flower beds, a cedar shed, and a small gazebo festooned with ivy, all enclosed by a concrete wall on one side and a picket fence on the other.

"This was given to us by Duncan's workmates," Peter says, pointing to a granite column with a brass sundial on top. My eyes are drawn to the inscription at its base: DUNKY, FROM THE BOYS AT EVE-CLAYDON.

We continue on to a row of rosebushes, still naked in early spring. "We plant a rosebush for each deceased family member. Over the last year and a half, Lesley's lost her uncle, mother, brother-in-law, son, and aunt."

I shake my head, a gesture that seems ridiculously inadequate. I read the names under each bush: Mark, Uncle Dennis, Mother, Ken, Duncan, and Auntie Ruth. We gaze at the bushes together. A cool breeze carries the distant sounds of children playing. Lengthening picket shadows put the rose bed behind bars. "Do you think you'll ever see Duncan again?" I ask.

"No," Peter says, still staring at the bushes. "I've thought loads and loads of times that I didn't even get to say goodbye to him. If Duncan's off to kill himself, then 'Cheerio, son, I've said goodbye to you,' you know? It doesn't happen, does it? You don't want to say goodbye knowing that that's it, do you?"

He turns and looks at me as if he isn't seeing me, the way people do when they're still caught up in what they've just said. Then his expression turns to mild surprise, as if he's noticing how affected I am by this achingly sad truth. He says, "I'm desperately trying to grab hold of something. I'm certainly not religious, I'm not looking for someone to save my soul at any stage in life. I think there's gotta be something greater than us but not as we know it. Not the Bible, nothing as we would like it to be. I would say, 'God, take my debts over' and 'Please, God, don't let this happen to me' because I don't know any other name to call it. That's the one that I've been brought up with. But I don't necessarily believe God's walked on water and He's resurrected. I mean, they're all hand-me-down things. You only gotta tell somebody, 'Oh, did you hear about Charlie Brown trying to rob a bank?' And then by the time it's gone 'round the block a few times, Charlie Brown not only tried to rob a bank but he blew it up afterwards. And then you think, you know, 'Over thousands of years, you're not going to tell me that it hasn't sort of been smartened up to make it more attractive.' Because it has, hasn't it? It's got to be."

I nod, not to be polite but because I share the same belief. Peter looks down at the spindly rosebushes.

"I would like to think that I will see Duncan again, but I don't believe I will. I honestly don't believe I'm going to. That is the end, that's finished. He was our creation, and it just went down the tubes."

There is no self-consciousness in the wake of these words, only the face of grief. I've never been one to use the word "love" lightly. I don't get how rock stars can shout "I love you" to anonymous faces in the audience, or how people can purport to fall in love at first sight. But standing there, returning Peter's gaze, I feel strangely like his son. Not Duncan, just some other son who loves him and is about to say goodbye.

ON THE RIDE BACK TO EASTBOURNE, I ask Nikki why she thinks her father was so adamant on the point of Duncan's sanity. "I think he was worried that if Duncan was found to be mad that it wasn't right," she says quietly. "Dad can be quite old-fashioned, Victorian really, with some things. I don't know if he thinks there's a stigma attached to it." She pauses. "I think he would like to think that Duncan made a man's decision. He was very, very brave. He made that decision, and he stood by it and did it."

I stare out the window. Peter wants and needs to believe that Duncan made a rational decision because madness carries a stigma. I want and need to believe that Conrad also made a rational decision. Why is that? To lighten what guilt I carry? To give Conrad the benefit of the doubt? Or do we melancholics of the world need to believe that people who felt confused and powerless in their lives were clear and assertive in the prosecution of their deaths because, subconsciously, that's how we would want to be remembered if our lives came to the same end? People see in suicide what they want and need to see.

In the center of Tunbridge Wells, we pass a densely wooded park threaded with meandering walkways. "The Common," Simon says. Farther down, Nikki points to a quaint tile-hung house fronted by a patch of lawn. "You might be interested in this. It's a restaurant but used to be the inn where William Thackeray wrote his books."

I don't much care. My mind is elsewhere. I feign interest and turn the conversation back to Duncan's suicide. "How do you think your parents are coping?" I ask Nikki.

"Dad seems to show it more. He tends to go quiet. He'll speak more softly. And he'll be quite down, whereas Mum, she's gotta be the brave one for the rest of us. So people will say, 'How's Pete?' or 'Lesley, you seem to be coping,' and a couple of times she's been really upset by that, because she says, 'I'm not necessarily coping.' " Nikki watches Simon with an air of reassurance, as if he is driving her to safety. "I think it's harder for Mum because she's home all day. The rest of us work. We have people to talk to, and we're away from the environment where Duncan would be. But Mum's at home, where Duncan was. She'd be cooking him his dinner or getting him up in the morning. There'd be this routine. So I really feel for Mum in that way.

"I'm sure if Simon and I weren't around, Mum and Dad wouldn't— If it had been just Duncan, you know, they might have done the same thing, because they felt that way after Mark died. That's why we said right on that night, 'None of us must do anything silly, because we've got to be here for each other, we've got to be strong for each other.' Mum and Dad have really pulled together. I have a lot of admiration for them. I don't know how they can cope, when you think of the horror of it, really."

AFTER MY VISIT WITH THE COPPERS, I review my notes of our conversation in an attempt to understand more fully why Kath's rejection triggered in Duncan such a drastic response. He obviously had a low opinion of himself. "He was quite shy in an unusual way," Nikki said, recalling a New Year's party where Duncan apparently sat at a table with Kath and her friends, looking down and saying little. Peter said, "Duncan, in a sense, thought he was a nobody. So much to offer and thought he had nothing to give." During the last four months of his life, what little self-regard Duncan had seemed to have been tied up in his relationship with Kath.

Nikki said that "when Duncan got into something, like *The Simpsons* or *X Files*, he wanted all of it: the books, the posters, the T-shirt . . . he was fanatical in that way."

Kath was another obsession. But he couldn't have all of her, because she didn't want much of him. Paralleling his all-or-nothing possessiveness was a black-and-white perceptual style. "He was very intense in that way," Peter said. "A person was guilty or not guilty, good or bad at their job. No middle road. No center." In what he called "a little bit of a pointer," Peter observed this same sort of rigidity when they played video games together. "Duncan would be shooting the enemy on his Sony PlayStation, wiping the floor of them all, and then when things started to go a little wrong—say he got trapped on the edge of a ravine—he'd say, 'Ah, blow it, kill meself,' and throw himself off the edge. Just a crashing instead of a rebooting. Just a closing down."

Then there was Duncan's drinking. Two years before his death, Peter went up to Duncan's garage to tinker with his son's car and saw a bunch of empty cigarette packs and a whiskey bottle on the floor. He asked Duncan if he had a problem. "No," he said. He'd gone through a bad patch but was over it. While cleaning out his room after his death, Peter and Lesley found empty beer bottles stashed in his closet. Whatever pain Duncan was trying to dull predated his relationship with Kath. A friend told Peter that several years before his death, Duncan had contacted a member of the Samaritans, who then met up with Duncan at Beachy Head.

SEVERAL MONTHS AFTER my meeting with the Coppers, they are still very much on my mind. Back home in Connecticut, I write to Peter and Lesley, sharing, for the first time, my regret that I had not taken my usual evening walk along the cliff top on the night of Duncan's death. Lesley writes back:

> It is odd that you told us in your letter that you often
> walked in the area at night and what seems even more strange
> is that we should meet later without us knowing any of what
> had maybe linked us together. We four believe in destiny and
> fate. What happened was meant to be and nothing would have
> or could have prevented it from happening. If you had been
> walking the cliffs that night, you might have been able to stop
> him but not forever. He was a free spirit. He did not go to use
> the phone that was there. He did not even go to the place where
> most people go. He knew just what he wanted to do and went
> for it as he would have said.
>
> We still keep asking why. How could this happen? There
> are if's, but's and maybe's, but we will never have all the
> answers. Perhaps it is for the best really. We may have ended up

feeling very bitter instead of being very proud and thankful for
having shared his life and all the good times of which there
were plenty.

I RETURN TO SEE THE COPPERS the following spring. They put me up in Duncan's bedroom, and we spend much of the weekend *not* talking about Duncan. Nikki and Simon join us for a lighthearted dinner at an Indian restaurant. One morning we go to the Pantiles, a colonnaded arcade of shops in the town center and home of the Chalybeate Spring, a small, stone-lined reservoir of spa water that drew swarms of visitors to Tunbridge Wells in the seventeenth century but now sits dry and forlorn in the early spring, its empty basin lined with scabrous deposits. We ramble past castles and manor houses to the outskirts of Winnie-the-Pooh country, where we stop for lunch at a quaint pub on the edge of Ashdown Forest. Sunday morning Peter and I drink ouzo while watching motorcyle racing on TV. And in the afternoon, before leaving for Nikki and Simon's for Sunday supper, we watch home videos of Duncan looking on quietly from a kitchen doorway as his relatives whoop and cut the cake during his aunt and uncle's twenty-fifth wedding anniversary; Duncan, beer in hand, telling a roving video camera to "Sod off!" during a retreat with friends; Duncan feeding ducks at the edge of a pond; Duncan fainting at his best friend's wedding; Duncan bungee jumping off the platform of a crane on his twenty-first birthday.

The videos elicit scattered endearments and funny asides but surprisingly little discussion, and that, I think, is a good sign.

I LIE IN DUNCAN'S BED, craving but resisting the oblivion of sleep. It is Mother's Day eve, the second anniversary of Duncan's death, my last night in England. Fragments of conversation reopen like daffodils along a twisting road. *You're a number seven, which makes you probably a bit of an introvert, somebody who is quite analytical.* The fortune-teller was right. I must take everything apart: the sudden-death reports, my attraction to Beachy Head, Duncan's death, and now, the Coppers' healing.

Lesley: *Peter should have retired in January but they asked him to stay on. Best thing he could ever do. Stay at work because he'd just sit here and rot.* "The only way to deal with it," Don Haffenden, the grieving widower, told me, "is to keep busy, stay a part of society."

Nikki: *My dad has changed a lot. He's more, "Life is short. You gotta do this, you gotta do that." He was always quite cautious with money and now he's like, "That's it. We'll get a new car. That's it. We'll go on holiday."* Yes. Grieving isn't loving. The Coppers don't wallow in grief to show how much they loved Duncan; they honor his life by living fully.

Peter: *Duncan died on his terms. Some people don't get that luxury. Duncan chose his time, where, and how it would be.*

Lesley: *That is one thing I'm grateful for—Duncan didn't have children, he hasn't left little ones.*

Nikki: *I'm glad he left a note.* The power of small consolations.

Peter: *Jaffa's been the best therapy. If it wasn't for him, I'm not sure I would have made it.*

Nikki: *I mean, we're all quite verbal, we all talk things through.*

Lesley: *This is helping a little, isn't it? We still don't know why. But speaking to somebody else is, you're listening, and we haven't really spoken to anybody else.* "Give sorrow words" Malcolm counseled Macduff, "The grief that does not speak / Whispers the o'er-fraught heart, and bids it break."

Lesley: *You know, on some level, there's nothing you did that caused him—even though you feel guilty and wonder two, three years ago that you didn't do what you should have done or whatever. You know it's nothing you did or didn't do.* A tough one—being realistic about what you could or should have done. Moses, ever the dutiful father, staying up until the small hours, shooting pool with Conrad in the basement and listening—lots of listening—then trudging off to work the next day exhausted; trying to get Conrad to see a therapist; finally getting him on antidepressants. For a week, he feels better, but then he stops taking the medication. Still, Moses thinks, *I could have done more. If only I hadn't been so wrapped up in my work, it might have made a difference.* My wife, too: *If I'd made more of an effort to get to know him when he was little, if I'd been better about keeping in touch with him while he was at college—if I'd nurtured our relationship, I might have been able to reach him.*

And me—I continue to wonder what might have been had Conrad gotten the help and support he needed during his last years. I imagine my wife and me writing him letters while he's at college. When he returns home, we visit more, not less, frequently. We knock on the door of his room. Maybe he doesn't come out, but at least our presence shows our love and concern and spares him the burden of feeling that he has driven us away. Maybe he does come out, and we talk. He agrees to see a therapist. He takes his medication faithfully—an antidepressant *and* an antipsychotic—because someone carefully monitors his compliance. The voices inside his head are quieted. He talks more. He feels less alone, less afraid, less ashamed. He feels more hopeful. He decides to give college another try—not Syracuse but a university closer to home. He gets his degree. He does the bookkeeping for his brother's landscaping business or starts his own business restoring old computers. Something manageable. He takes pride in his ability to work; it's a small miracle he's thankful for. On the evening of October 8, 1996, he comes home from work, eats dinner with his parents, and shoots pool with his father while he talks about his day. Later that night, he and his parents watch TV together on their bed. Abruptly, Conrad says good night. He's tired, and he has work the next morning. He goes to his bedroom. Minutes later, his parents hear, through their bedroom wall, the familiar click of his lamp.

But what's the point? Where do the what ifs get you?

I turn over and peek at the clock. Ten-fifty. The significance of the time occurs to me, and the what ifs start all over again. Duncan is sitting on his bed scribbling a suicide note. He leaves his room and heads down the stairs, wishing Lesley a happy Mother's Day. He drives to Beachy Head and parks in the Belle Tout parking area.

I'm taking my late-night walk along the cliff top. I see his car, and, drawing closer, I see him tipping back a bottle. I walk up to the car and knock on the rain-coated window. Startled, Duncan rolls it down. I ask if he's okay. He nods, but I don't believe him. His eyes are moist and his face tear-stained. His breath smells of alcohol. Small talk turns large, and after an hour of conversation, I offer to ride back home with him. He accepts. Fifty minutes later, we arrive at the Coppers' into a different future. Peter answers the door and throws his arms around Duncan. In the living room, a message crackles over a police radio, saying that they haven't found Duncan's car at Beachy Head. Lesley calls Nikki and tells her Duncan is home. A year later, there is no sudden-death report on Duncan Copper in the pile on Michael Davey's desk, and now it is Duncan, not me, sleeping in his bed.

EPILOGUE

Peter's car slowly pulls away, and I feel suddenly alone. A sign at the pub's entrance advertises Mother's Day luncheon specials. Behind the pub, a bright cloud lumbers across the azure sky, blanketing Edgar Williams's fields in shadow. A gust of wind rattles the stalks of antennae above the coast guard storage shed and fans the heavy smell of french fries across the coast road. I unzip my duffel bag, put on my fleece jacket, and head toward the cliffs, stepping across the crumbled foundations of the old radar station. I pass a young family gathered around a World War II monument, the two children dutifully listening to their father's history lesson. Yes, tell them about the women who tracked the movements of German warplanes from radar stations scattered across

Beachy Head and about the men who shot them down. And while you're at it, tell them that the chalk beneath the turf they're standing on was once the ocean floor, and that long before the Germans came, the turf was a battleground where heavily armored men fought with swords and shields.

Just don't mention the suicides.

I come to the edge of the cliffs—the very spot where, two years before, I watched the police helicopter recover the body of the London artist. Instead of looking down, I fix my gaze on the brightening horizon and breathe deep the cool morning air. I start walking toward Belle Tout until I come to the spot where Duncan jumped. It still amazes me that you can just walk off the edge of England. A fence would be ugly, some say, or impractical (it would fall into the sea every few years), or ineffectual (people would simply climb over). I look down at the hard-packed dirt around my feet. I would like to think that the turf has been worn bare by the feet of people who couldn't decide if they wanted to jump. A fence might have made a difference.

But not, I think, for someone like Conrad. He saw no prospect of restoring his life to the way it was before he began to break into a sweat at the sound of a clicking furnace or a creaking floorboard. So he started packing up his life as neatly as he had arranged it before it fell apart. Folding and labeling and discarding in the privacy of his parents' basement, he must have felt like his old self again: goal-driven and self-possessed. Some people who jump off Beachy Head may feel that they, too, are reclaiming for a brief moment a self that once knew clarity and purpose. Having read about their lives in the sudden-death reports, I've developed a deep respect for what the cabdrivers, bartenders, and police constables can't take away: a tenacious will to die, to forge from the passive, mangled syntax of their lives a concise, declarative statement. "We don't try to talk people out of jumping," Nancy the Samaritan told me. "We listen. We don't take away their self-determination."

I turn and head toward the pub. The parking lot is beginning to fill up with cars. Mothers in dresses filter into the pub with their families, and I follow. I find an empty stool at the bar and order a cup of coffee. Jazzy pop music plays softly in the background. I scan the dining area. I'm not looking for suspicious ones. I'm looking for a wife and daughter who remind me of my own.

Acknowledgments

A book of this nature isn't possible without the coopera-
tion of people willing to share their private pain with a
stranger. I offer my heartfelt thanks to the following people: Don Haffenden, who welcomed me into his home
when he was still reeling from the loss of his wife, Doris,
and gave generously of his time; Peter and Lesley Copper
and their daughter, Nikki, and son-in-law, Simon Manser,
who showed me what it means to grieve well, and who
treated me like a member of the family; and Bill Hull
for being willing to reopen a period of his life that he
may have preferred to keep closed. All of these people,
whom I once regarded as interview subjects, I now count
as dear friends whose generosity, courage, and strength
was a source of inspiration throughout the writing of
this book.

I owe a large debt of gratitude to the workers in and around Eastbourne who were willing to take time out from their busy days to share their stories. Most of what I know about cliff rescue and recovery I learned from Garry Russell, Bob Jewson, and Chris Turner, who endured numerous marathon interviews at the hands of a neophyte. Special thanks to Bob Jewson, who responded in detail to numerous follow-up e-mail queries. Thanks is also due to the Eastbourne police department, who made space for a curious, law-abiding noncitizen in its detention rooms and squad cars, and to police constables Ian Tubb, Julia Clasby, Steve Mosely, and Michael Jones, who filled up those spaces with enough tales to remind me why I could never be a police officer. I am especially grateful to Michael Davey for giving me access to the sudden-death reports, without which this book would have been incomplete.

A few miles from police headquarters, Sharon Debenham Edwards took time out from her crazy-busy day to reveal the inner workings of the Eastbourne morgue, showing, in the process, that there is room for laughter in the darkest of places. Thanks, also, to Kevin and Sandie Carlyon for their warm hospitality and for sharing their unique perspective on Beachy Head's allure. It was all too easy during my research to see Beachy Head as only a notorious suicide spot. But the residents of Beachy Head, in particular Brian Johnson and Mark and Louise Roberts, reminded me that Beachy Head is not merely a destination, but a home.

Of the vast amount of suicide literature I read during the writing of this book, five works were especially valuable: A. Alvarez's *The Savage God*, George Howe Colt's *The Enigma of Suicide*, Kay Redfield Jamison's *Night Falls Fast*, Edwin Shneidman's *The Suicidal Mind*, and Andrew Solomon's *The Noonday Demon*. Thank you all for helping me to understand this most complex of subjects. Two other writers deserve special mention: *Washington Post* reporter Steve Coll, who wrote the haunting article that introduced me to Beachy Head and cast the spell; and Dr. John Surtees, who, in generously sharing his Beachy Head research during the early stages of the project, got me launched.

My agent, Wendy Sherman, was an anchor in rough waters. Her encouragement and enthusiasm were two of the few constants during the long and winding road to publication. My editor, Susanna Porter, deserves far more thanks than I can give for her close readings and exquisite judgment. My copyeditor, Beth Thomas, was the best last line of editorial defense a writer could hope to have.

Finally, my family. I'd like to thank my sister Leslie and my brothers-in-law Raf and Joe for their timely reassurances and keen interest in the book; my parents-in-law Moses and Renee, for being willing to revisit the most painful chapter of their lives and for sacrificing their privacy for a cause they supported unwaveringly; and my parents, Tom and Susan Hunt, and my daughter, Eva, who rode with me all the way, sharing the many ups and downs, and fueling my efforts with a steady stream of support and sacrifice borne of love. A very special thanks to my beautiful wife, Gabriel, for her editorial guidance, patience, and belief. To my brother-in-law Conrad, thank you for the example of your courage. May you rest in peace.

NOTES

1. *The Last Stop Pub*

11 "The last line of defense" Steve Coll, "Keeping an Eye on the Suspicious Ones," *The Philadelphia Inquirer*, April 30, 1994.

2. *Southern Hospitality*

16 "The glory of these glorious Downs" Richard Jeffries, "The Breeze on Beachy Head." Quoted in David Arscott, *In Praise of Sussex* (Lewes: Pomegranate Press, 1996), p. 71.

18 "This beautiful place" Louis de Bernières, "Legends of the Fall," *Harper's Magazine*, January 1996, p. 79.

40 "It is a melancholy consideration" Quoted in George Howe Colt, *The Enigma of Suicide* (New York: Simon & Schuster, Touchstone, 1992), p. 180.

40 "There is a little murder" Quoted in Karl Men-

ninger, *Sparks,* L. Freeman (ed.) (New York: Thomas Y. Crowell Company, 1973), p. 142.

3. *Uncharted Territory*

46 "drawn by a horse" Granville Williams, quoted in A. Alvarez, *The Savage God* (New York: W. W. Norton and Co., 1971), p. 64.

47 "through his brain and thence" R. Cooper, *Reminiscences of Eastbourne* (London: Bath House, 1903), p. 55.

55 "a town conceived" Quoted in D. Robert Elleray, *Eastbourne: A Pictorial History* (Chichester, West Sussex: Phillimore & Co., 1995), p. 2.

55 "a graceful dame" *The Daily Telegraph,* December 14, 1893, quoted in Elleray, *Eastbourne,* p. 1.

62 "In the end each man" Karl Menninger, *Man Against Himself* (New York: Harcourt, Brace and World, 1938), p. viii.

4. *The Lure of Beachy Head*

66 "the vertical became the horizontal" de Bernières, "Legends of the Fall," p. 79.

66 "the suicidal tendency appears" Emile Durkheim, *Suicide* (New York: The Free Press, 1951), p. 65.

66 "because it was unwilled, regretted" Edward Hoagland, "Heaven and Nature," from *Tigers and Ice: Reflections on Nature and Life* (New York: The Lyons Press, 1999), p. 32.

66 "To a lesser degree" Durkheim, *Suicide,* p. 65.

70 "They are 100 percent certain" Alun Rees, "We Owe Our Baby to Jolly White Giant," *The Express,* April 5, 1998.

78 "When the mind is beginning" Quoted in J. M. Galt, *The Treatment of Insanity* (New York: Harper and Brothers, 1846), p. 212.

82 "In the consideration of the faculties" Edgar Allan Poe, *Complete Stories and Poems of Edgar Allan Poe* (New York: Doubleday, 1966), p. 271.

5. *Rescue and Recovery*

115 "I don't like these people" M. Williams, "Threaten to Jump from the Golden Gate; You'll Get Tough Love," *The Wall Street Journal,* September 10, 2001.

116 "a maladaptive action" Quoted in John Donnelly (ed.), *Suicide* (Amherst: Prometheus Books, 1998), p. 187.

116 "in every case of suicide" Edwin Shneidman, *The Suicidal Mind* (New York: Oxford University Press, 1996), p. 165.

116 "When it takes four hours" John Surtees, *Beachy Head* (Seaford, East Sussex: S.B. Publications, 1997), p. 99.

117 "And there are tribal societies" Celeste Fremon, "Love and Death," *Los Angeles Times Magazine*, January 27, 1991, p. 19.

118 "Something about acute self-destruction" Sherwin B. Nuland, *How We Die* (New York: Vintage Books, 1995), p. 151.

7. A Range of Reasons

135 "You can win a million dollars" Quoted in Colt, *The Enigma of Suicide*, p. 59.

136 "No one ever lacks" Cesare Pavese, *The Burning Brand: Diaries, 1935–1950*, trans. A. E. Murch (New York: Walker and Company, 1961), p. 99.

145 "when an individual commits suicide" Shneidman, *The Suicidal Mind*, p. 18.

146 "A man of inner worth" Quoted in Donnelly, *Suicide*, p. 55.

146 "relationship problems" Samaritans website, http://www. samaritans.org.uk/know/statistics_suic_at_popup.shtm.

152 "No neurotic harbors thoughts" Sigmund Freud, *Beyond the Pleasure Principle* (New York: W. W. Norton and Company, 1990).

152 "may be driven by delusions" Quoted in Angela Neustatter, "What Drives a Father to Kill His Entire Family?" *Guardian Unlimited*, May 2, 2001, p. 2.

152 "The overwhelming urge" Ibid.

165 "the ridiculous character of that habit" Albert Camus, *The Myth of Sisyphus, and Other Essays*, trans. J. O'Brien (New York: Alfred A. Knopf, 1955).

166 "I am totally willing to believe" Shneidman, *The Suicidal Mind*, pp. 162–164.

169 "obsessive suicides" Durkheim, *Suicide*, p. 64.

169 "I know that I am forever" Pavese, *The Burning Brand*, p. 48.

169 "A suicide's excuses" A. Alvarez, *The Savage God* (New York: W. W. Norton and Co., 1971), p. 123.

8. The Suicidal Mind

182 "veritable howling tempest" William Styron, "Darkness Visible," *Vanity Fair,* December 1989, p. 212.

182 "depression, in its extreme form" Ibid., p. 278.

182 "stuffed further and further" Sylvia Plath, *The Bell Jar* (New York: Bantam Books, 1971), p. 105.

182 "constantly vomiting" Andrew Solomon, "Anatomy of Melancholy," *The New Yorker,* January 1998, p. 48.

186 "We shrink in horror" Quoted in Donnelly, *Suicide,* p. 52.

186 "is an act of man" Primo Levi, "Shame," from *The Drowned and the Saved* (New York: Simon & Schuster, 1988).

187 "Unlike other animals" Daniel Callahan, *The Tyranny of Survival* (Lanham: University Press of America, 1985), p. 113.

188 "I believe only in this moment" Jane Kenyon, "Having It Out with Melancholy," from *Otherwise: New and Selected Poems* (Saint Paul, Minn.: Graywolf Press, 1996).

189 "The life of a man" David Hume, "On Suicide," from *Essays Moral, Political and Literary* (London: Oxford University Press, 1963), pp. 587.

189 "there is much in the world" Quoted in Donnelly, *Suicide,* pp. 53, 55.

190 "The suicide does not play" Joyce Carol Oates, "The Art of Suicide," from *The Reevaluation of Existing Values and the Search for Absolute Values. Proceedings of the Seventh International Conference on the Unity of the Sciences* (New York: International Cultural Foundation Press, 1978).

9. The Long Goodbye

219 "is so involved in an activity" Mihaly Csikszentmihalyi, *Flow: The Psychology of Optimal Experience* (New York: HarperPerennial, 1991), p. 5.

219 "information that conflicts" Ibid., p. 36.

BIBLIOGRAPHY

Alvarez, A. *The Savage God: A Study of Suicide.* New York: W. W. Norton and Co., 1971.

Arscott, David. *The Sussex Story.* Lewes: Pomegranate Press, 1992.

———. *Living Sussex.* Lewes: Pomegranate Press, 1994.

———. *In Praise of Sussex.* Lewes: Pomegranate Press, 1996.

Casey, Nell (ed.). *Unholy Ghost: Writers on Depression.* New York: William Morrow, 2001.

Colt, George Howe. *The Enigma of Suicide.* New York: Simon & Schuster, Touchstone, 1992.

Donnelly, John (ed.). *Suicide: Right or Wrong?* 2nd edition. Amherst: Prometheus Books, 1998.

Durkheim, Emile. *Suicide: A Study in Sociology,* trans. John A. Spaulding and George Simpson. New York: The Free Press, 1951.

Farberow, Norman (ed.). *The Many Faces of Suicide: Indirect Self-Destructive Behavior.* New York: McGraw-Hill, 1979.

Guinan, John, and Smolin, Ann. *Healing After the Suicide of a Loved One.* New York: Simon & Schuster, Fireside, 1993.

Holmes, E. *Seaward Sussex: The South Downs from End to End.* London: Robert Scott Roxburghe House, 1923.

Humphrey, George. *Wartime Eastbourne.* Eastbourne: Beckett Features, 1989.

Jamison, Kay Redfield. *Night Falls Fast: Understanding Suicide.* New York: Alfred A. Knopf, 1999.

Kant, Immanuel. *Lectures on Ethics,* trans. Louis Infield. New York: Harper and Row, 1963.

Kushner, Howard. *Self-Destruction in the Promised Land.* New Brunswick, N.J.: Rutgers University Press, 1989.

Lester, David. *Making Sense of Suicide.* Philadelphia: The Charles Press, 1997.

Lifton, Robert Jay. *The Broken Connection: On Death and the Continuity of Life.* New York: Simon & Schuster, Touchstone, 1980.

Miller, John (ed.) *On Suicide: Great Writers on the Ultimate Question.* San Francisco: Chronicle Books, 1992.

Nuland, Sherwin B. *How We Die: Reflections on Life's Final Chapter.* New York: Vintage Books, 1995.

Pavese, Cesare. *The Burning Brand: Diaries, 1935–1950,* trans. A. E. Murch. New York: Walker and Company, 1961.

Plath, Sylvia. *The Bell Jar.* New York: Bantam Books, 1971.

Shneidman, Edwin S. *The Suicidal Mind.* New York: Oxford University Press, 1996.

Solomon, Andrew. *The Noonday Demon: An Atlas of Depression.* New York: Scribner, 2001.

Surtees, John. *Beachy Head.* Seaford, East Sussex: S.B. Publications, 1997.

Williams, Mark. *Cry of Pain: Understanding Suicide and Self-Harm.* London: Penguin Books, 1997.